THE RUSSIAN VIEW
OF U.S. STRATEGY

THE RUSSIAN VIEW OF U.S. STRATEGY

Its Past, Its Future

Jonathan Samuel Lockwood
Kathleen O'Brien Lockwood

Transaction Publishers
New Brunswick (U.S.A.) and London (U.K.)

Eight paperback printing 2009
Copyright © 1993 by Transaction Publishers, New Brunswick, New Jersey.

This book is printed on acid-free paper that meets the American National Standard for Permanence of Paper for Printed Library Materials.

Library of Congress Catalog Number: 92-11344
ISBN: 978-1-56000-031-0 (cloth); 978-0-7658-0636-9 (paper)
Printed in the United States of America

Library of Congress Cataloging-in-Publication Data

Lockwood, Jonathan Samuel, 1955-
    The Russian view of U.S. strategy : its past, its future / Jonathan Samuel Lockwood, Kathleen O'Brien Lockwood.
        p. cm.
    Rev. ed. of: The Soviet view of U.S. strategic doctrine. c1983.
    Includes bibliographical references and index.
    ISBN 1-56000-031-7 (cloth); 0-7658-0636-3 (paper)
    1. Military doctrine—United States—History—20th century. 2. United States—Military policy. 3. Nuclear weapons—United States—History—20th century. 4. Military doctrine—Soviet Union—History—20th century. 5. Soviet Union—Military policy. I. Lockwood, Kathleen O'Brien. II. Lockwood, Jonathan Samuel, 1955- Soviet view of U.S. strategic doctrine. III. Title. IV. Title: Russian view of US strategy. V. Title: Russian view of United States strategy.
UA23.L63   1992   92-11344
355.02'17' 0973—dc20   CIP

*This book is dedicated to the memory of David Henry Feick
(1958-1991), my best friend since childhood.
His life was short but full.*

Contents

Acknowledgments

For this expanded, second edition, there are a number of people to whom I wish to express my thanks and gratitude. First of all, my sincere thanks to Dr. Leon Goure, Dr. William F. Scott and Harriet Fast Scott for their contributions to this volume. As my dissertation committee chairman, Dr. Goure first stimulated my interest in this field and has shown his interest in my research and career ever since. The Scotts also lent me a considerable amount of material from their personal library to help expedite my research, as well as provided encouragement and insightful comments.

I also wish to thank Dr. Roy Godson of the Consortium for the Study of Intelligence for inviting me to present my research proposal at a seminar at Bowdoin College, Brunswick, Maine in August 1991. This seminar, which encouraged young as well as experienced scholars to explore the field of intelligence studies as an academic discipline, was immensely helpful to me. Of particular value were the comments of Col. David Glantz, Director of the Foreign Military Studies Office at Fort Leavenworth; Tom Diaz, Senior Research Fellow at the National Strategy Information Center; and Dr. H. Bradford Westerfield, Damon Wells Professor of International Studies at Yale University.

–Jonathan Samuel Lockwood

Introduction

In my 1983 book, *The Soviet View of U.S. Strategic Doctrine: Implications for Decisionmaking*, I had argued that the available evidence of Soviet perceptions of U.S. strategic doctrine indicated that the Soviets most feared a "mirror-image" of their own strategic doctrine.[1] The U.S. lacked a credible strategic defense (and still does). The Soviets believed their own strategic offensive nuclear forces provided them with significant political leverage over U.S. doctrine and foreign policy. Accordingly, anything that neutralized the military effectiveness of their offensive strategic missiles would be the most powerful, effective, and credible political deterrent from the Soviet perspective. I had therefore recommended the deployment of a three-tiered strategic defense comprised of civil defense, ground-based surface-to-air missile (SAM) and antiballistic missile (ABM) defense, in addition to space-based defense. Although President Ronald Reagan's declaration of the Strategic Defense Initiative (SDI) in March of 1983 emphasized a space-based rather than a three-tiered defense, the effect on the Soviet perception was predictably dramatic and in ways not generally understood in the West.

Not so predictable was the virtual collapse of the Soviet-led Warsaw Pact alliance in 1990, accompanied by the overthrow of Communist regimes throughout Eastern Europe. As of this writing, the former Soviet Union has been wracked by internal dissension and impending economic collapse, its Marxist-Leninist ideology is bankrupt and repudiated publicly by Mikhail Gorbachev, its empire is gone, and its republics have spun away from the authority of the central government with centrifugal force; its economic capacity to support its massive military infrastructure had been outrun by the grandiose ambitions of Soviet military leadership prior to Gorbachev's ascension to power. With the new formation of a Commonwealth of Independent States by Russian republic President Boris Yeltsin incorporating most of the former Soviet republics, one might be tempted to think that the millennium had arrived.

But even in the midst of what appeared at first to be the final triumph of democracy (if not of capitalism), the current situation within the nascent Commonwealth gives us no cause to become either euphoric or smug over their current turmoil. Henry Kissinger warned precisely against such an attitude:

All democratic leaders—President Bush actually less than most—relish the zephyrs blowing from Moscow and are reluctant to disturb the cordial atmosphere by raising underlying issues of policy. But how prudent is it to base long-range policy on the premises of permanent Soviet good will? Sooner or later, the Soviet domestic turmoil will resolve itself. And at that point—even before a full Soviet economic recovery—the Soviet Union may choose to return to a more traditional Russian pattern and assert its still huge military strength and the weight inherent in its vast territory and large population.[2]

Aleksandr Solzhenitsyn warned, too, back in 1980 of the dangers involved in too rapid a transition from totalitarianism to democracy in his book *The Mortal Danger: How Misperceptions About Russia Imperil America:*

But this letter was a genuine address to very real rulers possessed of immeasurable power, and it was plain that the very most one could hope for would be concessions on their side, certainly not capitulation: neither free general elections nor a complete (or even partial) change of leadership could be expected. The most I called for was a renunciation of communist ideology and of its most cruel consequences so as to allow at least a little more breathing space for the national spirit; for throughout history, only national-minded individuals have been able to make constructive contributions to society. *And the only path down from the icy cliff of totalitarianism was the slow and smooth descent via an authoritarian system. (If an unprepared people were to jump off that cliff directly into democracy, it would be crushed into an anarchical pulp.)* This "authoritarianism" of mine also drew immediate fire in the Western press.[3] [Emphasis added.]

Even though the Soviet Union no longer exists, Kissinger is correct in asserting that there are signs that the current turmoil may not "resolve itself" in ways favorable for U.S. foreign policy and security. According to some optimists among us, the Soviet economic conversion from a defense to a consumer-oriented economy was to have been well underway by this time. But not only has this not taken place, it has met with substantial opposition from the Soviet defense establishment.[4] Moreover, the collapsing Soviet economy brought out the radical, ultra-conservative elements in Soviet politics who opposed the reforms made by Gorbachev and who desired the formation of a "national patriotic front" to save the homeland.[5] Alexander Yakovlev, a key leader and architect of the Soviet reform movement who quit the Communist Party on 16 August, 1991, had warned of the preparation of a potential coup by a "Stalinist" core of the party leadership.[6] According to Alexander Prokhanov, a right-wing newspaper editor who recently co-signed a letter with leading military and Communist party leaders lambasting the Gorbachev government, a movement allying "Marxist-Leninists, Marxist-Stalinists, Russian Communists, social democratic liberals, extremist pro-fascist organizations, writers, artists, the military, industrialists, monarchists, and pagans" had been forming to prevent the disintegration of the union and its economy.[7] Even though Gorbachev managed to survive the subsequent coup attempt in August 1991, he was powerless to prevent the virtual disintegration of the former Soviet Union in December 1991 into its individual republics, a number of which not only wished to form their own indigenous military forces, but to claim the nuclear weapons residing within their territories as well.[8]

Regardless of the eventual resolution of the internal conflict within the former Soviet Union, however, it is paramount that we be aware of past Soviet perceptions of U.S. strategy and policy and the factors that influenced that policy. In the first edition of this book, it was demonstrated that Soviet analysts and commentators consistently fell into the mirror-imaging fallacy in their assessments of U.S. strategic doctrine and intentions; they projected their own strategic concepts, mindset, and cultural outlook onto U.S. planners and policy-makers. This gave them something in common with U.S. analysts and policy-makers, who had been doing virtually the same thing for most of the postwar period, and who still engage in this kind of faulty thinking on occasion, despite the large body of evidence to the contrary.

The consequences of this mutual mirror-imaging have been radically different for the course of U.S. and Soviet doctrine and force development during the postwar period. Mirror-imaging promises to continue to push the U.S. and the Soviet Union along divergent paths in the future, the recent experience of Operation Desert Storm notwithstanding. In fact, although the mirror-imaging phenomenon has been noted by such scholars as Raymond Garthoff and Stephen Gibert,[9] the full implications of this phenomenon have not been fully appreciated. This is a mistake; just because the Soviet mindset may differ in important respects from our own, it is cavalier to dismiss it as mistaken and therefore unworthy of further notice. Rather, we should try to interpret events through the prism of this mindset in order to appreciate what constitutes an effective deterrence strategy from the Soviet perspective. The importance of understanding the mirror-imaging phenomenon and its significance in the U.S.-Soviet relationship was illustrated in an August 1991 article in *Newsweek*:

> The Bush administration has been laboring to convince the Soviet military that the Cold War is really over. General Colin Powell, chairman of the Joint Chiefs of Staff, delivered that message on his visit to Moscow last week. But his counterparts believe the West is poised to exploit Soviet weakness ruthlessly. General Mikhail Moiseyev, chief of the Soviet General Staff, claimed earlier that Pentagon spending was growing (it's expected to shrink 20 percent by 1995). "They can't believe we are not going to take advantage of our victory—just as they would in our shoes," a top NATO Soviet intelligence analyst said.[10]

In spite of the obvious importance of understanding the Soviet perspective in a comprehensive historical context, aside from my first book, there still has been no comparable effort to analyze the Soviet perspective regarding the development of U.S. strategic doctrine since John Foster Dulles first enunciated the doctrine of "massive retaliation" in 1954.[11] Fritz W. Ermarth first stated the need for this kind of study in the fall 1978 issue of *International Security*:

> The next five to ten years of the U.S-Soviet strategic relationship could well be characterized by mounting U.S. anxieties about the adequacy of our deterrent forces and our strategic doctrine. There seems to be little real prospect that the SALT process, as we have been conducting it, will substantially alleviate these anxieties. Even if a more promising state of affairs emerges, however, it is hard to see us managing it with calm and confidence unless we develop a more thorough appreciation of the differences between U.S. and Soviet strategic thinking. Things have progressed beyond the point where it is useful to have the three familiar schools of thought on Soviet doctrine arguing past each other; one saying, "Whatever they say, they think as we do"; the second insisting,"Whatever they say, it does not matter"; and the third contending, "They think what they say, and are therefore out for superiority over us."[12]

A comprehensive understanding of how the Soviet leadership perceived our strategic doctrine and the ways in which this perception influenced Soviet defense programs and employment of military power is of vital importance, even during this period of revolutionary transition for the former Soviet Union. Not only can an analysis of the Soviet perception give us an indication of the probable future direction of its defense programs (or at least that of the Russian republic), but the first edition demonstrated that such analysis can provide clues as to how best to influence the behavior of the separate republics in ways favorable to such U.S. objectives as nuclear arms control. Ermarth set forth a number of questions he believed any study of comparative strategic doctrine ought to address. Although this book deals primarily with the Soviet perception of U.S. strategic doctrine, some of the questions he raises (in modified form) are useful:[13]

- What are the prevailing concepts, beliefs, and assertions that appear to constitute the Soviet view of U.S. strategic doctrine in a particular period?
- What are the hedges and qualifications introduced in Soviet pronouncements that modify the main theses of their stated thinking?
- What propagandistic purposes, if any, are likely to motivate certain Soviet pronouncements on U.S. doctrine? Do the Soviets recognize distinctions between what ought to be true of U.S. doctrine and what actually is?
- What perceptions have the Soviets held regarding the development of U.S.doctrine, and what effect, if any, have these perceptions had on Soviet doctrine and associated defense programs? What implications do these views have for the Strategic Arms Reduction Talks (START)?
- How does the Soviet perception oi U.S. strategic doctrine correlate with the use of Soviet military power in support of foreign policy objectives?

Erroneous assumptions have been made before by U.S. analysts about what the Soviet view was. The first school of thought described by Ermarth is best described as the mirror-imaging school, which assumes that the Soviet perspective is largely similar to our own, and that any observed differences or discrepancies are merely the result of a lack of intellectual sophistication or failure to understand fully the logic of the U.S. position. Former Defense Secretary Robert McNamara, former arms control negotiator Paul Warnke, and (to a certain extent) noted analyst Raymond Garthoff are the most prominent members of this school.[14] Yet there are a number of studies, some quite recent, that offer substantial evidence of significant differences between U.S. and Soviet strategic thinking, and that these differences are based on a set of rational assumptions rather than mere backwardness or lack of understanding.[15]

The second school of thought contends that the sources of Soviet strategic thought are not to be found in their writings at all. This school is best characterized as the "historical continuity" argument. In this view, Soviet strategic thinking and behavior can be explained as the natural continuation of tzarist policies. Having been invaded numerous times in their history, the peoples of the Soviet republics, but particularly the Russians, have developed paranoia regarding the threat of invasion from without. It is this fear of invasion, coupled perhaps with a sense of collective insecurity and inferiority vis-à-vis the West, that compelled the former Soviet leadership to maintain large standing military forces of all types, just as the tzars had. Foreign ambitions are deemed to be an extension of tzarist ambitions, and the role of ideology is downplayed or disregarded altogether.

What the members of this latter school do not consider is that current national behavior cannot always be explained in terms of historical precedent. There are instances in which a nation's foreign policy outlook has been irrevocably changed by a watershed event in its history—an occurrence of such magnitude that a radical change in outlook occurred out of either necessity or a change in national values. A prime example of the former can be found in U.S. history. Prior to the outbreak of the Second World War, the U.S. international outlook was predominantly isolationist in character. The United States had supposedly fought the "war to end all wars" back in 1917-1918; the source of evil had been cleansed from the world (or so Americans liked to think), and America could go back to "business as usual." But the experience of the Second World War and its immediate aftermath—establishing the Soviet Union's Eastern European empire—convinced U.S. leadership that a policy of isolationism could no longer be afforded. Thus the "internationalist" school of thought came to dominate American foreign policy.

The Russian Revolution of 1917, on the other hand, was an example of how a nation's foreign policy outlook could be radically altered as a result of a change in national values or, if you will, ideology. When the Bolsheviks came to power in 1917, they had a significant threat of outside invasion with which to contend. But they also brought with them something the tzars never possessed—an ideological orientation that was universal in scope and which gave the messianic strain in the Russian national character a dangerous new outlet in the form of a world revolutionary vision. The scope of tsarist ambitions was largely defined by the desire to unite the Slavic peoples under Russian rule (Pan-Slavism) and to acquire warm-water ports for Russia's navy and commercial shipping; under Marxism-Leninism, the scope of Soviet ambition became unlimited. Therefore, to attempt to explain the recent strategic outlook of the former Soviet Union (let alone the present or future outlook of the separate republics) in terms of tzarist tradition, without reckoning with the historical discontinuity resulting from the Russian Revolution, is as illogical as attempting to explain the current foreign policy outlook of the United States in terms of its historical situation in 1793.

This book, then, bases its methodology (with certain qualifications) on the assumption of the third school of thought described by Ermarth, which is that the Soviets mean substantially what they say. The reasoning behind this position has been most cogently stated in the monograph *Soviet Strategy for the Seventies: From Cold War to Peaceful Coexistence*:

> The members of the ruling hierarchy provide through their public utterances a substantially accurate picture of what they are up to and why, at least in a strategic sense. This is due to the requirement for uniformity that is so vital to the Soviet political system. Not only must those at the top speak with a single voice, but the entire hierarchy must echo that voice. Words are a critical factor in holding the system together . . . . The only way in which the regime can carry forward a program or effect a change in direction without creating confusion and uncertainty is to talk about it.[16]

The danger in attempting to analyze open-source Soviet writings, of course, is to have a means for distinguishing those statements reflecting the "real" Soviet perception from those which are merely part of the overall Soviet strategy of *desinformatsiya* (disinformation) against a particular U.S. strategic doctrine or program during any given period. The primary hypothesis of this book is that the real Soviet perception of any given U.S. strategic doctrine was reflected in their own "mirror-image" projections of their own strategic thinking and priorities onto U.S. doctrine and policy. All statements, analyses, and conclusions that were consistent with this "mirror-image" projection reflected the actual Soviet view; those statements that were clearly at odds with the Soviet "mirror-image" logic were part of the Soviet *desinformatsiya* strategy.[17] The authors firmly believe that this methodology has significant predictive potential as an intelligence tool; present and future Russian strategic priorities can be discerned by careful examination of their analyses of U.S. strategy. What might appear to the casual reader to have been merely a "misreading" of U.S. strategy and intentions was in fact either an unconscious or veiled discussion of Soviet strategy and intentions. As will be seen in the concluding chapter, this predictive methodology has profound implications for forecasting likely scenarios for the sovereign Commonwealth republics.

Soviet *desinformatsiya* statements can be identified largely by their intended purpose: to discredit or otherwise reduce the credibility of U.S. strategic doctrine's deterrent value against Soviet use of military power in support of its foreign policy goals. This practice could also be called "declaratory deterrence."[18] By publicly denying the validity of U.S. doctrine, the Soviets were in effect saying to the U.S., "We are not going to 'play by your rules'; since we will not react in the manner in which your doctrine assumes we will react, it is therefore invalid."

As an additional check to verify the validity of the "real" Soviet view of U.S. strategic doctrine, Soviet foreign policy behavior during each period of U.S. doctrinal development was compared with Soviet analyses of U.S. doctrine. This comparison helped determine whether stated Soviet perceptions were consistent with their actual behavior, as well as to what degree U.S. doctrine affected Soviet doctrine and force structure.

Sources used in this book consist mainly of open Soviet publications. These are periodical publications for the most part, supplemented by representative books, pamphlets, and newspaper articles from each period. Translations of some of these sources into English were done either by the Soviets themselves or by translation services such as the Foreign Broadcast Information Service (FBIS), the Joint Publications Research Service (JPRS), RAND Corporation, and the U.S. Air Force. The selection of periodicals and books was intended to provide as wide and diverse an array of military and political viewpoints as possible within the highly structured Soviet system. The most valuable and authoritative periodical, particularly as a check against more "open" Soviet sources, has been the formerly classified Soviet General Staff journal *Voennaya Mysl'* (Military Thought), a complete collection of which was recently made available to the general public through the services of East View Publications. Some articles from Soviet periodicals such as *Kommunist Vooruzhennykh Sil* (Communist of the Armed Forces), *Mirovaia Ekonomika i Mezhdunarodnaya Otnosheniia* (World Economy and International Relations), *Voenno-Istoricheskii Zhurnal* (Military-Historical Journal), as well as certain later issues of *Voennaia Mysl'*, have been translated by the authors. Other periodicals used were *New Times, International Affairs* (Moscow), *SShA: Ekonomika, Politika, Ideologia* (USA: Economics, Politics, Ideology), and *Soviet Military Review*.

These sources have been used by scholars such as Raymond Garthoff, Herbert Dinerstein, Thomas Wolfe, Leon Goure, Roman Kolkowicz, William Kintner, William Scott, and Harriet Scott in assessing Soviet strategic doctrine. Some of these analysts have done research similar in nature to this book, although the analyses have covered a much shorter period of time. Most of the early analyses, for example, were done by the RAND Corporation in the late 1950s and early 1960s, with Dinerstein, Goure, Wolfe and Kolkowicz providing the bulk of such studies. Later efforts by other authors include Kintner and H. Scott, *The Nuclear Revolution in Soviet Military Affairs;* S. Gibert, *Soviet Images of America;* L. Frank, *Soviet Nuclear Planning: A Point of View on SALT;* and Goure, Kohler, and Harvey, *The Role of Nuclear Forces in Current Soviet Strategy.* The works of these authors dealt with the Soviet perspective from a contemporary point of view rather than the evolutionary perspective used in this book. By focusing on too narrow an historical period, it is not possible to gain a true sense of the continuity and change in the overall Soviet perspective over time. We believe that this research avoids that mistake.

One final word on methodology is needed. Given the greater access in recent years to Soviet military officers and political spokesmen, which ostensibly has been brought about by Gorbachev's policy of *glasnost,* the reader may wonder why we have not taken advantage of these opportunities to interview high-ranking Soviet military officers. We do not believe that such interviews would lend our research any greater scholarly authenticity, for one thing. It is highly unlikely that one is going to obtain authoritative perceptions and analyses from isolated interviews with individual officers or political spokesmen. For another thing, the motives of the interviewees would be extremely suspect, to say the least, given the well-known history of Soviet *desinformatsiya* practices. Probably the best argument against the use of interviews in this context was given by journalist Tom Diaz, formerly an editor of the *Washington Times:*

> Journalists understand the concept of manipulation in the abstract. In fact, they often sit around and talk among themselves about the motivations of sources. But none ever thinks or is willing to admit that he has been manipulated himself.[19]

As in the first edition of this book, the research concerning the Soviet perspective is organized chronologically, for the most part. The only exceptions to this are in Part I, which is comprised of a doctrinal overview of both U.S. and Soviet strategic doctrinal development. This is designed to give the reader an appreciation of the strategic mindsets of both sides before exploring the perception of the Soviets vis-à-vis U.S. strategy. Parts Two through Four take the reader through an evolutionary examination of the Soviet viewpoint of U.S. strategic doctrine, as well as describing the Soviet *desinformatsiya* themes used during any given period. Part Five discusses the Soviet perspective on SDI, and closes with a chapter projecting the future of U.S. and Russian strategic doctrine based on the foregoing analysis. In addition, in light of the recent U.S. experience in Operation Desert Storm, we have decided to introduce a new theory we have developed which explains the impact of Ballistic Missile

Defense (BMD) on the future of operational warfare. We hope that it will provide the basis for much sober discussion about just where the U.S. is headed in a world of increasing nuclear proliferation and decreasing political stability.

Notes

1. See Jonathan Lockwood, *The Soviet View of US Strategic Doctrine: Implications for Decisionmaking* (New Brunswick, N.J.: Transaction Press, 1983), 179-82. I also recommended that the US freeze additional development of offensive strategic forces in order to accelerate the development and deployment of the three-tiered strategic defense. I believed then, and still believe, that additional offensive nuclear forces do not significantly enhance deterrence from the Soviet perspective as decisively as would strategic defense, particularly since the US still possesses no deployed strategic defense.
2. Henry Kissinger, "Soviet Good Will—Don't Count On It," *Washington Post*, A27, August 13, 1991.
3. See A.I. Solzhenitsyn, *The Mortal Danger: How Misperceptions About Russia Imperil America*. Cited in E.P. Hoffmann and R.F. Laird, *The Soviet Polity in the Modern Era* (New York: Aldine Publishing Company, 1984), 31.
4. See Jim Hoaglund, "The Other Cold War Goes On," *Washington Post*, 13 August 1991. See also John Barry and Karen Breslau, "All Unhappy on the Eastern Front," *Newsweek*, August 5, 1991, 38.
5. Barry and Breslau, "All Unhappy," 38.
6. Cited in David Remnick, "Reformist Yakovlev Quits Communist Party," *Washington Post*, August 17, 1991.
7. Ibid.
8. See Fred Hiatt, "Soviet Republics See A-Weapons as Bargaining Chips," *Washington Post*, 24 October, 1991, A41.
9. See Raymond Garthoff, *Deterrence and the Revolution in Soviet Military Doctrine* (Washington D.C.: The Brookings Institution, 1990), 24-28. Garthoff acknowledges the existence of different mindsets, but dismisses them as "misperceptions" rather than projections of their own mindset onto U.S. doctrine.
10. Barry and Breslau, "All Unhappy," 38.
11. An analysis of the Soviet perspective of the United States over a range of issues and areas, including a section on U.S. doctrine, is found in Stephen Gibert *Soviet Images of America* (New York: Crane, Russak, 1978). Its main problem, like that of Garthoff and other analysts, is its contemporary perspective; the analysis does not go back farther than the period of realistic deterrence beginning in 1969 and tends to focus primarily on that period.
12. Fritz W. Ermarth, "Contrasts in American and Soviet Strategic Thought," *International Security*, 3 (Fall 1978): 140.
13. Ibid., 140-1. The questions have been paraphrased slightly to suit this subject.
14. See R. Garthoff, *Deterrence and Revolution*. Garthoff's latest work provides a premier example of this line of thinking. He contends that the latest revolution in Soviet military doctrine has resulted in greater similarity between U.S. and Soviet strategic thinking, and hence greater common ground for arms control negotiations.
15. Two useful recent works that discuss all three schools of thought are W.C. Green and T. Karasik, eds., *Gorbachev and His Generals: The Reform of Soviet Military Doctrine* (Boulder, Colo.: Westview Press, 1990), S.M. Lynn-Jones, S.E. Miller,

and S.V. Evera, eds., *Soviet Military Policy* (Cambridge, Mass.: MIT Press, 1989). A direct counterpoint to Garthoff's thinking is found in H.F. Scott and W.F. Scott, *Soviet Military Doctrine: Continuity, Formulation, and Dissemination* (Boulder, Colo.: Westview Press, 1988).

16. F.D. Kohler, et al., *Soviet Strategy for the Seventies: From Cold War to Peaceful Coexistence* (Coral Gables, Fla.: Center for Advanced International Studies, 1973), 5.

17. The Soviet practice of declaratory *desinformatsiya* in their public pronouncements as an integral part of Soviet strategic deception has been extensively documented in recent years. Excellent works on the subject are R.H. Shultz and R. Godson, *Dezinformatsia: Active Measures in Soviet Strategy* (Washington, D.C.: Pergamon-Brassey's, 1984); L. Bittman, *The KGB and Soviet Disinformation: An Insider's View* (Washington, D.C.: Pergamon-Brassey's, 1985); B.D. Dailey and P.J. Parker, eds., *Soviet Strategic Deception* (Lexington, Mass.: D.C. Heath & Co., 1987); and C. Andrew and O. Gordievsky, *KGB: The Inside Story* (New York: Harper Collins Publishers, 1990).

18. The terms "declaratory deterrrence" and "desinformatsiya" are used interchangably throughout the book.

19. Attributed to Tom Diaz (in an interview, of course!), "Seminar on Research About Intelligence", August 1991, sponsored by the Consortium for the Study of Intelligence.

Part I

DOCTRINAL OVERVIEW

1
The Development of U.S. Strategic Doctrine

The term "massive retaliation" first came into vogue as a result of a speech made by then Secretary of State John Foster Dulles on January 12, 1954, in which he stated that "local defenses must be reinforced by the further deterrent of massive retaliatory power." This marked the first official enunciation of an official strategic doctrine by an American administration. Dulles's statement, remarkable enough by itself, gained further importance from other statements within the context of his speech, which implied that primary reliance would be placed on strategic power for deterring local aggression.[1]

Actually, the idea of massive retaliation as a strategic doctrine did not originate with Dulles' statement in 1954. Prior to his speech, the Eisenhower administration had in 1953 inaugurated the so-called "New Look," which was a strategic program based largely on economic considerations. Not wishing to spend enormous sums of money for defense for fear of damaging the national economy in the long run, the administration decided that severe budget constraints should be placed on the military in general. In addition, the main effort was to be made in developing strategic air power in hopes of maximizing deterrence at minimum cost.[2]

The strategic rationale behind massive retaliation was also fairly straightforward. Its deterrent value rested "upon a great capacity to retaliate, instantly, by means and at places of our own choosing."[3] This stressed the importance of seizing and retaining the strategic initiative, a distinctively military consideration. Deterrence would be achieved by forcing the Soviet Union to consider the possibility that any local aggression they initiated might provoke a nuclear response by U.S. strategic air power on cities in the Soviet heartland.[4]

The major difficulties of the massive retaliation doctrine as a credible strategy were twofold. The first difficulty lay in the reasoning behind the doctrine itself. A doctrine of massive retaliation served mainly to deter a direct attack against the United States itself, and in retrospect arguably acted as a deterrent against a Soviet invasion of Western Europe. However, for conflicts short of such magnitude, it was clear that the Soviets were not completely convinced of the credibility of the American threat. The outstanding example of this was the Korean War. Well before the formal declaration of massive retaliation, the Korean conflict was a precedent that rejected the tenets of that doctrine. Not only had the United States not seized the strategic initiative in that conflict, it deliberately sought to keep the conflict limited by deliberately not attempting to carry the war beyond the bounds of the Korean peninsula to the Soviet Union, or even to the Peoples Republic of China (PRC). Given such a precedent, the declaration of massive retaliation in 1954 made little sense other than as a repudiation of engaging again in Korean-style intervention in response to local aggression. Nevertheless, the Soviets did not consider this threat credible enough to prevent them from intervening in Hungary in 1956 or from indulging in "saber rattling" exercises in the Suez and Berlin crises.[5]

The credibility of massive retaliation depended heavily on the belief that the United States would remain relatively invulnerable to retaliatory strikes by the Soviet Union. While the United States had an atomic monopoly from 1945 to 1949, this belief was well founded. However, once the Soviet Union had begun to develop and stockpile atomic and hydrogen bombs, it possessed the makings of a strategic deterrent, no matter how few and unreliable the early means of delivery might be. Even though Soviet bombers of the mid- to late 1950s could only have reached the continental United States on one-way missions, this alone nullified the basic assumption of massive retaliation— the assumption that the United States could launch a major nuclear attack on the Soviet Union and emerge totally unscathed.[6] Once the United States' leadership realized this, there was a gradual move toward the advocacy of "tactical" use of lower-yield nuclear weapons as a more "believable" response to local aggression.[7]

The other major problem with massive retaliation was that the United States did not actually have, at least until the late 1950s, the capacity to inflict a decisive degree of absolute damage on the Soviet Union. Until the acquisition of the B-52 bomber in 1955, the workhorse of U.S. strategic air power was the B-29, followed by the B-36 and B-47 medium-range bombers, all of which had to be based overseas in Great Britain and Western Europe in order to be within range of the Soviet heartland. The preponderance of U.S. strategic air power in relative terms arguably would not have been enough by itself to prevent the Soviet Army from occupying Western Europe, thus depriving the United States of most of its bases.[8] And there is little doubt that the Soviet Union could have done so if war occurred, since NATO forces were insufficient in number to be much more than a "trip-wire" to verify the fact of invasion.

The predominant attitude behind the strategy of massive retaliation was one that saw the nuclear weapon as an *absolute* weapon, capable of deciding the outcome of a war by itself. As will be seen in a subsequent chapter, the Soviets did not agree with this view. In order for U.S. strategic doctrine to have any credibility, it was necessary to have means for dealing with Soviet sponsored aggression that could not be adequately deterred by strategic air power alone. It was thus that the doctrine of limited war evolved.

The U.S. Rationale for Limited War

In the October 1957 issue of *Foreign Affairs*, the Secretary of State, John Foster Dulles, announced a modification in the strategic doctrine of the United States. Instead of a doctrine of pure massive retaliation, the new concept was later to be known as "graduated deterrence."[9] Subsumed under this concept was the use of limited war as an instrument of the policy of "containment."[10] Dulles characterized the need for additional nuclear deterrence on a smaller scale in an article where he stated:

> However, the United States has not been content to rely upon a peace which could be preserved only by a capacity to destroy vast segments of the human race. Such a concept is acceptable only as a last alternative . . . .
> In the future it may be thus feasible to place less reliance upon deterrence of vast retaliatory power. It may be possible to defend countries by nuclear weapons so mobile, or so placed, as to make military invasion with conventional weapons a hazardous attempt. Thus . . . the nations which are around the Sino-Soviet perimeter can possess an effective defense against full scale conventional attack and thus confront any aggressor with the choice between failing or himself initiating nuclear war against the defending country . . . .[11]

There were several important considerations that justified the development of a doctrine of limited war. Henry Kissinger, in his book, *Nuclear Weapons and Foreign Policy*, published in 1958, listed the following three reasons:

1. Limited war represents the only means for preventing the Soviet bloc, at an acceptable cost, from overrunning the peripheral areas of Eurasia.
2. A wide range of military capabilities may spell the difference between defeat and victory in an all-out war.
3. Intermediate applications of U.S. power offer the best chance to bring about strategic changes favorable to the United States.[12]

The employment of limited wars, as explained by Kissinger, provided a means for the United States to enforce its policy of containment as an acceptable cost. Although the massive retaliation doctrine had done an acceptable job of deterring a Soviet attack on the United States or western Europe, it was becoming less and less effective against lesser forms of aggression because of the growing Soviet capability to retaliate against the United States.[13] Under the massive retaliation doctrine, the United States could respond to limited acts of aggression only with either inaction or all-out war. Massive retaliation relied primarily on the credibility of the U.S. threat to strike the Soviet homeland in order to reduce the change of local aggression ever occurring, which would permit the U.S. to spend minimal amounts of her resources on the strengthening of conventional forces.[14] Once the Soviets had developed an intercontinental ballistic missile (ICBM) capability, this threat was less believable because of increased U.S. vulnerability to retaliation. An alternative to either waging all-out war or simply doing nothing was therefore needed in order to strengthen U.S. deterrent power.

A limited war strategy required a wider range of military capabilities than under the massive retaliation doctrine, capabilities that Kissinger argued could provide victory even in the event of an all-out war. Since it was possible that a nuclear exchange might result in the exhaustion of the strategic stockpiles of both sides, a premium would then be placed on other elements of military power in order to decide the victor. A capacity to wage limited war would therefore be valuable in the event of escalation to general war as well as in fighting limited wars. This reasoning would subsequently provide the basis for the even broader requirements of the later doctrine of flexible response.

Limited war was not supposed to replace the threat of massive retaliation. Instead, the idea was to shift the risk of initiating an all-out war with the Soviet Union by using the U.S. capability for massive retaliation as a "shield" against Soviet initiation of nuclear war. This would enable the U.S. to fight local actions on its own terms, inflicting local reverses against attempted Soviet gains.

Such a strategy was not without its weaknesses, however; although it reduced the chances of escalation to general nuclear war, it increased the likelihood of local aggression. This was because the Soviets, since they did not have to fear the threat of massive retaliation if they initiated a local war, would therefore be less discouraged from engaging in less risky forms of conflict. On the other hand, though the massive retaliation strategy theoretically minimized the chance that a local act of aggression would ever occur (assuming, of course, that the Soviets believed the threat to be completely credible), it also maximized the probability of escalation to general nuclear war. Given the fact that the massive retaliation strategy was becoming less effective, the necessity of engaging in local conflicts in order to enforce containment was a more palatable choice.

Limited war, then, involved the imposition on oneself of limited means in order to attain correspondingly limited goals. This strategy became readily accepted in the United States, mainly because the thought of actually having to employ nuclear weapons in an all-out conflict had become an unthinkable prospect, according to analysts such as Bernard Brodie.[15] The concept of limited war was the first step taken by the United States in the direction of more limited uses of military power in order to support a foreign policy of containment. It would remain the centerpiece of the subsequently declared doctrine of flexible response during the Kennedy administration.

The U.S. Doctrine of Flexible Response

The principles of flexible response were formally declared by Defense Secretary Robert S. McNamara in a speech before the American Bar Association on February 17, 1962.[16] The real doctrine of flexible response, however, can be said to have been laid by General Maxwell D. Taylor. In his book, *The Uncertain Trumpet*, first published in 1959, Taylor postulated a U.S. need to have the capability to "react across the entire spectrum of possible challenge." The reasoning behind Taylor's assertion was that "it is just as necessary to deter or win quickly a limited war as to deter general war. Otherwise, the limited war which we cannot win quickly may result in our piecemeal attrition or involvement in an expanding conflict."[17] Taylor's motivation was also a more realistic effort on behalf of the recently neglected active Army. By formulating a strategic doctrine that recognized that the nuclear boundary was too easily reached, he could cause more attention to be given to building up conventional forces. Among the military services, all vying for limited funds, the U.S. Army would be the chief beneficiary.[18]

In the January 1961 issue of *Foreign Affairs,* General Taylor was the first to actually use the phrase which was the keynote of the new Kennedy administration's strategic doctrine. Addressing the problem of a strategic doctrine outmoded by an unfavorably altered military balance, Taylor said:

> What are the principles which need to be asserted and accepted as the platform for a new military balance? The most obvious one, perhaps, is that world conditions have changed drastically since the adoption of the New Look in 1953 and its supporting strategy of massive retaliation, and that a new program is needed which will take the changes into account. Such a program needs to be based on a flexible military strategy designed to deter war, large or small, and to assist the West in winning the cold war.[19]

McNamara further defined the need for "balanced forces":

> As we develop a balanced, modern non-nuclear force, ready to move rapidly against aggression in any part of the world, we continue to inhibit the opportunities for the successful conduct of Khrushchev's "local wars" [i.e., "wars of national liberation"]. It is tempting to conclude that our conventional forces will leave us free to compete with communism in the peaceful sphere of economic and social development, where we can compete most effectively.[20]

McNamara then described the threat from Communist "insurgency" movements in Third World countries and outlined the proposed strategy of "counterinsurgency." It is obvious that the doctrine of flexible response, in trying to respond to the complete spectrum of conceivable threats, required far larger military expenditures across the board than the massive retaliation strategy under the Eisenhower administration.

At the same time that flexible response was officially adopted as doctrine, however, there was a movement sponsored by the newly ascendant "systems analysis" school in the Defense Department. These analysts were looking for a more "organized" approach to the question, "How much is enough?" This produced a clash between the flexible response doctrine, which tended to push the requirements for strategic forces upwards, and the cost-effectiveness calculations of the systems analysts, which pushed such requirements downwards.[21]

However, the chief test of flexible response was to be the war in Indochina, which initially proved frustrating for the advocates of flexible response and ultimately proved a serious setback. The major change in U.S. strategic doctrine after this period, though still emphasizing the desirability of a wide range of options as a response and deterrent to Soviet aggression, would deemphasize the requirement for the participation of U.S. combat forces. Instead, it would be the nations under attack that would bear the main burden of providing the manpower.[22]

The McNamara Concepts

During the period of flexible response, McNamara devised several strategic nuclear concepts that were to influence U.S. strategic doctrine long after the demise of the flexible response doctrine itself. These concepts—called counterforce, damage limitation, and assured destruction—therefore deserve special attention. The first concept was enunciated by McNamara in an address at Ann Arbor, Michigan, on June 16, 1962.[23] The concepts of damage limitation and assured destruction were explained by McNamara in statements before the Committee on Armed Services and the Subcommittee on Department of Defense of the Committee on Appropriations, U.S. Senate, February 24, 1962.[24]

Another concept gained prominence during this period, although it was not officially a part of U.S. strategic doctrine. This was the concept of escalation, an idea given its theoretical birth by Herman Kahn in his book, *On Escalation*. The principal feature of this work was the 44-step "escalation ladder," which ran the gamut of levels of conflict from "pre-crisis maneuvering" to the ultimate paroxysm of violence, called "spasm war."[25] Although this concept was quite influential, it had been intended only as a descriptive model rather than a prescriptive guideline for policy. It is mentioned here because the Soviets mistakenly perceived it as an actual tenet of U.S. strategic doctrine. This nature and consequences of this error will be discussed in a later chapter.

In outlining the counterforce strategy, McNamara was assuming that the United States, along with NATO, had "overall nuclear strength adequate to any challenge confronting it," and that "this strength not only minimizes the likelihood of major nuclear war but makes possible a strategy designed to preserve the fabric of our societies if war should occur." McNamara stated the essence of the counterforce strategy in the following passage:

> The United States has come to the conclusion that, to the extent feasible, basic military strategy in a possible general nuclear war should be approached in much the same way that more conventional military operations have been regarded in the past. This is to say, principal military objectives, in the event of a nuclear war stemming from a major attack on the alliance, should be the destruction of the enemy's military forces, not of his civilian population.[26]

There were two important implications of the counterforce strategy as outlined by McNamara. The more significant was the implication that the United States would initiate a "preemptive strike" on Soviet nuclear forces in response to a "major attack on the alliance" and not merely as a response to a surprise attack on the United States. Any references to a first strike were subsequently downplayed in favor of a retaliatory posture. Nevertheless, given this kind of statement, it is not surprising that Soviet analysts would see their own idea of the "preemptive blow" in the counterforce strategy, since counterforce lent itself easily to the idea of a first strike (after all, a counterforce attack would be more effective before the enemy launched his missiles). Also implicit in McNamara's statement was the idea of "city avoidance," that is, not targeting civilian population centers as ends in themselves.

Counterforce remained the dominant concept in U.S. nuclear strategy for only a short while. It began to lose prominence after 1964 with the rise of the damage limitation and assured destruction strategies. McNamara outlined these new ideas in his speech before the Senate Committee on Armed Services in February, 1965:

> The first of these capabilities required to deter potential aggressors we call "assured destruction," i.e., the capability to destroy the aggressor as a viable society even after a well-planned surprise attack on our forces. The second capability we call "damage limitation," i.e., the capability to reduce the weight of the enemy attack by both offensive and defensive measures and to provide a degree of protection for the population against the effects of nuclear detonations.[27]

However, there was a serious contradiction between these two ideas. A damage limitation approach, when taken in conjunction with a strategy of counterforce, most resembled a nuclear warfighting doctrine based on having an ability to survive a nuclear war. On the other hand, assured destruction led in the opposite direction to a "war avoidance" strategy that relied on the threat of being able to inflict "unacceptable damage" on the Soviet Union. Since an assured destruction strategy was obviously cheaper to implement than a nuclear warfighting strategy, it was deemed a more cost-effective solution by McNamara. Indeed, McNamara later defined unacceptable damage as "the capability to destroy one-quarter to one-third of [the enemy's] population and about two-thirds of [the enemy's] industrial capacity."[28] This was a retreat only in degree from the initial definition of assured destruction, which was the ability "to destroy the enemy as a viable society." This pragmatic but still morally empty line of thinking was the major strategic consequence that the systems analysis school of thought was to have for U.S. strategic doctrine.

The assured destruction strategy, which was later to evolve into the doctrine of mutual assured destruction, was also as much an arms-control concept as it was a strategy. As it became more dominant, coupled with the growth of Soviet strategic forces to near parity by 1969, counterforce and damage limitation were discarded. Since assured destruction later called for only a "minimum" capability to inflict unacceptable damage, force level requirements were correspondingly lowered. This was the reasoning behind the decision to freeze ICBM deployment at 1,054 and submarine-launched ballistic missiles (SLBMs) at 656 after 1965.[29]

Also implied in the strategy of mutual assured destruction was McNamara's assumption that "both sides have the same general strategic objectives." From this followed the reasoning that "our assured destruction problem is the other side's damage limiting problem, and our damage limiting problem is their assured destruction problem."[30] As will be seen in the following chapter on Soviet doctrinal development, however, this assumption was incorrect.

The general course of U.S. nuclear strategy during the 1960s, therefore was marked by a gradual transition from the warfighting-oriented strategies of counterforce and damage limitation to the war avoidance strategy of mutual assured destruction by the late 1960s and early 1970s. This strategy was to heavily influence subsequent developments in U.S. strategic doctrine.

The U.S. Doctrine of Realistic Deterrence

On February 17, 1972, Secretary of Defense Melvin R. Laird formally outlined in detail the tenets of the new strategic doctrine that had, in effect, been adopted shortly after the accession of President Nixon to office in January of 1969. The new doctrine, although given the name realistic deterrence by Laird in his 1972 statement, had earlier been known as the "Nixon Doctrine."[31] Secretary Laird stated the necessity for a "new" approach to national security strategy:

> Successful implementation of the strategy of realistic deterrence is, I believe, the most difficult and challenging national security effort this country has ever undertaken. This is so because we most move forward in an environment of virtual balance in the strategic nuclear field, and in a period of vigorous Soviet military expansion at sea, on the land, in the air, and in s pace. In addition, we must pursue our goal with due regard for the influences of today's other constraining realities—realities which I will discuss at some length.[32]

According to Secretary Laird, the defense strategy of the United States was to be based on the following three main aspects of the Nixon Doctrine:

1. The United States would keep all of its treaty commitments.
2. The United States would "provide a shield" if any nuclear power threatened the freedom of a nation allied with the United States or of a nation whose survival the United States considered vital to its security.
3. In cases involving "other types of aggression" the United States would furnish military and economic assistance when requested and as appropriate. The United States, however, would "look to the nation directly threatened to assume the primary responsibility for providing the manpower for its defense.[33]

In other words, realistic deterrence would place primary emphasis on U.S. strategic power only for deterring strategic nuclear war between the United States and the Soviet Union. For theater nuclear and other conventional conflicts, the United States should share the burden of deterrence with its allies. Deterrence of communist insurgency wars was to be the main responsibility of the country being threatened, with the United States providing only logistical support except in those cases where the United States believed a vital interest was at stake.[34]

For the purpose of this book, it is best to concentrate on the portion of realistic deterrence that was concerned with deterrence of strategic nuclear war between the superpowers. From the standpoint of how much offensive strength was needed for a believable deterrent, the requirement had been steadily declining. From a requirement for "superiority" during the 1950s and early 1960s, this had changed to "parity" in 1964, and again to "sufficiency by 1969.[35] In addition to the concept of MAD, the term "crisis stability" was now added. This simply meant the maintenance of "an adequate second strike capability to deter an all-out surprise attack" on U.S. strategic forces with the objective of "providing no incentive for the Soviet Union to strike the United States first in a crisis."[36]

Another part of the requirement for sufficiency was the retention of the ability to inflict roughly equal amounts of damage vis 'a vis the Soviet Union. The idea was to prevent the Soviets "from gaining the ability to cause considerably greater urban/industrial destruction than the United States would inflict on the Soviets in a nuclear war." Although the stress was still on targeting cities, counterforce gradually began to receive greater attention as a way of dealing with lesser challenges short of an all-out exchange.[37] However, these efforts were impaired by the U.S. lack of a significant ability to destroy Soviet missile silos. And while the possible effectiveness of the Soviet civil defense program might be open to question, there is little doubt that it would have been more effective than the comparatively nonexistent U.S. civil defense capability. This raised significant doubts about the ability of the United States to achieve assured destruction against Soviet cities.[38]

The other side of the sufficiency coin was the ability to defend "against damage from small attacks or accidental launches."[39] This need was supposedly taken care of by the installation of the Safeguard antiballistic missile system (ABM) which however, was abandoned after the construction of only the early-warning sites.[40]

Thus, the doctrine of realistic deterrence neither served to foster the kind of strategic flexibility deemed necessary by President Nixon,[41] nor appreciably affected the U.S. force posture and defense programs. The criteria of parity, sufficiency, and eventually "essential equivalence" were all attempts to apply rigid rules emphasizing statistical strengths as opposed to comparative capabilities. Using these criteria, arms-control efforts became vital to the defense posture, and not merely convenient or desirable.[42] Although some half-hearted attempts had been made to move away from the pure retaliatory posture of MAD, no important proposed changes were to be declared until the announcement of the Schlesinger Doctrine in January 1974.

The Schlesinger Doctrine and Limited Nuclear Options

In his annual Defense Department report to the Congress for fiscal year 1975, Defense Secretary James Schlesinger set forth principles for a new U.S. strategic doctrine. Schlesinger outlined the main features of the proposed new strategic posture as follows:

1. A capability sufficiently large, diversified, and survivable also as to provide us at all times with high confidence of riding out even a massive surprise attack and of penetrating enemy defenses, and with the ability to withhold an assured destruction reserve for an extended period of time.
2. Sufficient warning to insure the survival of our heavy bombers together with the bomb alarm systems and command control capabilities required by out National Command Authorities to direct the employment of the strategic forces in a controlled, selective, and restrained fashion.

3. The forces to execute a wide range of options in response to potential actions by an enemy, including a capability for precise attacks on both soft and hard targets, while at the same time minimizing unintended collateral damage.
4. The avoidance of any combination of forces that could be taken as an effort to acquire the ability to execute a first-strike disarming attack against the Soviet Union.
5. An offensive capability of such size and composition that all will perceive it as an overall balance with the strategic forces of any potential opponent.
6. Offensive and defense capabilities and programs that conform with the provisions of current arms-control agreements and at the same time facilitate the conclusion of more permanent treaties to control and, if possible, reduce the nuclear arsenals.[43]

It was the second and third features of the proposed posture that were to cause the greatest interest and consternation among Soviet analysts. These particular tenets were calling for increased nuclear targeting flexibility so as to create a greater number of options for a U.S. president to choose from in the event of a confrontation. In arguing for such flexible options, Schlesinger pointed out that credible deterrence must rest on the possession of a wide range of options with matching capabilities:

> Threats against allied forces, to the extent that they could be deterred by the prospect of nuclear retaliation, demand both more limited responses than destroying cities and advanced planning tailored to such lesser responses. Nuclear threats to our strategic forces, whether limited or large-scale, might well call for an option to respond in kind against the attacker's military forces. In other words, to be credible and hence effective over the range of possibility contingencies, deterrence must rest on many options and on a spectrum of capabilities to support these options.[44]

Schlesinger further argued that "flexibility of response is also essential because, despite our best efforts, we cannot guarantee that deterrence will never fail, nor can we forecast the situations that would cause it to fail." His rationale for limited nuclear options under these circumstances was based on his assertion that "if deterrence fails, we may be able to bring all but the largest nuclear conflicts to a rapid conclusion before cities are struck. Damage may thus be limited and further escalation avoided."[45]

It is interesting that Schlesinger referred to the formerly discarded concept of damage limitation, particularly within the context of a warfighting scenario if deterrence failed. Although the assured destruction strategy was still in use, it was no longer an arbitrary measure of population fatalities. Instead, it was to be a gauge in terms of postwar political objectives that were relevant to a nuclear war. Deterrence was now also a function of postwar political objectives;

mainly, a reduction of the enemy's ability to recover quickly from the effects of a nuclear war and to attain a superior political-military position. The Schlesinger doctrine would therefore seem to lend itself more to a nuclear warfighting doctrine than the deterrence-oriented strategy of MAD.[46]

Ironically enough, the concepts then being resurrected by Schlesinger had previously been abandoned in order to exercise a self-restraint that, it had been hoped, the Soviets would imitate, only to be reconsidered later precisely because of the lack of any such restraint on their part. Indeed, the Soviet buildup rendered the U.S. assured destruction capability highly questionable except as a deterrent to the threat of a massive Soviet attack on U.S. cities as well as on U.S. strategic forces. The continuous growth of the Soviets' strategic power coupled with their steadfast rejection of the notion of mutual assured destruction eventually forced the U.S. to reconsider its strategic doctrine.[47]

The logic behind the strategy of limited nuclear options (LNO) was two-fold. First, it was designed to introduce more flexibility into the available range of options for the use of strategic nuclear weapons so that, in a crisis, the president could theoretically order the *selective* use of nuclear weapons on military targets in the Soviet Union. The idea was to create the greatest uncertainty possible in the minds of Soviet leaders about what action the United States would be likely to take in response to a Soviet move that threatened an American vital interest. Ideally, this uncertainty would be so great that the Soviet leadership would be inhibited from making any aggressive moves. Second, the purpose was to strengthen the overall credibility of the U.S. deterrence strategy, which was correctly believed to have been eroded by continued reliance on an all-out nuclear response as embodied in the concept of MAD.

However, once Schlesinger was fired by President Ford in 1976, the issue of whether to modify U.S. strategic doctrine in the direction of a nuclear war-fighting strategy was temporarily sidetracked. After the demise of LNO, there was essentially a hiatus in U.S. doctrinal development until President Carter announced a change in U.S. strategy in August 1980.

Presidential Directive 59

In a speech to the Naval War College on August 20, 1980, Defense Secretary Harold Brown explained the Carter administration's new concept of nuclear strategy:

> The overriding objective of United States strategic nuclear forces is to deter nuclear war, for which three requirements must be met. First, we must have strategic nuclear forces that can absorb a Soviet first strike and still retaliate with devastating effect. Second, we must meet our security requirements and maintain an overall strategic balance at the lowest and most stable levels. Third, we must have a doctrine and plans for the use of our forces (if they are needed) that make

clear to the Soviets the hard reality that, by any course leading to nuclear war, they could never gain an advantage that would outweigh the unacceptable price they would have to pay. The ability of our forces to survive a surprise attack is the essence of deterrence.[48]

PD 59 was not, in fact, anything new or innovative when compared with previous strategic doctrine, and Secretary Brown conceded as much. "It was a refinement," Brown said, "a codification of previous statements of strategic policy. PD 59 took the same essential strategic doctrine and restated it more clearly, more cogently in the light of current conditions and current capabilities."[49]

The state of U.S. strategic doctrine, therefore, was then at an impasse. Although the inherent weakness of a doctrine based merely on the threat to punish the enemy if he initiates nuclear war had been duly recognized, if reluctantly, the U.S. leadership was still unable to bring itself to the point of wholehearted adherence to a nuclear warfighting doctrine. However, during the Reagan administration, this would change drastically.

The Strategic Defense Initiative

In the closing remarks of President Reagan's 23 March, 1983 speech, he outlined the basic rationale for the Strategic Defense Initiative:

> ... What if free people could live secure in the knowledge that their security did not rest upon the threat of instant U.S. retaliation to deter a Soviet attack, that we could intercept and destroy strategic ballistic missiles before they reached our own soil or that of our allies?
>
> ... I clearly recognize that defensive systems have limitations and raise certain problems and ambiguities. If paired with offensive systems, they can be viewed as fostering an aggressive policy, and no one wants that. But, with these considerations firmly in mind, I call upon the scientific communities in our country, those who gave us nuclear weapons, to turn those great talents now to the cause of mankind and world peace, to give us the means of rendering those nuclear weapons impotent and obsolete.
>
> Tonight, consistent with our obligations of the ABM Treaty and recognizing the need for closer consultation with our allies, I'm taking an important first step. I am directing a comprehensive and intensive effort to define a long-term research and development program to begin to achieve our ultimate goal of eliminating the threat posed by strategic nuclear missiles. This could pave the way for arms control measures to eliminate the weapons themselves. We seek neither military superiority nor political advantage. Our only purpose-one all people share-is to search for ways to reduce the danger of nuclear war.[50]

President Reagan undoubtedly never thought that he was proposing a revolution in U.S. strategic doctrine; the U.S. had long been experimenting with strategic defense of one form or another against nuclear attack, with President

Nixon's abortive attempt from 1970-1974 to deploy the Safeguard ABM system as merely the most recent and unsuccessful. Nevertheless, the Strategic Defense Initiative represented a repudiation of the doctrine of Mutual Assured Destruction as the basis of strategic deterrence. This touched off a strategic debate on both sides of the Atlantic which is still going on today, even with the ostensible elimination of the strategic nuclear threat from the former Soviet Union. Indeed, in a recent article in *Defense 91*, Dr. Henry Cooper, Director of the Strategic Defense Initiative Organization, outlined the rationale for the newer Global Protection Against Limited Strikes (GPALS) system, based on lessons learned from the Desert Storm operation:

- We cannot rely on the threat of retaliation to deter potential adversaries from acquiring and using ballistic missiles. Indeed, Patriot was of strategic political importance because it helped frustrate Saddam Hussein's apparent strategy to break up the alliance by provoking Israeli retaliation; defense and continued restraint was a better Israeli option.

- Preemptive strikes against mobile missile launchers, before they send their weapons of terror on their way, are not completely effective.

- Thus, missile defenses are needed to protect our forces, citizens and friends against the not unlikely use of ballistic missiles in possible future regional conflicts.

- Space-based sensors are very important to achieving effective ground-based defenses, even for theater applications.

- Defenses do not need to work perfectly to be useful; at the same time it is clear that future defenses must improve on the demonstrated Patriot capability.

- The value of defended areas and of enabling policy options must be considered when calculating the cost-effectiveness of missile defenses. The fact that Iraqi Scuds cost far less than the allied efforts to counter them had little relevance to the now well-understood value of Patriot.[51]

With the recent success of the Patriot ATBM system against Iraqi Scuds in Operation Desert Storm, the Strategic Defense Initiative seemingly received a new lease on life. Even the Soviet leadership, albeit for unique reasons of its own, had become willing to consider the notion of joint strategic defense against ballistic missile attack.[52] And in a future world of increasing nuclear proliferation, reduced U.S. military forces, and shifting alliances, strategic defense will undoubtedly occupy a more central role in American defense policy.

Notes

1. B. Brodie, *Strategy in the Missile Age*, (Princeton, N.J.: Princeton University Press, 1959), 248.
2. Ibid., 250. For an example of how the massive retaliation doctrine was justified during the period, see P. Peters, *Massive Retaliation: The Policy and Its Critics*, (Chicago: Foundation for Foreign Affairs, 1959).
3. Brodie, *Strategy*, 250.
4. Judging by the statements made by Sokolovskiy et al in the editions of *Voennaia Strategia* (Military Strategy), published during the 1960s, the Soviets apparently understood this point very well. See V.D. Sokolovskiy, Soviet Military Strategy, ed. and trans. by Harriet Fast Scott, (New York: Crane, Russak & Company, Inc. 1968), 56-57.
5. Brodie, *Strategy*, pp. 251-253. See also R. Garthoff, *Soviet Military Policy: A Historical Analysis*, (London: Faber & Faber, 1966), 112-114.
6. R. Bonds, ed., *The Soviet War Machine*, (New York: Chartwell, 1976), p. 202.
7. Brodie, *Strategy*, 261-63.
8. E. Bottome, *The Missile Gap* (Cranbury, NJ: Associated University Presses, 1971), 221-24. For a discussion of the U.S. contingency plan for a projected war with the Soviet Union in 1957, see: A. Brown, ed., *Dropshot: The United States Plan for War with the Soviet Union in 1957*.
9. Dulles stated the broad outlines of the new policy in "Challenge and Response in U.S. Policy," *Foreign Affairs* 36, 1, (Oct 1957): 30-33.
10. For the details of the overall policy of containment and its rationale, see X (George Kennan), "The Sources of Soviet Conduct," *Foreign Affairs* 25, 4 (July 1947): 566-82.
11. Dulles, "Challenge and Response in U.S. Policy," 31.
12. H. Kissinger, *Nuclear Weapons and Foreign Policy*, (Garden City, NY: Doubleday, 1958), 125.
13. A.W. Buzzard, "Massive Retaliation and Graduated Deterrence," *World Politics* 8, 2 (January 1956): 232.
14. M.W. Hoag, *On Local War Doctrine* (Santa Monica, Calif.: The RAND Corporation, P-2433, August 1961), 6.
15. Brodie, *Strategy*, 312-14.
16. Excerpts from McNamara's speech are in J.E. Endicott and R. W. Stafford, Jr., eds., *American Defense Policy*, (New York: Johns Hopkins University Press, 1977), 71-73.
17. General M.D. Taylor, *The Uncertain Trumpet* (New York: Harper, 1959), 5-7. Quoted in J.M. Collins, *American and Soviet Military Trends since the Cuban Missile Crisis* (Washington, DC: Center for Strategic and International Studies, 1978), 158.
18. It should be noted that the Defense budget was allocated vertically, by service, rather than horizontally, by function.
19. General M.D. Taylor, "Security Will Not Wait," *Foreign Affairs* 39, 2 (January 1961): 175.
20. Endicott and Stafford, 73.
21. Bonds, *US War Machine*, 61.
22. Collins, *Military Trends*, 159-66.
23. Endicott and Stafford, 77. Excerpts from McNamara's speech, 74-75.
24. Ibid., 76-77.

25. See H. Kahn, *On Escalation: Metaphors and Scenarios* (New York: Praeger, 1965), 37-195, for a detailed description of the rungs of the escalation ladder.
26. Endicott and Stafford, 74-75.
27. Ibid.
28. Ibid.
29. Bonds, *US War Machine*, 61-62. See also Collins, *Military Trends*, 84, 94.
30. Endicott and Stafford, 75.
31. Ibid., 78.
32. Ibid.
33. Ibid., 79. Although the Nixon Doctrine included the strategy of realistic deterrence, it was intended as a general statement of degrees of defense or security commitments that the realistic deterrence strategy itself did not cover .
34. Ibid.
35. Collins, *Military Trends*, 83.
36. Endicott and Stafford, *American Defense*, 80. See also Bonds, *US War Machine*, 65.
37. Collins, *Military Trends*, 83.
38. Ibid., 85-88. See also Goure, *War Survival in Soviet Strategy* (Coral Gables, FL: Center for Advanced International Studies, 1976), 7.
39. Endicott and Stafford, *American Defense*, 80.
40. Collins, *Military Trends*, 130.
41. Endicott and Stafford, *American Defense*, 80.
42. Collins, *Military Trends*, 80-84.
43. Endicott and Stafford, *American Defense*, 87-88. See also Bonds, *US War Machine*, 65-66.
44. Endicott and Stafford, *American Defense*, 85.
45. Ibid. See also Collins, *Military Trends*, 80-81.
46. Bonds, *US War Machine*, 66.
47. Ibid.
48. Stewart Menaul, "Changing Concepts of Nuclear War," *Conflict Studies* 125 (December 1980): 4.
49. Ibid.
50. Speech by President Ronald Reagan on March 23, 1983, as cited in H. Waldman, *The Dictionary of SDI* (Wilmington, Delaware: Scholarly Resources, 1988), 176-177.
51. H.F. Cooper, "The Changing Face of SDI," *Defense* 91 (May-June 1991): 4.
52. S. Schmemann, "Gorbachev Matches U.S. on Nuclear Cuts and Goes Further on Strategic Warheads," *New York Times*, October 6, 1991, 1.

2
The Evolution of Soviet Strategic Doctrine

The period from the end of World War II through the death of Stalin in 1953 was characterized by stagnation in Soviet military thinking. Most of the commentary in Soviet publications reiterated the lessons of the past war and continually expounded on what came to be known as Stalin's "permanently operating factors" of war. Stalin's view, promulgated in 1942 after it had become apparent that the Germans had not achieved victory in their initial campaign, was that war was a massive social phenomenon in which the strengths of two or more societies were pitted against each other. Since war was a social phenomenon, it followed that it was subject to the laws that governed the development of the society itself. Within this context, the permanently operating factors would decide the outcome of the war, and not such "transitory factors" as surprise. These permanently operating factors were "the stability of the rear, the morale of the army, the quantity and quality of divisions, the armament of the army, the organizational ability of the army commanders."[1] Whichever side was superior in the permanently operating factors would be victorious.

Such a concept was a truism. Its relevance applied primarily to the world wars. In a nuclear war, it would certainly be important to have superiority in the permanently operating factors, but the question of the potential influence of the nuclear weapon on a future war was never discussed. In this sense, Stalin's ideas prohibited any serious discussion of foreign military thought until 1954.[2]

Of course, one must consider the immediate postwar strategic situation that confronted Stalin. The twin problem Stalin perceived was how to restrain the United States from reacting strongly to Soviet political moves and from attempting to exploit East European unrest. In the longer run, the larger problem he faced was how to get the Soviet Union safely through a period in which it would be vulnerable to U.S. strategic power. Stalin's solution was to downplay publicly the significance of the nuclear weapon and to emphasize instead the elements of military power in which the Soviets had the biggest advantage; namely, land power as embodied in mass armies.[3] Furthermore, by deploying large numbers of Soviet ground forces in Eastern Europe, thus giving the impression that the Soviets were preparing to invade Western Europe if war with the United States occurred, Stalin made Soviet land power an effective "counterweight" to U.S. strategic air power. By holding Western Europe hostage, so to speak, the Soviet Union had a credible deterrent against U.S. initiation of war.[4]

Soviet discussion of foreign military thought was quite limited and superficial during this period, confined for the most part to propagandistic rhetoric accusing the United States of preparing a "nuclear blitzkrieg" against the Soviet Union. Not unexpectedly, this alleged reliance on a so-called atomic blitzkrieg was decried for ignoring the permanently operating factors governing the outcome of war, and thus was doomed to failure.[5] Soviet commentary did not depart from this basic line until after the death of Stalin.

Emergence of Soviet Nuclear Strategy

After the death of Stalin, Soviet military theorists were able to express disagreement with the concept of the permanently operating factors governing the outcome of war, which had been virtually unchallenged up to that time. The first step taken in this direction was an article in *Voennaia Mysl'* by its editor, Major General N.A. Talensky, in September 1953. Although he did not completely break with Stalin's concepts, Talensky did speak of the possibility of the "decisive defeat in a limited time of one or another opponent." This opened up the discussion concerning the question of the validity of the permanently operating factors, which culminated in the rejection of the concept as "old-fashioned" three years later.[6]

This transition period was marked also by a recognition of the potential decisiveness of nuclear weapons in helping to determine the outcome of a war. This is not to say that the Soviets at any time adopted anything resembling the American notion that the nuclear weapon was an *absolute* weapon able to decide the outcome of a war by itself. Indeed, the Soviets clearly rejected such an idea, asserting that nuclear weapons could aid in achieving decisive results, but not attributing all-powerful qualities to them.[7]

There also seems to have been some early debate during the early to mid-1950s among Soviet military analysts over how much emphasis should be placed on the use of nuclear weapons. On the one hand, there were those who argued that heavy reliance should be placed on nuclear weapons as a means of achieving decisive results on the battlefield. On the other hand, there were those, such as Lieutenant General Krasilnikov of the Soviet General Staff, who claimed that "weapons of mass destruction not only require mass armed forces, but require their inevitable increase."[8] Once Nikita Khrushchev was firmly in power in 1955, however, the emphasis was to be in favor of preparation for a nuclear war, with a corresponding deemphasis on land forces.[9]

The greatest change, however, was in the Soviet estimation of the value of strategic surprise. The initial contentions were somewhat inconsistent; they simultaneously claimed the primacy of the permanently operating factors, while suggesting that a surprise attack with nuclear weapons might determine the course, and possibly the outcome, of the entire war. This debate was not entirely resolved until publication of the May 1955 issue of *Voennaia Mysl'*, in which it was stated editorially that "the task is to work out seriously all sides of this question [of surprise] and above all to elaborate ways and means of warning of surprise attack by the enemy and of dealing to the enemy preemptive blows on all levels-strategic, operational, and tactical."[10] In other words, the Soviets had settled on the adoption of a preemptive strike strategy to be used in the event that an attack by the United States appeared imminent. Although the Soviets still did not regard surprise as a sufficient prerequisite for victory by itself, it was nevertheless considered potentially decisive enough by the Soviets for them to want to deny the advantages of surprise to the United States.

Soviet delivery capabilities in 1955 were so poor, however, that one wonders why the Soviets even bothered with a preemptive strategy. The answer to this is that the Soviets, from their standpoint at least, did not have any more desirable alternatives. One alternative was the avoidance of war at any cost, no matter what concessions had to be made. The problem with such a course of action is that it had failed miserably in 1941 in attempting to ward off a German invasion of the Soviet Union. Besides, the Soviets were now in a much stronger relative position vis-à-vis their major adversaries; furthermore, the Eisenhower Administration posed no threat comparable to Hitler's. The other alternative, initiating a preventive war with the United States, was even more undesirable. Given the much weaker Soviet delivery capabilities at that time, there was little chance of the Soviet Union's being able to inflict sufficient damage on American military bases to prevent major retaliation. The requirements for a successful preemptive strategy, chief among them being reliable advance warning of an enemy attack, were at least unequivocal and possibly attainable. Seen in this light, a preemptive strategy was undoubtedly the best of a bad set of choices.[11] Once the Soviet Union attained an ICBM capability in 1957, however, the preemptive strategy became much more feasible; the means of surprise attack now had become nearly invulnerable and unstoppable.

Soviet Doctrinal Development in the 1960s

The development of Soviet military doctrine during the 1960s can be divided into two main periods: (1) the period from Khrushchev's initial enunciation of his strategic doctrine in January 1960 to his ouster in 1964, and (2) the Brezhnev-Kosygin period of doctrinal development to 1970. The first period differed significantly in doctrine and force requirements from the latter.

The declaration of Soviet strategic doctrine by Khrushchev on January 14, 1960, in addition to those made by then Defense Minister Malinovskiy on January 14 and 19 of the same year, placed its main emphasis on the decisiveness of nuclear weapons in a future war. Referred to mistakenly by one Western analyst as Khrushchev's version of "massive retaliation,"[12] its implication was that any U.S. attempts at limiting armed conflict would not succeed, and that all wars between the capitalist and socialist camps would quickly escalate to all-out war.[13] Defense Minister Malinovskiy concisely stated the nature of a future world war:

> A future world war, if the imperialists succeed in unleashing it, will be a decisive armed clash of the opposed social systems . . . it inevitably will be thermonuclear, a war in which the main means of its delivery to the target will be the rockets . . . Now war might arise without the traditional clearly threatening period, by surprise, as a result of the mass use of long-range rockets armed with powerful nuclear warheads.[14]

Just because the above passage stressed the "single-option" strategy of immediate escalation to strategic nuclear war is not to say that the Soviets categorically denied the possibility of limited wars ever taking place. Certain statements made during Khrushchev's tenure give reason to conclude that Soviet willingness to escalate to all-out conflict was declaratory rather than real: an exercise in declaratory deterrence, if you will. One Soviet military analyst conceded that "limited wars have occurred in the past; they may also occur in the future." The chance of a protracted war was also not ignored, because strategic capabilities of both sides were still relatively small in 1960.[15]

There has been some disagreement by Western analysts over the nature of Soviet doctrinal development during the Khrushchev period. Some claimed that a "debate" occurred between two schools of thought said to exist within the Soviet military. One school was referred to as the "traditionalist" school, which supposedly affirmed the necessity for the maintenance of multimillion-man armies for the purpose of replacing the enormous losses inherent in nuclear warfare. The other alleged school of thought was called the "modernist" view, which was ostensibly for a radical adaptation of modern technology to military affairs to the extent of placing the main emphasis on nuclear weapons. It was further contended by such analysts as Thomas Wolfe that the debate resulted in the emergence of a "centrist" viewpoint that was a compromise between the two schools.[16]

The idea of a doctrinal debate between factions of the Soviet military has not been without its critics. William F. Scott, a former U.S. military attache to the Soviet Union, had argued in 1971 in *Strategic Review* that the basic emphasis of Soviet military doctrine throughout the 1960s had always been and continued to be oriented around the notion of the primacy of nuclear weapons. Since the declaration of a particular doctrine can precede the deployment of forces for carrying it out by as much as 10 years (mainly because of the long lead times involved in the development of modern weapons systems), the large Soviet nuclear forces of today were actually the result of decisions made at the beginning of the 1960s.[17]

In truth, there was no contradiction between the idea that the nuclear weapon was to be the decisive weapon and the claim that multimillion-man armies were required in order to sustain the anticipated losses of a nuclear war; both concepts could easily coexist within the same doctrine without conflict. It should be noted that the fact that manpower levels were being reduced did not mean a rejection of the notion that multimillion-man armies should be maintained, even with Khrushchev's actual as well as planned reductions in manpower taken into account. The lowest figure for Soviet manpower levels projected by Khrushchev was 2.4 million men, which still constituted a fairly large army, and was hardly an outright rejection of the so-called traditionalist school. The *actual* reductions, furthermore, resulted in an overall decrease of 2.7 million men from 5.7 million men in 1955 to approximately 3 million by the time of Khrushchev's ouster in 1964.[18] The main point that should be emphasized is that there was no debate in the sense of an actual conflict over *doctrine* during the period from 1960 to 1964. What argument that existed was not over whether one was to have multimillion-man armies or not, but over how large those armies were to be. In other words, the disagreements were over implementing doctrine, as distinguished from doctrine itself. The primacy of nuclear weapons was to remain the predominant theme in Soviet strategy throughout the 1960s. It is important to remember that any evidence of "debates" in Soviet military journals was not a sign that the Soviet military was challenging the political authority of the CPSU, since these debates took place within carefully prescribed and authorized limits defined by the party.[19] In Khrushchev's opinion, 2.4 million men was the level of manpower adequate for the purpose of maintaining a multimillion-man army. He also claimed that any reduction in manpower would be made up by the increase in firepower from nuclear weapons:

> A reduction of the numerical strength of our armed forces will not prevent us from maintaining the country's defensive power at the proper level. We shall have all the means required for the defense of our country, and our enemy

will know it very well. In case he does not, we are warning him and telling him outright: by reducing the numerical strength of our armed forces, we shall not be diminishing their firepower. On the contrary, their firepower will increase many times over in terms of quality.[20]

With the removal from power of Khrushchev in 1964, some modifications in doctrine were made, although the nuclear emphasis remained unaltered. Soviet doctrine began moving away from the assertion that war between the capitalist and socialist states must inevitably escalate to general nuclear war. Indeed, there were increasing indications in public Soviet journals, as well as in the following passage from the Soviet General Staff publication *Voennaia Mysl'*, that the Soviets were recognizing the need to be prepared for conflicts that were less than all-out war:

Consequently, according to the means of conducting warfare, consideration is given both to nuclear and non-nuclear, and according to its scales-world and local.[21]

Public recognition of the necessity to be prepared for nonnuclear conflict was made by then Minister of Defense Marshal A.A. Grechko in a speech to the All-Army Conference of Young Officers in November 1969:

Much attention is being devoted to the reasonable combination of nuclear rocket weapons with perfected conventional classic armaments, to the capability of units and subunits to conduct combat actions under nuclear as well as nonnuclear conditions. Such an approach ensures the high combat capabilities of the troops and their constant readiness for action under conditions of variously shaped circumstances.[22]

A theme that remained constant throughout the 1960s, and was in fact a carryover from the resolution of the debate over the role of surprise in *Voennaia Mysl'* in 1955, was the Soviet emphasis on a preemptive strike strategy in the event of war. The idea of a preemptive strike was not directly stated in public pronouncements, but the implication was nonetheless clear that the Soviets intended to launch the first strike in the event of total war. They perceived this strategy as the best for achieving survival and, therefore, also for achieving victory. Soviet capabilities were still not up to the requirements of doctrine, however. The best example of this kind of statement was in the third edition of Sokolovskiy's *Military Strategy*:

. . . Possibilities of averting a surprise attack are constantly growing. Present means of reconnaissance, detection, and surveillance can opportunely disclose a significant portion of the measures of direct preparation of a nuclear attack by the enemy and in the very first minutes locate the mass launch of missiles and the take-off of aircraft belonging to the aggressor and, at the right time, warn the political leadership of the country about the impending danger. Thus, possibilities exist not to allow a surprise attack by an aggressor, to deliver nuclear strikes on him at the right time.[23]

The strategy of a preemptive strike was to be one of the main components of the Soviet emphasis on a nuclear warfighting strategy during the 1960s and 1970s. The essence of Soviet thinking regarding its warfighting strategy was expressed in an article in a September 1965 issue of *Kommunist Vooruzhennykh Sil* (KVS) by Lieutenant Colonel E. Rybkin, then a doctoral candidate of philosophical science. At the time, Rybkin's article was regarded by Western analysts such as Roman Kolkowicz and William Zimmerman as an aberration on the side of militancy, rather than as evidence of a consensus within the Soviet military. These analysts interpreted Rybkin's article as indicating the existence of a hawkish fringe element within the Soviet military as opposed to the more moderate views expressed by Talensky in the May 1965 issue of *International Affairs*. Talensky claimed that "there is no more dangerous illusion than the idea that thermonuclear war can still serve as an instrument of politics" and appeared to oppose the notion "that it is possible to find acceptable forms of nuclear war."[24] These analysts were unfamiliar with Soviet *desinformatsiya* techniques, however, and overlooked the fact that Talensky was a retired major general at the time, writing his article for *International Affairs*, a publication not directed toward a Soviet military audience. On the other band, Rybkin was writing for *KVS,* a military theory journal published by the Main Political Administration, thus indicating that Rybkin's views had the prior approval of the CPSU. Rather than being representative of a hawkish element in the Soviet military, therefore, Rybkin's article demonstrated that the Soviets were pursuing a line of strategic thinking much different from the one that would lead the United States into a strategy relying on mutual assured destruction.[25]

In his assessment of "imperialist" military theory, Rybkin asserted that "until recently, militarist ideologues have altered the interpretation of this formula in order to relate and unite the concepts of war and politics and have even 'overturned' Clausewitz's formula to mean that 'politics is war.'" Rybkin naturally disagreed with the alleged "imperialist" view, claiming that "it is clear that it is definitely incorrect to identify the concept of 'a continuation of politics' with that of 'an instrument of politics.' War is always the continuation of politics, but it cannot always serve as the latter's instrument." Rybkin eschewed the position taken by Talensky concerning the nonutility of nuclear war as an instrument of state policy on the grounds that "an a priori rejection of the possibility of victory is harmful because it leads to moral disarmament, to a disbelief in victory, and to fatalism and passivity."[26] For Rybkin to have said otherwise would have meant opposing the ideological assertions of many

Soviet leaders and commentators who held that a future nuclear war would result in the final destruction of capitalism, thus implying the survival of the Soviet Union and the triumph of socialism. From Rybkin's standpoint, then, Talensky's statements were both militarily and politically unpalatable. (One must also take into account, however, the likelihood that the Soviets were setting up a false debate as part of their *desinformatsiya* strategy to mislead Western analysts.)

Rybkin, though, was not a "superhawk" (as erroneously contended by Kolkowicz and Zimmerman) in the sense of being more willing to wage a nuclear war than his supposedly more moderate colleagues. In the following passage, Rybkin qualified his disagreement with Talensky:

> Nuclear war because of its consequences transcends the framework of previous ideas regarding the correlation of politics and war. Though nuclear war still represents a continuation of politics *it is now circumscribed as an instrument of politics because of the effects of atomic weapons.* This fact does not negate either the possibility of the aggressors unleashing a war *or the possibility of our victory in the war.* The chief conclusion derived from the analysis of this problem is that it is necessary to do everything in order to avert a world nuclear war . . . . Moreover, the CPSU Program and the decisions of the party and the government *obligate our Armed Forces to be constantly in the state of complete readiness and by their decisive actions to bring to naught the schemes of the aggressors and to inflict upon them a retaliatory, all-crushing blow.*[27] [Emphasis added.]

It is clear, therefore, that Rybkin not only was arguing that it was possible for the Soviet Union to fight and win a nuclear war, but he was also advocating a preemptive strike strategy as part of a nuclear warfighting doctrine should war occur.

The objective of victory in a nuclear war was confirmed in the third edition of Sokolovskiy's *Military Strategy.* Although the editors of the third edition had altered their statement regarding war between the Soviet Union and the imperialists to read that "such a war might take the nature of a world war with the majority of the countries in the world participating in it,"[28] they still emphasized the possibility of attaining victory via a nuclear warfighting strategy should war occur:

> The ability of a nation's economy to engage in mass production of military equipment, especially nuclear rocket weapons, to create a superiority over the enemy in modern means of armed combat determines the material prerequisites of victory. *A decisive factor for the outcome of a future war will be the ability of the economy to assure the maximum strength of the Armed Forces, in order to inflict a devastating strike upon the aggressor during the initial period of the war.*"[29] [Emphasis in original]

The main points of Soviet thinking during this period regarding a nuclear warfighting doctrine can be summarized as follows:

- Nuclear war is possible.
- If nuclear war is possible, it should be fought to achieve victory.
- Correct capabilities and strategies make it possible to attain victory.
- Adherence to mutual assured destruction deprives Soviet strategic forces of their political and military utility and gives the United States a free hand in the conduct of limited wars.

The development of Soviet strategic doctrine during the 1960s thus involved elements of continuity from the 1950s, mainly the ongoing emphasis on the importance of surprise and a preemptive strategy with the objective of victory in the event of general nuclear war. The decade of the 1960s was further characterized by a shift in emphasis following the forced retirement of Khrushchev from a single-option strategy relying on a "minimum deterrence" posture to a doctrine that recognized the need for greater flexibility in military capability across the spectrum of conflict, and therefore called for a greater buildup in conventional as well as nuclear capability. The decade was especially marked by the rapid growth of Soviet strategic forces to the point where they began to exceed those of the United States; the Soviets would perceive this development as decisive in terms of its effect on the evolution of U.S. strategic doctrine.[30]

Soviet Doctrinal Developments in the 1970s

The orientation of Soviet strategic doctrine throughout the 1970s and early 1980s remained that of a nuclear warfighting/war survival doctrine. The assumption underlying this doctrine was that the better prepared the Soviet armed forces were to fight and win a nuclear war, the more effective they would be as a deterrent to an attack on the Soviet Union as well as an "umbrella" under which the Soviets could pursue a more aggressive foreign policy. Deterrence, therefore, was an implied goal of Soviet strategic doctrine, and was not treated separately from a warfighting doctrine. Rather, it remained an inseparable part of Soviet doctrine.[31]

Implicit in the Soviet warfighting strategy was the notion of war "survival," with civil defense one of the main means of achieving it. The Soviets reasoned was that no country could rationally threaten another with nuclear war if both know that such a war would be suicidal for the country that initiated it. Furthermore, a Soviet war survival capability increased the credibility of Soviet deterrence by undermining a (until very recently) fundamental tenet of U.S. strategic doctrine: being able to threaten the Soviet Union with assured destruction. This also provided the Soviets with greater opportunity to exploit their military power for the pursuit of foreign policy goals, since it increased the likelihood that the United States would make concessions in the face of Soviet-supported advances, rather than run the risk of confrontation or war.[32]

Still another aspect of Soviet doctrine unchanged since 1955 has been the role of the preemptive strike as the best means of maximizing the chances of survival in a nuclear war, and thus attaining victory.[33] This intention was again expressed in an August 1972 issue of *KVS*:

> In the current phase, the Armed Forces should be capable of stopping a surprise attack by the aggressor in any situation and use rapid, crushing blows to destroy his main nuclear missile weapons and troop formations, thus securing favorable conditions for further conduct of and victorious conclusion to the war.[34]

This assumption was also reflected in the fifth edition of *Marxism-Leninism on War and Army*, published that same year:

> Soviet military doctrine proceeds from the assumption that the imperialists are preparing a surprise nuclear attack against the USSR and other socialist countries. At the same time they consider the possibility of waging military operations escalating into military actions involving the use of nuclear missile weapons. Therefore, the chief and main task of the Armed Forces consists in being constantly ready to repel a sudden attack of the enemy in any form, to foil his criminal intentions, no matter what means he might use.[35]

The rationale behind the preemptive strike strategy also remained substantially unaltered; it contended that "the first massive nuclear strikes are able largely to predetermine the subsequent course of the war and to inflict such heavy losses in the rear and among the troops that they may place the people and the country in an extraordinarily difficult position." Even so, the Soviets still did not believe that nuclear weapons could determine the outcome of a war by themselves. Instead, they argued that "final victory over the aggressor can be achieved only as a result of the joint actions of all the arms of the services, which must utilize in full measure the results of the nuclear strikes at the enemy and fulfill their specific tasks."[36]

During the 1970s, however, the Soviets had begun emphasizing an even more ambitious requirement for Soviet doctrine, the capability for projecting Soviet military power into distant areas of the globe. Although Leonid Brezhnev had cautiously hinted at this new change in his address to the Twenty-fourth Party Congress in March 1971,[37] it was more directly stated in a book published by the Institute for World Economy and International Relations in 1972:

Greater importance is being attached to Soviet military presence in various regions throughout the world, reinforced by an adequate level of strategic mobility of its armed forces.

In connection with the task of preventing local wars and also in those cases wherein military support must be furnished to those nations fighting for their freedom and independence against the forces of international reaction and imperialist interventions, the Soviet Union may require mobile and well-trained and well-equipped forces . . . .

Expanding the scale of Soviet military presence and military assistance furnished by other socialist states is being viewed today as a very important factor in international relations.[38]

This theme was reaffirmed as an official addition to Soviet military doctrine by Marshal Grechko in 1974. In a leading party theoretical journal, he wrote:

At the present state the historic function of the Soviet Armed Forces is not restricted to their function in defending our Motherland and the other socialist countries. In its foreign policy activity the Soviet state purposefully opposes the export of counterrevolution and the policy of oppression, supports the national liberation struggle, and resolutely resists imperialists' aggression in whatever distant region of the planet it may appear.[39]

Although Soviet strategic doctrine had undergone these new modifications during the 1970s, the essence of Soviet strategic doctrine had remained basically unchanged since 1960. The emphasis was still on the decisiveness of the nuclear weapon in determining the course and outcome of a future world war. Such a doctrine was a clear rejection of the concept of mutual assured destruction, since the Soviets contended that they "are not for peace at any price and . . . are not, of course, for any freezing of social-political processes taking place inside the countries."[40] Brezhnev continued:

War can and must be banned as a means for resolving international disputes. But we must not "ban" civil or national liberation wars, we must not "ban" uprisings and we by no means "ban" revolutionary mass movements aimed at changing the political and social status quo.[41]

Soviet Doctrinal Developments in the 1980s

The principal change in Soviet strategic doctrine during the 1980s was Gorbachev's declaration of the doctrine of "reasonable sufficiency" in 1985. Gorbachev's initial statements on the new doctrine were vague, leading some Western analysts to conclude that either the Soviet leadership was engaging in strategic deception, or that the doctrine represented only minimal changes from previous Soviet doctrine:

The USSR and the U.S. will have to reach a common understanding of what level of weapons on each side could be considered relatively sufficient . . . We are convinced that the level of this sufficiency is much lower than that which the USSR and the United States in fact possess at the moment. This means that weighty practical steps for the limitation and reduction of weapons are perfectly possible, measures that not only will not lessen, but will strengthen security both for the USSR and the U.S., and the entire strategic stability of the world.[42]

Once the concept of "reasonable sufficiency" began to be explained in greater detail by various Soviet military and political leaders, however, it showed that there was still a great deal of continuity between it and previous Soviet strategic thinking. Most noteworthy was the following statement by Col (Ret.) L. Semeyko in October 1987 concerning the importance of nuclear strategic parity in the new doctrine:

Sufficiency does not preclude but, on the contrary, presupposes the presence of strategic parity; that decisive factor in preventing war. It is necessary to have within the framework of parity a reasonably sufficient military potential capable of reliably ensuring the security of the USSR and its allies. This means that under contemporary conditions we are obliged to have a guaranteed potential for nuclear retaliation designed to prevent an unpunished nuclear attack under any, even under the most unfavorable, nuclear attack scenarios. In any situation, an answering strike must unacceptably damage the aggressor.[43]

Even though one could find considerable continuity between "reasonable sufficiency" and previous Soviet doctrinal declarations, there was one real difference: "reasonable sufficiency" did not call for the kind of capability for projecting military power to intervene in distant areas of the globe as previous doctrine had under Brezhnev. This omission was more than just an oversight; it represented a conscious decision on the part of Gorbachev to curtail the active role of the Soviet military in supporting USSR foreign policy objectives, at least until his policy of *perestroika* had a chance to work. This was confirmed in his announced decision of February 8, 1988 to withdraw Soviet troops from Afghanistan beginning May 15. Later that same year on December 7, Gorbachev would announce a unilateral reduction of 500,000 men in the Soviet armed forces, in spite of considerable public opposition and criticism by senior officers of the Soviet military. Later withdrawals from Eastern Europe would follow, although not entirely of Gorbachev's own volition.[44]

Soviet Doctrine in the 1990s: Collapse and Transition

The debacles suffered by Soviet arms, training, and tactics, most notably in Afghanistan and Operation Desert Storm, have caused the senior Soviet military leadership to undergo their own agonizing reappraisal of their own theory and doctrine. Indeed, some officers such as Colonel General I.N. Radionov of the USSR Armed Forces General Staff Academy have gone so far as to say that "a thoroughly developed doctrine does not exist."[45]

In spite of this apparent doctrinal quandary and the ongoing internal economic and political upheavals that will further constrain the ability of the Soviet military to implement new doctrine, this has not prevented the military leadership from discussing the need for reform in its strategic doctrine. Instead, the economic weakness of the republics in general, and the Russian republic in particular, will dictate that the former Soviet military develop its future doctrine by emphasizing areas in which it is comparatively the most competitive: nuclear weapons and the military exploitation of space. Because of the collapsing economy within the former Soviet Union, there will be (as in the early 1960s) a significant lag between any declared doctrine and its later manifestation in the military force structure. With this in mind, we should take note of the words of General Major V. Ivanov in August 1990, when he declared that any military reform should:

> . . . include the currently existing Strategic Rocket Forces, and units and large units of Military Aviation, the Navy, and Air and Anti-Satellite Defense forces, equipped with nuclear weapons and weapon delivery vehicles which are to be consolidated into Nuclear Forces and also *Space Forces, whose units and large units will be provided with systems capable of destroying the enemy's installations from space.'*[46] [Emphasis added.]

The evolution of U.S. and Soviet strategic doctrine has proceeded along two entirely different paths since the end of World War II. The United States, operating under the assumption that nuclear war was unthinkable and unwinnable, evolved toward a war-avoidance strategy, and only recently has begun to devote serious attention to strategic defense. The Soviet Union, however, still adhering to the idea that nuclear war could serve as a continuation of state policy (albeit in a somewhat circumscribed fashion) eventually developed a nuclear warfighting doctrine based upon the concepts of war survival and the preemptive strike; even now its individual republics still tacitly acknowledge the primacy of nuclear forces as an instrument of political leverage. Each side has perceived the other's strategic doctrine within the context of its own strategic mindset; the consequences of this, however, has been quite different for Soviet than for U.S. planning.

Notes

1. H.S. Dinerstein, *War and the Soviet Union* (New York: Praeger, 1959), 6-7.
2. R. Garthoff, *Soviet Strategy in the Nuclear Age* (New York: Praeger, 1958), 70.

3. Bonds, ed., *The Soviet War Machine,* (New York: Chartwell, 1976), 202. See also H. Kissinger, *Nuclear Weapons and Foreign Policy* (Garden City, N.Y.: Doubleday, 1958), 93-96.

4. T. Wolfe, *Soviet Power and Europe, 1945-1970* (Baltimore: Johns Hopkins Press, 1970), 32-35.

5. A. Dallin, *Red Star on Military Affairs, 1945-1952* (Santa Monica, Calif.: RAND, RM-1637, February 10, 1956), 21.

6. Dinerstein, *War and the Soviet Union,* 41, 53-54.

7. Garthoff, *Soviet Strategy,* 76-78.

8. Ibid., 79.

9. Bonds, *Soviet War Machine,* 204.

10. Cited in Garthoff, *Soviet Strategy,* 85.

11. Discussed in Dinerstein, *War and the Soviet Union,* 200-2.

12. H.S. Dinerstein, *Soviet Strategic Ideas: January 1960* (Santa Monica, Calif.: RAND, RM-2532, February 19, 1960), 25.

13. H.F. Scott and W.F. Scott, *The Armed Forces of the USSR* (Boulder, Colo.: Westview, 1978), 45. See also Dinerstein, *Soviet Strategic Ideas,* 28-29.

14. R. Malinovskiy, *Bditel'no Stoyat Na Strazhe Mira (Vigilantly Stand Guard Over the Peace)* (Moscow: Voyenizdat, 1962), 24-27. Quoted in Scott and Scott, *Armed Forces,* 45.

15. Cited in L. Goure, *Soviet Limited War Doctrine* (Santa Monica, Calif: RAND, P-2744, May 1963), 3. See also D. Palevich and I. Pozynak, "The Peculiarities and Nature of a World Nuclear-Rocket War," *KVS* 20, October 1964, 78-79. V.D. Sokolovskiy, *Soviet Military Strategy,* ed. and trans. by H.F. Scott (New York: Crane, Russak, 1975), 64-69, for discussion in detail of the limited war concept.

16. T. Wolfe, *Soviet Power,* 161-2.

17. W.F. Scott, "Soviet Military Doctrine and Strategy: Realities and Misunderstandings," *Strategic Review,* 3, 3, (Summer 1975): 60-62.

18. Wolfe, *Soviet Power,* 164-6.

19. H.F. Scott, *Soviet Military Doctrine: Its Continuity, 1960-1970* (Menlo Park, Calif.: Stanford Research Institute, SSC-TN-8974-28, 17 June 1971), 65-69. See also Scott and Scott, *Armed Forces,* 41-56. The role of the Main Political Administration in Soviet party-military relations has been comprehensively examined in M.J. Deane, *Political Control of the Soviet Armed Forces* (New York: Crane, Russak, 1977). For a more recent exposition, see also J.J. Dziak, *Soviet Perceptions of Military Power: The Interaction of Theory and Practice* (New York: National Strategy Information Center, 1981).

20. Cited in H.F. Scott, *Soviet Military Doctrine: Its Continuity, 1960-1970,* 78.

21. S. Ivanov, "Soviet Military Doctrine and Strategy," *Voennaia Mysl'* 5 (May 1969), trans. in FBIS, FPD, No. 01 16/69, 18 December 1969, 49.

22. A.A. Grechko, "The Growing Role, Tasks, and Obligations of Young Officers at the Contemporary State of the Development of the Soviet Armed Forces," *Krasnaya Zvezda,* 27 November 1969. Cited in Scott and Scott, *Armed Forces,* 55. See also G. Semenov and V. Prokhorov, "Scientific-Technical Progress and Some Questions of Strategy," *Voennaia Mysl'* 2, (February 1969), trans. in FBIS, FPD, No. 0060/69, 18 June 1969, 29; N. Vasendin and N. Kuznetsov, "Modern Warfare and Surprise Attack," *Voennaia Mysl'* 6, (June 1968), trans. in FBIS, FPD, No. 0005/69, 16 January 1969, 45.

23. Sokolovskiy, *Soviet Military Strategy,* 280. See also N. Krylov, "The Nuclear-Missile Shield of the Soviet State," *Voennaia Mysl',* 11, (November 1967), trans. in FBIS, FPD. No, 0157/68, 18 November 1968, 18-19, passim.

24. N. Talensky, "The Late War: Some Reflections," *International Affairs,* 5, (May 1965), 15.

25. R. Kolkowicz, *The Red "Hawks" on the Rationality of Nuclear War* (Santa Monica, Calif.: RAND, RM-4899-PR, March 1966). See also W. Zimmerman, *Soviet Perspectives on International Relations, 1956-1967* (Princeton: Princeton University Press, 1969), 233.

26. E. Rybkin, "On the Essence of a World Nuclear-Rocket War," *KVS* 17, (September 1965), 51-55.

27. Ibid., p. 56.

28. Sokolovskiy, *Soviet Military Strategy,* 208.

29. Ibid., 209.

30. Wolfe, *Soviet Power,* 451-457.

31. L. Goure, F. Kohler, and M. Harvey, *The Role of Nuclear Forces in Current Soviet Strategy* (Coral Gables, Fla.: Center for Advanced International Studies, 1975), 47. See also B. Lambeth, *The Political Potential of Equivalence: The View from Moscow and Europe* (Santa Monica, Calif.: RAND, P-6167, August 1978).

32. L. Goure, *War Survival in Soviet Strategy* (Coral Gables, Fla.: Center for Advanced International Studies, 1976), 6-24.

33. Garthoff, *Soviet Strategy,* 84-87. See also Goure, Kohler, and Harvey, *Nuclear Forces,* 102-12. The Soviet "preemptive strike" strategy was reaffirmed during the late 1960s and early 1970s in the following articles from the classified Soviet General Staff journal *Voennaia Mysl':* S. Lukonin and A. Migolat'yev, "The 24th CPSU Congress on Current Problems in the Building of Communism and the Strengthening of the Defensive Might of the *USSR,"* *Voennaia Mysl'* 5, (May 1971), trans. in FBIS, FPD No. 0016/74, March 18, 1974, 13; Editorial, "The Tasks of Soviet Military Science in Light of the Decisions of the 24th CPSU Congress," *Voennaia Mysl',* 8, (August 1971), trans. in FBIS, FPD No. 001 1/74, February 28, 1974, 6; Editorial, "On Guard for Peace and the Building of Socialism," *Voennaia Mysl',* No. 12, December 1971, trans. FBIS, FPD No. 0003/74, January 17, 1974, 8.

34. I. Forofonov, "The 24th CPSU Congress on Missions of the Soviet Armed Forces in the Current Phase," *KVS,* 15, (August 1971): 77. Quoted in F. Kohler et al, *Soviet Strategy for the Seventies,* 87.

35. *Marxism-Leninism on War and Army* (Moscow: Progress Publishers, 1972), trans. under the auspices of the U.S. Air Force (Washington, D.C.: U.S. Government Printing Office, 1972) 305.

36. Ibid, p. 304.

37. Quoted in Scott and Scott, *Armed Forces,* 56. See also Kohler et al., *Soviet Strategy for the Seventies,* 93-95.

38. V.M. Kulish, *Voennaia Sila i Mezhdunarodnie Otnoshenia (Military Force and International Relations)* (Moscow: International Relations Publishing House, 1972), 137, quoted in Scott and Scott, *Armed Forces,* 57.

39. A.A. Grechko, "The Leading Role of the CPSU in Building the Army of a Developed Socialist Society," *Problems of History of CPSU,* May 1974. Quoted in Scott and Scott, *Armed Forces,* 57. See also Editorial, "The Party of Lenin: The Fighting Vanguard," *Voennaia Mysl',* 3, (March 1971), trans. in FBIS, FPD No. 0020/74, March 29, 1974, 6-7.

40. *Pravda,* January 30, 1974. Quoted in Goure, Kohler, and Harvey, *Nuclear Forces,* 62-63.
41. *Izvestia*, September 11, 1973. Quoted in Goure, Kohler, and Harvey, *Nuclear Forces,* 63.
42. *Pravda*, November 28, 1985, 1-2. Cited in *Gorbachev and His Generals: The Reform of Soviet Military Doctrine* (Westview Press, Boulder, Colorado, 1990), 42-43.
43. *Izvestia,* August 13, 1987, 5. Cited by W.F. Scott in *Gorbachev and His Generals,* 4, "Soviet Military Doctrine: Continuity and Change?"
44. W.F. Scott, *Gorbachev and His Generals,* 221-3.
45. Attributed to Colonel General I.N. Radionov, Commander, USSR Armed Forces General Staff Academy, 9 May 1991. Cited in briefing by F.X. Kane and J.R. Howe, "Emerging Soviet Views on Future Warfare," 27 August 1991.
46. Attributed to General Major V. Ivanov, Academy of the General Staff, August 1990. Cited in Kane and Howe, "Emerging Soviet Views on Future Warfare."

Part II

MASSIVE RETALIATION PERIOD
(1954-1960)

3
The Soviet View of Massive Retaliation

What was the Soviet perception of the massive retaliation doctrine during the period when it was currently in force? In answering this question, Soviet declarations must be considered in conjunction with Soviet foreign policy behavior and military programs. In addition, one must look carefully at statements that are not in consonance with Soviet strategic doctrine, since these are part of the Soviet declaratory deterrence strategy to mislead Western analysts.

Actual Soviet interpretations of U.S. doctrine during this period reveal a preoccupation with the problem of deterring the "worst possible case," a preemptive nuclear strike by the United States. This was largely a mirror-imaging by the Soviets of their own estimation of the value of surprise as a decisive factor in determining the outcome of a war; it was also a reflection of the fact that the Soviets had little corresponding capability to threaten the United States in the same way until the development of the Soviet ICBM. From the Soviet perspective, the key to undermining the massive retaliation doctrine lay in negating the U.S. perception of its own invulnerability by using propagandistic rhetoric as well as by striving to attain an intercontinental capability as soon as possible.

This goal was confirmed in the military programs of the Khrushchev regime. Roughly 2,000 of the Tu-16 bombers were produced in the years after their entry into service in 1954. The range of this bomber made an intercontinental capability possible only with one-way missions or in-flight refuelling, but it was sufficient to give the Soviets some capability, however unreliable.[1] It is interesting that only about 300 of the longer-range Tu-20 bombers were produced after its entry into service in 1957, since Khrushchev may have decided to devote more attention to the nascent Soviet ICBM program.[2]

Since the Soviets placed such a high value on the potential decisiveness of surprise in determining the outcome of a war, it is logical that they would do everything in their power, whether through propaganda or through their military programs, to undermine the credibility of a U.S. strategic doctrine they perceived as depending on surprise attack. The tactics of bluff and deception practiced by the Soviets regarding their own ICBM capability were intended to discourage such an attack as well as to reap possible political gains. Yet the Soviets realized that their "superiority" was an illusion, so they did not attempt to press their advantage when it appeared that their bluff might be called.

The Soviets might have *publicly* questioned the credibility of the massive retaliation doctrine during the period when it was officially in force (1954-1960), but with the exception of the Soviet intervention in Hungary in 1956 (where the Soviets obviously believed they were forced to take risks), there was no instance in which they actually *committed* an act of local aggression that might have called for the carrying out of the threat implied by massive retaliation. To be sure, several times during this period the Soviets made both implied and direct threats to use their strategic capability.[3] For example, during the 1956 Suez crisis, the Soviets threatened both Great Britain and France with nuclear weapons. In 1958, after the Quemoy-Matsu crisis, Khrushchev threatened to retaliate against the United States if she attacked China. And, of course, the period from 1957 to 1962 was characterized by exaggerated claims and veiled threats regarding Soviet ICBM capability and possible employment. The Soviets also used military manuevers frequently during this period, as typified by the Soviet announcement in 1958 of military manuevers in the Transcaucasus and Bulgaria in response to the U.S. intervention in Lebanon (see Appendix B). None of these responses were direct uses of military power against the West; the Soviets were deterred in large measure from local aggression during this period. This, however, was a combination of Soviet strategic weakness and respect for the relatively massive U.S. capability, rather than a genuine belief in the credibility of the massive retaliation doctrine itself. This skepticism was reinforced by the lack of a strong U.S. response to the Soviet intervention in Hungary.[4]

All of this ought to be considered within the context of the "peaceful coexistence" policy as espoused by Khrushchev. The main points of this policy were as follows:

- War is no longer "fatalistically" inevitable.
- Neither general nor local war is desirable.
- A peaceful way is possible and preferable for the attainment of socialism.
- War among capitalist states is no longer a likely "midwife of revolution."
- In any event, the Soviet Union and the socialist camp do not require war of any kind to win on a world scale.
- Already the correlation of forces is moving relentlessly in favor of the Soviet Union.

• The Soviet Union can expect the shift in the correlation of world forces to accelerate because of changing attitudes and new opportunities for Moscow in the Third World.[5]

According to Khrushchev, the focus of the competition between the United States and the Soviet Union was now the economic rather than the military sphere. He appeared to have little doubt at the time that the Soviet Union would be the ultimate victor in such a competition, provided it was allowed to proceed without the occurrence of a nuclear war in which, he contended, there would be no possibility of triumph for either side.[6] The Soviet perception of the massive retaliation doctrine was quite rational when considered within the framework of Soviet nuclear strategy and the foreign policy of peaceful coexistence. A logical outgrowth of this perception was the Soviet effort to discredit the massive retaliation doctrine with their declaratory deterrence strategy.

The Soviet Propaganda Line

It should be kept in mind that the primary objective of Soviet declaratory deterrence statements during this period was to confuse U.S. observers about Soviet intentions and strategic capabilities. The major points of this propaganda line were seldom, if ever, repeated in later Soviet analyses of massive retaliation, since the Soviets probably believed that it was safer to comment candidly on a particular U.S. doctrine only when it was no longer in force. The four major themes of Soviet declaratory deterrence are summarized below.

1. *The Soviets denied that the United States could achieve decisive results in a nuclear war with the Soviet Union (i.e., attain victory) by relying on the use of surprise in its doctrine of massive retaliation.*

The claim that the U.S. could not achieve decisive victory in a nuclear war with the Soviet Union was advanced more often during the early part of the massive retaliation period. For example, it was argued in the Soviet *New Times* that if the United States "embarked on atomic aggression," the only result would be to "bring down incalculable misery on their own country." The launching of a so-called preventive war, it was claimed, "can earn its initiators nothing but tremendous loss of moral and political prestige."[7]

It is important to note that this did not mean that the United States would actually lose such a conflict, but rather that the cost would be so excessive that any victory would be meaningless. Obviously, the purpose here was to discourage the United States from trying to enforce massive retaliation with its nuclear arsenal. The assumption was also apparently made by the Soviets that victory in a nuclear war, rather than pure deterrence, was the United States' objective.

From the ideological standpoint, it was only natural for the Soviets to say that the massive retaliation doctrine indicated a U.S. desire to initiate a nuclear war with the Soviet Union and that the United States was therefore engaging in deception regarding its allegedly defensive intentions. Since massive retaliation suggested a defensive posture within the context of a "grand strategy" of containment,[8] this ran counter to the Soviet claim that U.S. "imperialism" was "inherently aggressive" and was the "source of all wars." Assuming that the Soviets were not inclined to fly in the face of ideological principle, they had no real alternative as far as their public declarations were concerned. Either they had to claim that the United States was lying about its defensive intentions, or they would have to concede that United States "imperialism" was not inherently aggressive. This would then have raised the ideologically nettlesome question of why an inherently "aggressive" state was adopting a defensive posture vis-à-vis an inherently "peace-loving" state.

The Soviets' public denial of the decisiveness of the factor of surprise had another motivation as well. As noted previously, the Soviets themselves placed a great deal of emphasis on surprise, going so far as to have approved the adoption of a preemptive strike strategy in the May 1955 issue of *Voennaia Mysl'*.[9] Given the high value the Soviets placed on surprise, their public efforts to discredit a preemptive strike strategy had two likely reasons. One was that the Soviets intended the denial as a deterrence statement of sorts in an attempt to dissuade the United States from reliance on what the Soviets perceived as a strategy of surprise attack. The other possibility was that the Soviets lacked confidence in their own capabilities for mounting an effective preemptive strike and therefore were not anxious to see the United States adopt such a strategy.

2. U.S. discussions of a preemptive strike strategy meant that the United States was actually planning a preventive war against the Soviet Union.

The predominant Soviet propaganda line was that the United States was actually planning to undertake a preventive war against the Soviet Union. This was a distortion of the admittedly fine line between the two concepts of a preemptive strike and preventive war. A preemptive strike involves attacking an enemy who is about to mount an attack himself. The preemptive strike is thus designed to wrest the strategic initiative from an opponent. A preventive war, on the other hand, is based more upon longer-range political considerations, rather than an imminent threat of attack. A preventive war may be undertaken in order to defeat more easily a perceived long-term enemy while the military balance is still in one's own favor, thus ensuring a less costly victory.

The ideological problem posed for the Soviets by U.S. discussion of a preemptive strike was a significant motivating factor in the public Soviet attribution to the United States of an intent to undertake a preventive war. Preemptive strike is a strategy that presumes that the opponent has already made a political-military decision in favor of declaring war, thus making a preemptive strike a defensive measure forced upon one out of sheer necessity. For the Soviets to have conceded publicly any necessity for the United States to adopt such a strategy would have been tantamount to admitting the possibility that the Soviets would start a war. The Soviets denied this possibility, since it was contradictory to the allegedly peace-loving nature of their social system and, consequently, contradictory to their foreign policy and strategic doctrine. Moreover, if the United States were planning to employ a preemptive strike strategy only if threatened with imminent attack, and the Soviets were basically peaceful, then there was no actual threat of U.S. aggression, since the Soviets alone controlled the trigger cause for war. For ideological reasons, then, it was necessary for the Soviets to equate publicly the alleged U.S. concepts of preemptive strike and preventive war. As shown below, however, the Soviets well understood the difference between the two concepts, even while using them interchangeably in describing U.S. intentions.

In the following excerpt from an article from an April 1958 issue of *Krasnaya Zvezda*, the terms "preemptive blow" and "preventive war" were used in such a manner as to blur the distinction between them. Yet it can be seen from these passages that the author himself knew the difference:

> The ideas of preventive war, *and the dealing of a preemptive blow as a means of attack and of unleashing war*, are incompatible with socialist ideology. These ideas do not correspond to the interests of the Soviet people who are building communism.
>
> But the Soviet Union has never threatened anyone with *an attack, "preventive war," or dealing a preemptive blow.* Always, beginning with the first days of the existence of the Soviet Union, the leaders of the Communist Party and of our state have said that, in the event of an attack upon us, an immediate retaliatory blow will be dealt to the aggressor.
>
> Naturally, the idea of dealing a retaliatory blow *does not mean conducting only defensive actions.* If any aggressor tried to make an attack upon us, *the Soviet armed forces would conduct the most resolute aggressive action upon him.* [Emphasis added.][10]

The last paragraph is especially significant, since the Soviets publicly denied that a preemptive strike was part of their doctrine in the event of war. The wording of the last paragraph was such that it implied that the Soviets would not wait for an attack to be accomplished but would instead "conduct the most resolute aggressive action." This, of course, was the very essence of the so-called preemptive blow the Soviets denied they planned to use.

The most noteworthy example of Soviet distortion of the distinction between preemptive blow and preventive war appeared in the December 1960
issue of *International Affairs* (Moscow). The authors used Bernard Brodie's
Strategy in the Missile Age as the documentation for their arguments:

> It goes without saying that the advocates of a "preventive" war, or, *what is
> in effect the same thing, a "preemptive" nuclear attack on the Soviet Union,*
> do not, as a rule, venture to make public their cannibalistic views. Brodie writes
> that "those in favour have had grounds for considering it impolitic to express
> their views too publicly, especially if they happened to be in the public ser-
> vice. [Emphasis added.][11]

In the footnote of their citation of Brodie, the authors also explained that
"the advocates of a 'preventive' war *often try to disguise it as a 'preemptive'
one,* i.e., a war in which the aggressor strikes the first blow *when he 'becomes
convinced' that the other side is preparing to attack.*" [Emphasis added.][12] It
is clear, therefore, that the Soviets recognized the difference between a preemptive strike and a preventive war.

3. *The development of the Soviet ICBM negated U.S. strategic superiority.
The implication was that the Soviet Union now had at least parity, and that
the United States would be unable to avoid significant destruction in a nuclear
war with the Soviet Union.*
The record of Soviet ICBM claims has already been well documented
elsewhere; an extensive reiteration of Soviet claims is not necessary.[13] The purpose
of their claims, however, was to cast doubt in the minds of U.S. readers about
the strategic superiority of the United States over the Soviet Union. The Soviets
argued that because of the arrival of the ICBM, neither participant in a future
war "can now avoid the destructive force of an adversary possessing these
weapons."[14] This argument was used as part of a declaratory deterrence effort
against the U.S. strategy of using Western European bases as launchpoints
for its medium-range bombers; it contended that U.S. strategy "is obviously
premised on the assumption that the main retaliatory blow will be delivered
against the bases in Europe, not against U.S. territory."[15]
Soviet propagandists also capitalized on the debate in the United States over
the merits and disadvantages of the massive retaliation doctrine. One of the
reasons the Soviets cited for the debate was the alleged shift in technological
superiority in favor of the Soviet Union:

> In recent years the American press has given increasing space to the views of
> those who claim that the strategic conception of so-called "massive retaliation"
> . . . and related building of military bases abroad no longer conform to the new
> political and strategic situation. Moreover, they have pointed out that the main
> factor which brought about this changed situation was the collapse of the myth
> of the technical superiority of the United States over the Soviet Union. Now

the question is no longer whether the United States has fallen behind the Soviet Union in technical achievement, but how big the lag is.[16]

The Soviet strategic bluff reached its zenith by the beginning of the 1960s, typified by such claims as one in an issue of *International Affairs* (Moscow), that asserted that "the Soviet Armed Forces possesses all modern weapons, including a whole range of ballistic missiles, intercontinental and intermediate range, short range and large number of tactical missiles." Of course, these were claimed to have the capability "for striking a crushing retaliatory blow at the aggressor."[17]

Soviet ICBM claims were intended to mislead the U.S. about the actual level of strategic forces in the Soviet Union; in addition, the Soviets were attempting to undermine the credibility of the U.S. deterrent by asserting that the ICBM had rendered U.S. bombers obsolete. Since the United States "had now lost any superiority with regard to means of delivery," the problem thus posed for the United States to regain its superiority or invulnerability was not going to be solved simply by catching up with the Soviet Union in numbers of missiles. Therefore, argued one analyst, "the assurances of many American authors that the 'problem' will be solved when the United States overtakes the Soviet Union in rocketry and matches it in strategic striking power, are meaningless.[18] This was an attempt to dissuade the United States from attempting to gain strategic superiority in missiles by publicly downgrading the value of such superiority.

4. The Soviets claimed that they had sufficient forces to inflict a "crippling blow" on the United States, regardless of which side struck first.

The Soviet claim that a kind of "mutual deterrence" existed between the United States and the Soviet Union grew out of their ICBM claims. Their line of argument was that since the Soviet Union possessed a capability for inflicting a crippling retaliatory strike, regardless of whether the United States struck first, an all-out nuclear war was no longer a viable option for the United States. According to one Soviet analyst, this was so because the United States no longer possessed the clear supremacy that U.S. analysts such as Henry Kissinger said would be required for victory in a nuclear war.[19]

Henry Kissinger, the notorious American theoretician of nuclear war, supposes that the concept of "total retaliation," which is the main element of the entire "atomic age strategy," can be considered "reasonable" only while the United States possesses clear supremacy in the event of unlimited war. But if the United States does not have that clear supremacy, then is it possible to talk of any "equalization" or "balance"? After all, the basic consequence of the radical change in the world strategic situation which followed the advent of the rocket age lies in the tilting of the scales—and not to the advantage of the United States.[20]

The implication of this statement was that *any* change in the perceived strategic balance against the United States negated the kind of superiority required to make a massive retaliation strategy credible. This led to the argument that U.S. strategic doctrine had been based on an incorrect estimation of the so-called correlation of forces between the United States and the "socialist camp," but especially the Soviet Union. The Soviets, however, had been stressing relative military factors such as the Soviet development of an ICBM capability as having played a leading role in "forcing" the United States to consider modifying its doctrinal stance. Thus, while the Soviets certainly considered other factors in the calculus of the correlation of forces, the Soviets assigned (and, as of this writing, still assign) a leading role to military power in such a calculation, particularly strategic nuclear power.[21] Also, as pointed out earlier, the Soviets were significantly more restrained in the use of their military power during this period than the United States was, which indicates that the Soviet leadership did not believe their own propaganda about the alleged "non utility" of nuclear superiority.

Soviet propagandists frequently made use of the writings of their own prominent military men in an effort to give their declaratory deterrence statements more credibility. Major General N. Talensky wrote an article in the July 1960 issue of *International Affairs* that combined elements of the "real" Soviet view with deterrence propaganda:

> Rocket and nuclear weapons, or rather Soviet superiority in this field, strategically deflates one of the keystones of American military policy- The system of aggressive military blocs and military bases associated with it. United States territory has ceased to be invulnerable. America's military economic and political centers are no longer beyond reach. Moreover, the strategy of modern and total nuclear and rocket war would make them the first and principal objectives in the event of hostilities. Should the U.S.A. start another war, no amount of blocs or bases would be able to save it. *Neither would preventive war or sudden attack. The stocks of rocket missiles, their distribution and method of use are now such that the side subjected to a surprise attack would always be left with sufficient means of dealing the aggressor a mortal blow.* [Emphasis added.][22]

In view of the number of ICBMs estimated to have been deployed by the Soviet Union at that time (35 ICBMs as compared to 18 for the United States),[23] it is doubtful that the author seriously believed his own claim of mutual deterrence, especially considering the relative preponderance of U.S. strategic air power. Rather, the statement was designed to take advantage of apparent U.S. uncertainty over Soviet ICBM strength.[24] It is still more questionable when one remembers that Soviet strategic doctrine was based on the execution of a preemptive nuclear strike and not, as was publicly claimed, on a retaliatory second strike.

The effect of the Soviet declaratory deterrence strategy was twofold and mutually reinforcing. The first effect was to help undermine the credibility of U.S. deterrence by creating an inflated picture of Soviet strategic capabilities vis-à-vis the United States. The other effect of Soviet declaratory deterrence was to enhance the deterrence capability of Soviet strategic power by publicly discrediting the massive retaliation doctrine.

The Actual Soviet View of Massive Retaliation

The actual Soviet view of massive retaliation can be derived from a combination of Soviet hindsight analyses from later periods and Soviet mirror-imaging of their own strategic concepts onto U.S. strategic doctrine, as well as from a comparison of Soviet evaluations against declared U.S. doctrine. The Soviet perception consisted of four main themes.

1. *Massive retaliation envisaged preparation for only one type of war against the Soviet Union: a total nuclear war. As part of this preparation, the United States was relying chiefly on strategic air power while its European and Asian allies were supplying the troops.*

This first theme was essentially accurate.[25] Given the U.S. desire during this period to achieve maximum deterrence at minimum cost, and that the New Look policy of the Eisenhower Administration did not give the U.S. military establishment the kind of power projection capability that would have been required with a more flexible doctrine, it is difficult to dispute the validity of this Soviet perception. Although one could argue that the later statements by John Foster Dulles were moves away from a pure massive retaliation doctrine,[26] the emphasis of U.S. military programs proved that the original concept of massive retaliation was the one that dominated U.S. defense policy.[27]

The Soviets were also accurate in observing that the U.S. was placing its chief reliance on strategic air power while relying on its allies to provide the bulk of the troops. In the August 1956 issue of *International Affairs* (Moscow), there appeared a professional assessment of massive retaliation by Colonel A. Konenenko, author of several analyses of U.S. military strategy. He described U.S. strategy as patterned after the theories of Douhet, an Italian military theorist who argued that air power would be the all-decisive arm in a future major war. Konenenko asserted that future U.S. strategy would concentrate on the civilian population centers, with particular importance being attached to "suddenness of action by the strategic air force."[28]

Quoting then commander of U.S. Strategic Air Command General Curtis LeMay's remarks in *US News & World Report,* Konenenko cited the main tasks of the strategic air force as: (1) to win the battle in the air in the initial stage of war by destroying the enemy's vitally important centers, air bases, atomic plants, and air and ground striking forces, (2) total and systematic destruction of the enemy's industry and the sources of his economic strength through coordinated attacks on targets chosen in advance; (3) readiness to support the ground forces in the theater of operations.[29]

Konenenko also took note of the controversy of the "doctrinal differences" between the U.S. Army and the U.S. Air Force in their approach to future strategy:

> [American military leaders] publish proposals for cutting down the ground forces considerably, on the assumption that the future war will be short and that it will be fought by the United States chiefly with aircraft and atomic weapons. According to this view, the tactical use of atomic weapons should enable relatively small forces to cope with tasks which formerly had to be assigned only to big land armies. The proponents of this view hold that it is sufficient for the United States to have small mobile ground forces chiefly for exercising police functions in occupied enemy territories.[30]

On the other hand, Konenenko perceived two arguments being used by the Army in defense of maintaining large ground forces. For the military aspect of the argument, he cited General Matthew Ridgway's opinion that "armies are an essential element in our ability to conduct global war successfully, regardless of whether or not atomic and hydrogen bombs are used. The importance of the Army's role in geographically limited wars is equally clear."[31]

However, according to Konenenko, the U.S. Army was also considering the political value of keeping American ground forces stationed in Europe and Asia:

> Ridgway and other American generals are against reduction of land armies also for political reasons, in view of the situation in European and Asian countries where the people are resolutely opposing war. Ridgway emphasizes the police functions of American troops in allied countries . . . Morale of the U.S. allies in Europe, for example, is said to depend largely on the presence of American divisions, as concrete evidence that the U.S.A. is firmly committed to defense of that area. In Asian countries . . . it is still more important to keep big American ground forces in constant combat preparedness for fighting the national-liberation movement.[32]

Konenenko concluded that the Air Force view had won out, since the emphasis of the military programs of the Eisenhower Administration "is paying attention principally to aviation," particularly to strategic air power. This argument, incidentally, was corroborated in various earlier issues of *Voennaia Mysl'* and other Soviet sources. The idea of the United States "fighting with other people's hands" has been a long-held Soviet view; hence, Konenenko's reiteration of it was not surprising. The Soviet leadership must have thought privately that the United States had a good idea, considering the extent to which the Soviets later made use of Cuban and East European "proxy troops." The emphasis on air power was seen by Konenenko as "the cardinal objective and is based on the wide use of atomic and thermonuclear weapons, which is fully in line with the demands of Dulles' (sic) 'new policy'."[33]

2. *Massive retaliation assumed that the United States would be relatively invulnerable to any sort of retaliatory strike by the Soviet Union and that the United States possessed superior delivery capability.*

At least before the development of the Soviet ICBM in 1957, it appears, the Soviets had tacitly conceded this sort of relative invulnerability. For example, one Soviet general, on the pretext of attacking U.S. overseas bases as "offensive springboards," implied such U.S. invulnerability in a March 1955 issue of *New Times*:

> The aggressive elements in the United States calculated—and largely do now—being able to deliver a massive atomic attack on the vital centres of the Soviet Union and other peaceable countries. They believed, moreover, that the United States would be relatively invulnerable to retaliation. The imperialist strategists are not in the least perturbed by the generally recognized vulnerability of their satellites in Western Europe and other areas where the United States has military bases.[34]

Since the author did not attempt to refute U.S. invulnerability by claiming a Soviet retaliatory capability against the United States, but instead implied Soviet retaliation against Western European bases, it is apparent that the Soviets were admitting their own inability at that time to retaliate effectively against U.S. territory. (The mainstay of the Soviet bomber force in 1955 was the TU-4, which possessed a range of no more than 2,000 miles and thus could not have reached most of the continental United States.)[35]

Even the later Soviet claims about the effects of ICBM development on U.S. doctrine admitted that the United States had been invulnerable from their point of view. It was stated in the November 1965 issue of *Soviet Military Review* that "the Soviet Union's achievements in creating powerful nuclear weapons and intercontinental and other missiles reduced to naught America's quondam 'invulnerability,' bringing about the utter collapse . . . of the 'strategy of massive retaliation'."[36] The same admission was also made by Sokolovskiy in *Voennaia Strategia,* conceding that "previously the United States could, with almost complete immunity, threaten the unrestrained use of nuclear weapons in any incident, even in local military conflicts which might possibly arise." In retrospect as well as at the time, therefore, the Soviets clearly recognized U.S. immunity prior to their development of the ICBM.[37]

Much the same sort of validity can be attributed to the Soviet contention regarding the U.S. assumption of superior delivery capability. Soviet analysts had argued that the development of the Soviet ICBM meant that the United States "had now lost any superiority with regard to means of delivery," which of course implied that the United States had been superior prior to that time.[38]

The authors of *Voennaia Strategia* also stated as much in their argument that the United States "was assuming that the countries of the socialist camp would not dare to take this step [i.e., initiate a nuclear war] because of their unfavorable position with respect to offensive nuclear forces."[39]

3. *The strategy of massive retaliation placed a significant emphasis on surprise, particularly in light of U.S. discussions of a preemptive strike strategy.*

As stated earlier, the Soviets themselves had significantly upgraded their own estimation of the value of surprise, proof of which was their endorsement of a preemptive strategy in the May 1955 issue of *Voennaia Mysl'*:

> Modern wars begin as a rule by surprise. The role of surprise in war as a whole, in the strategic and operationsl dimensions, has grown especially with the appearance of weapons of mass destruction. This obligates the armed forces to many things. The matter is not only to understand the significance of the factor of surprise in its entirety, to study the facts and examples of the use of surprise in the past wars. The task consists in a serious study of all sides of this question and above all in working out the ways and means of preventing surprise attack by the enemy and inflicting on the opponent preemptive blows in all dimensions—strategic, operational, and tactical.[40]

An earlier author concluded that "the duty of the Soviet armed forces is not to permit an enemy surprise attack on our country" by the use against him of a surprise "preemptive blow."[41] This suggests that the Soviets believed U.S. doctrine to be based on a surprise first strike. Indeed, the massive retaliation doctrine was apparently alluded to in the following passage:

> The military figures of the United States and Britain openly declare that they intend to open war against us by means of surprise strategic blows with atomic and hydrogen weapons on the vitally important targets deep in the rear of the countries of the camp of peace and democracy, calculating in a few days to knock out the basic industrial targets, to paralyze transport, to demoralize the population. The American-British strategists suppose that, utilizing these weapons, they can defeat the enemy as a result of an initial strike, and seize the initiative in the war.[42]

It was further contended that "surprise attack is a favorite means of the aggressor for unleashing war and proceeds from the very nature of the imperialist states."[43] But "surprise attack" as embodied in the concept of the preemptive blow already had become an accepted part of *Soviet* military strategy. One can only conclude that the Soviets were projecting their own strategic thinking onto the United States.

Furthermore, since the discussion and acceptance of a preemptive strategy took place in *Voennaia Mysl'*, a restricted journal not intended for foreign dissemination, it is clear that the Soviets did not want to admit publicly that they had adopted such a strategy. The most obvious reason was that since the Soviets believed U.S. doctrine to have been founded on surprise attack, they may have feared that admitting such a strategy on their part might have provoked the United States into a first strike. One should also consider that the Soviets probably had little confidence in their ability to execute a preemptive strike because of their unreliable intercontinental capability at the time.

Although the Soviets did not admit publicly to a preemptive strategy except in the most oblique terms, they did openly express their view that U.S. doctrine was in fact based on similar considerations. An example of this is found in the March 1957 issue of *MEMO*:

> A future war, in their opinion, appears to be of short duration, yet exceptionally destructive. The outcome of it will be decided with the aid of aviation and guided jet missiles, and yet even so, large scale land forces will be brought into action. The land forces and military-naval fleets should only consolidate successes attained as a result of the activities of strategic aviation.

> Proceeding from this, American propagandists of the air war theory draw the following conclusion: the military-air forces, particularly strategic aviation and atomic weapons, will play the decisive role at the outbreak of war; for *in order to win in contemporary war, it is necessary to deal a first surprise attack and to take the initiative in one's own hands.*[44] [Emphasis added]

A further indication of the value placed by the Soviets on surprise was an article in the August 1958 issue of *International Affairs* by Talensky. In it he stated that "surprise attack as a factor giving great advantage to those who employ it, making it possible in many cases to compensate in some degree for an unfavourable correlation of other factors determining the outcome of war, will always be very tempting to the aggressors."[45] The implication was that considerable advantage is entailed in the use of a surprise attack, no matter which side decides to use it. If great advantages could be had by the side judged to be inferior in the overall correlation of forces, how much more advantageous might such an attack be for the side in whose favor the correlation of forces was allegedly shifting? Thus it is evident, both from Soviet pronouncements in their own doctrine and from their assessments of the alleged emphasis on surprise in U.S. strategic doctrine, that the Soviets were mirror-imaging their own concepts of surprise and the preemptive strike onto U.S. doctrine. As will be shown in subsequent chapters, this mirror-imaging tendency has significant implications for U.S. doctrinal planning.

4. *The development of the Soviet ICBM undermined the basis of the massive retaliation doctrine by rendering the United States vulnerable to a Soviet retaliatory strike. Once the United States realized that it was no longer invulnerable to a Soviet retaliatory strike, it was forced to adopt a different doctrine.*

The Soviets could find support for this contention among U.S. analysts, since U.S. vulnerability was being admitted by Bernard Brodie and Henry Kissinger in their respective analyses of massive retaliation.[46] Not only did Soviet analysts regard Soviet ICBM deployment as a decisive factor, but they still regarded it as such later on, claiming that "the achievement of superiority by the Soviet Union over the imperialist aggressors in the might of nuclear ammunition and the possibility of the inexorable and accurate delivery of them to the designated target forced the military and political leadership of the imperialist states to openly recognize the need to 'reassess values'."[47]

The Soviets were quick to exploit their launching of an ICBM in August 1957. Indeed, for the next four years, the Soviets would engage in a very successful exercise in strategic bluffing, convincing most U.S. observers that they were proceeding with ICBM production and deployment at a rate far greater than was actually the case. Khrushchev, in his public statements, found it useful to suggest two apparently contradictory theses: that the Soviets were rapidly acquiring a force capable of destroying the United States, and that they would take steps to acquire such a force if U.S. behavior did not become less hostile.[48] Ultimately however, the Soviet leaders must have regretted their reliance on such a bluff for so long, since it resulted only in a redoubled U.S. ICBM effort in the early 1960s, which produced a larger, if temporary, margin of U.S. strategic superiority than before.

Typical of Soviet statements contending that the Soviet ICBM capability was forcing the United States to reconsider its strategic doctrine was an article in the January 1960 issue of *International Affairs*: the author correctly observed that the United States had lost the near-absolute invulnerability to nuclear attack upon which the massive retaliation doctrine had been based:

> The program and aims of the United States remained unchanged even after it had lost its nuclear monopoly. The American rulers thought that, having the bombs and also the "near-absolute power of delivery," the United States would for a long time retain decisive predominance in this field, as well as *a monopoly of invulnerability* and hence "freedom of action" in time and space. This was an illusion. American military authorities now have to acknowledge that the 'atomic age strategy' is in a state of deep crisis.[49] [Emphasis in original.]

The implication of this Soviet perception is quite critical since it represented a means by which the Soviets could exert influence on U.S. strategic doctrine without having to rely on anything not under Soviet control. In later Soviet analyses, this was to be regarded as a major qualitative shift in the overall "correlation of forces" between the United States and the Soviet Union.

Conclusions

The main idea to remember concerning this period of the Soviet perception of U.S. strategic doctrine is that the Soviet views of the utility of strategic power were formulated during this period and eventually became the basis for later Soviet versions of a nuclear warfighting doctrine. The Soviets perceived themselves as restrained by U.S. nuclear superiority during this period, although they admitted this publicly only in retrospect. They also saw a great deal of similarity between U.S. strategic doctrine and their own, which also contributed significantly to the inhibition of the use of Soviet military power. With the exception of the Soviet suppression of the Hungarian Revolution in 1956, the Soviet use of military power during the period of the massive retaliation doctrine was confined to threats and military manuevers (see Appendix B).

At this particular stage of U.S. strategic doctrine, it is difficult to see the significant effect that U.S. doctrine and strategic power was eventually to have on Soviet military programs. Once the United States began to formulate strategic concepts advocating more "limited" uses of military power, however, Soviet analysts were confronted with a new problem.

Notes

1. Bonds, *The Soviet War Machine*, 86, 105.
2. Ibid., 86, 106. This opinion is shared by Wolfe in *Soviet Power and Europe, 1945-1970*, 178-84.
3. Examples of such behavior are given in Garthoff, *Soviet Military Policy*, 110-30; Horelick and Rush, *Strategic Power and Soviet Foreign Policy*, 105-56.
4. See Horelick and Rush, *Strategic Power*, 30-31.
5. F.D. Kohler, et al., *Soviet Strategy for the Seventies: From Cold War to Peaceful Coexistence* (Coral Gables, Fla.: Center for Advanced International Studies, 1973), 32-38.
6. Ibid., 39.
7. F. Isayev, "Fallacies of the Policy of Strength," *New Times* 10 (March 1955): 9.
8. X [G. Kennan], "The Sources of Soviet Conduct," *Foreign Affairs* 25, 4, (July 1947): 566-82.
9. Garthoff, *Soviet Strategy*, 85.
10. V. Kurasov, "On the Question of the Preemptive Blow," *Krasnaia Zvezda*, April 27, 1958, trans. by H.S. Dinerstein (Santa Monica, Calif.: RAND, T-87, May 12, 1958).
11. L. Gromov and V. Strigachov, "The Arms Race: Dangers and Consequences," *International Affairs* 12 (December 1960): 15. Brodie did not help matters by referring to "preemptive strike" as merely a variation of "preventive war," which is incorrect. As pointed out in the text, the motivational emphasis for the two strategies is different. See Brodie, *Strategy in the Missile Age*, 241-2.
12. Gromov and Strigachov, "The Arms Race," 15.
13. Horelick and Rush, *Strategic Power*, 35-102.
14. N. Talensky, "Military Strategy and Foreign Policy," *International Affairs*, 3, (March 1958): 27.
15. M. Mil'shtein, "Bases and Security," *New Times* 6 (February 1958): 6.
16. B. Teplinksy, "Military Bases and American Strategic Doctrine," *International Affairs* 9 (September 1959): 84.
17. Ibid., 85.

18. I. Yermashov, "The Crisis of American 'Atomic Age Strategy'," *International Affairs* 1 (January 1960): 54.
19. Kissinger, *Nuclear Weapons*, 106-7.
20. Yermashov, "Atomic Age Strategy," 53.
21. See M. Harvey, L. Goure, and V. Prokofieff, *Science and Technology as an Instrument of Soviet Policy* (Coral Gables, Fla: Center for Advanced International Studies, 1972), 4-5. See also M. Deane, *The Soviet Concept of the "Correlation of Forces"*, (Arlington, Va: Stanford Research Institute, Strategic Studies Center, 1976).
22. N. Talensky, "The Military Aspect of Coexistence," *International Affairs* 7 (July 1960): 65-66.
23. Bonds, *Soviet War Machine*, 210. For examples of the widely varying public estimates of the strategic balance at the time, see E. Bottome, *Missile Gap*, 227-8.
24. This was the opinion of Horelick and Rush about another article of a similar nature by Talensky. See *Strategic Power*, 80.
25. The following sources provide virtually identical analyses: R. Simonyan, "Doctrine of the American Aggressors," *Soviet Military Review* 1 (January 1969): 50; V.V. Glazov, "The Evolution of U.S. Military Doctrine," *Soviet Military Review* 11 (November 1965): 56; I. Potapov, "The Evolution of the Strategic Concepts of Imperialism in the Postwar Period," *Voenno-Istoricheskii Zhurnal* 5 (May 1971): 57; S. Konstantinov, "The Military Doctrine of American Imperialism," *KVS* 23 (December 1962): 78-85; V.D. Sokolovskiy, *Soviet Military Strategy*, trans. and ed. by H.F. Scott (New York: Crane, Russak, 1975), 54.
26. Bottome, *Missile Gap*, 25.
27. Brodie, *Strategy in the Missile Age*, 249.
28. A. Konenenko, "U.S. Military Doctrines," *International Affairs* 9 (September 1956): 63.
29. Ibid.
30. Ibid., 64-65.
31. Ibid., 65.
32. Ibid.
33. Ibid., 66. Konenenko reiterated these same views in more detail in his later book *Atomnoe Oruzhie v Voennykh Planakh SSHA* (Atomic Weapons in the Military Plans of the USA) (Moscow: Voennoe Izdatelstvo, 1957), 18-70.
34. F. Isayev, "Fallacies of the Policies of Strength," *New Times* 10 (March 1955): 4.
35. Sokolovskiy, *Soviet Military Strategy*, 54.
36. Ibid., 56-57.
37. Glazov, "U.S. Military Doctrine," 56.
38. Yermashov, "Atomic Age Strategy," 54.
39. Scott, *Soviet Military Strategy*, 54.
40. "World-wide Historic Victory of the Soviet People," *Voennaia Mysl'* 5 (May 1955): 12-13. Trans. by J. R. Thomas, (Santa Monica, Calif.: RAND, T-110, 1959), 25. Khrushchev, in retrospect, admitted early Soviet weakness in the mid-1950s in *Pravda*, August 12, 1961. Quoted in Horelick and Rush, *Strategic Power*, 30.
41. P. Rotmistrov, "On the Role of Surprise in Contemporary War," *Voennaia Mysl'* 2 (February 1955): 14. Quoted in Dinerstein, *War and the Soviet Union*, 187.
42. Rotmistrov, "Role of Surprise,", 19. Quoted in Garthoff, *Soviet Strategy*, 120.
43. Ibid.
44. M. Mil'shtein and A. Slobodenko, "The Aggressive and Adventuristic Character of US Strategic Concepts," *MEMO* 3 (March 1957): 80. Translation by L. Goure,

Some Soviet Views on Air Strategy (Santa Monica, Ca.: RAND, T-84, April 3, 1958). See also A. Horelick, *Some Soviet Views on the Nature of a Future War and the Factors Determining Its Course and Outcome* (Santa Monica, Ca.: RAND, T-97, September 15, 1958)

45. N. Talensky, "Prevention of a Surprise Attack," *International Affairs* 8 (August 1958): 54.

46. Kissinger, *Nuclear Weapons*, 41-42; Brodie, *Strategy in the Missile Age*, 261-3.

47. N. A. Lomov, ed., *Scientific-Technical Progress and the Revolution in Military Affairs*, trans. by U.S. Air Force (Washington, D.C.: U.S. Government Printing Office, 1973), 253. See also Sokolovskiy, *Soviet Military Strategy*, 56-57; V. Larionov, "The Development of Armed Means and Strategic Concepts of the USA," *MEMO* 6 (June 1966): 75.

48. See Horelick and Rush, *Strategic Power*, 42-81, for a chronological account of Soviet ICBM claims and the corresponding U.S. reaction to them.

49. Yermashov, "Atomic Age Strategy," 48.

4

Limited War: Can "U.S. Imperialism" Restrain Itself?

Soviet analysts had difficulty initially with the implications of the U.S. concept of "limited war" enunciated in 1957 by Secretary of State John Foster Dulles. The image of an inherently aggressive capitalist state publicly announcing its intentions to limit its own uses of military power in support of foreign policy objectives must have seemed contradictory to the Soviet leadership, not to mention highly suspicious. Soviet commentators nevertheless resolved the apparent contradiction in a way that was entirely compatible with the Soviet strategic mindset.

The lessons to be drawn from the Soviet interpretation of limited war are several. The first is that the Soviets perceived limited war as a necessary concession to the qualitative and quantitative growth of Soviet strategic power. Once U.S. "invulnerability" to nuclear attack had been clearly compromised by the development of the Soviet ICBM, the idea of "limiting" conflict was seen by the Soviets as a necessary adjustment for the United States in order to improve the credibility of U.S. deterrence. Khrushchev was so convinced of the decisiveness of the shift in relative strategic power that he felt confident enough to rely principally on a "minimum deterrence" posture based mainly on Soviet nuclear retaliatory capability as the foundation for an aggressive political strategy against the West.

Another relevant lesson was that the Soviets and Khrushchev in particular, saw both little possibility of an actual U.S. initiation of a total war with the Soviet Union, and a corresponding U.S. reluctance to escalate to dangerous levels in a crisis situation. The main reason behind such an appraisal was the consistent U.S. failure to react with the degree of military force implied in its doctrines of massive retaliation and limited war to Soviet provocations (in addition to the major instance of Soviet local intervention in Hungary) before the Cuban missile crisis in October 1962. This failure probably contributed as much to the weakening of the credibility of U.S. deterrence against acts of aggression as did the actual strengthening of the Soviet strategic deterrent.

In fact, this perception was undoubtedly the predominant influence on Khrushchev's decision to emplace intermediate-range missiles in Cuba in 1962, since he was already beginning to realize the political leverage value of nuclear weapons. This explains in large measure the Soviet evaluation of limited war as a lower-risk alternative for the United States.

This was confirmed by the military policy of the Khrushchev regime. With their primarily nuclear emphasis (and correspondingly low flexibility), Soviet military programs reflected a belief in the decisiveness of the nuclear weapon both as a warfighting instrument and as a restraint upon U.S. escalation. As a result of this belief, conventional forces were given a much lower priority. This was demonstrated in Khrushchev's 1960 speech in which he asserted the primacy of the nuclear weapon over other types of armament and contended that a future nuclear war would be of short duration. This was used as the rationale for an announced reduction by Khrushchev of the Soviet armed forces from 3.6 to 2.4 million men.[1] The "nuclearization" of Soviet theatre forces in Europe was both a reflection of Khrushchev's new strategic stance and a carry-over from the Stalinist strategy of holding Western Europe "hostage" as a guarantee of U.S. good behavior. In the event of war, Soviet theatre nuclear weapons would have been used in massive retaliation against NATO Europe. In fact, despite the claims of some Western analysts to the contrary, the nuclear emphasis of Soviet theatre doctrine had never been altered.[2]

It should be stressed that the tendency of Soviet analysts to fall into the mirror-imaging fallacy of projecting their own strategic culture and mindset onto the United States was a source of considerable difficulty for them. For example, they placed great weight on the pronouncements of such academics as Kissinger, Brodie, et al., as well as on statements by U.S. military and political figures, in an attempt to determine true U.S. strategic intentions. These analysts assumed that there was a degree of government control over the U.S. press similar to that in the Soviet Union. Therefore, under this assumption, no opinion or pronouncement on U.S. doctrine would have been published unless it had the backing of some U.S. political figure or government agency. This assumption led to trouble for Soviet analysts then and later; they were often confronted with a bewildering array of contradictory pronouncements. This being the case, these analysts apparently selected those U.S. pronouncements or analyses that most readily conformed to their own preconceived notions concerning the nature of U.S. strategic doctrine.

From the ideological standpoint, the U.S. limited war concept must have seemed peculiar. From the standpoint of a revolutionary state bent upon permanent alteration of the international status quo in its favor, it was difficult to comprehend that its principal adversary actually intended to limit itself regarding the use of force in a future war. Most Soviet analysts would probably have expected the United States to take its struggle with the Soviet Union with all the seriousness it deserved and therefore to see things in the same "rational" manner as they did. Their projection onto U.S. doctrine of their own strategic concepts such as the value of surprise in a nuclear war, was illustrative of such an attitude.[3] Given this kind of thinking, the logical conclusion for Soviet analysts to draw was that the limited war strategy was a forced development brought about by the growth of Soviet strategic power as perceived by the U.S. leadership.

The Soviet Propaganda Line

As in the case of the massive retaliation doctrine, Soviet declaratory deterrence efforts were aimed at discrediting the U.S. limited war strategy. They sought to achieve this by casting doubt in the minds of the U.S. leadership about the likely Soviet reaction to a limited use of military power by the United States, particularly if the United States contemplated using tactical nuclear weapons in a "limited" nuclear war in Europe.

1. *It is impossible to use nuclear weapons on a limited tactical scale because of their highly destructive nature.*

Major General N. Talensky, writing in January 1955 against NATO's then recently announced "trip-wire" strategy involving the use of tactical nuclear weapons, argued that the very nature of nuclear weapons militated against the likelihood of their being used on a tactical scale. He claimed this even though the Soviets were pushing early for their own tactical nuclear weapons,[4] thus causing one to doubt the general's sincerity:

> Atomic weapons, on the other hand, by the very nature of their combat properties, are designed, above all, for action against big economic and political. centres, against big cities, against the civilian population. An atomic bomb, an atomic rocket or an atomic shell can be of little efficacy against troops, operating in present-day, highly dispersed battle order, which are able to take cover in specially equipped trenches and shelters built by modern engineering methods in a relatively short time. In any case, such weapons are much less effective when used against troops in the field than against cities and economic centres, that is, ultimately against the civilian population.[5]

The statement that nuclear weapons are designed only for use against "economic and political centers" was aimed not only at the United States. Although Talensky was correct at the time because of the high yield and poor accuracy of then so-called tactical weapons, it is likely that he was also directing his criticism at those in the Soviet Union who emphasized the role of nuclear weapons on the battlefield and tended to view a future war in terms of a nuclear exchange. Since his article was written in January 1955, well before the Soviet enunciation of its preemptive strike strategy in the May 1955 issue of *Voennaia Mysl'* and years before Khrushchev's endorsement of the decisive role of the nuclear weapon in his January 1960 speech to the Supreme Soviet, there was still apparently room for criticism. It was Khrushchev who was to come around to the views of those criticized by Talensky in the Soviet leader's subsequent efforts to "nuclearize" Soviet European theatre forces while cutting back sharply on manpower.[6] Even so, for purposes of declaratory deterrence the Soviets made statements designed to dissuade the United States from relying on tactical nuclear weapons. An example of this is an article by Major General Isayev in the March 1955 issue of *New Times*:

> That tactical atomic weapons -or "small atomic weapons," as the NATO politicians and strategists also call them- would be used on a small scale is hardly likely because *that would be inexpedient from the purely military and tactical standpoint. Small-scale tactical tasks can be achieved no less successfully with conventional weapons.* Hence, what the Pentagon strategists have in mind is the employment of "tactical" atomic weapons on a massive scale, and in that case, no matter what name they are given, remain weapons of mass destruction.[7] [Emphasis added]

The above statement is interesting because it represents a counterpoint of sorts to the statement made by Talensky. The idea of massive use of theatre nuclear weapons was later to become a central theme in Soviet theatre doctrinal writings, particularly Colonel Sidorenko's 1972 work, *The Offensive*. As the Soviets acquired their own tactical nuclear weapons, however, this theme of Soviet declaratory deterrence receded in prominence.

2. *The use of nuclear weapons in a limited war may escalate into their use on a strategic scale.*

This theme of Soviet *desinformatsiya* had been stated ever since NATO introduced tactical nuclear weapons into its arsenal in the mid-1950s and was long a prominent theme of Soviet propaganda, as evidenced by the later Soviet reaction to President Reagan's remarks concerning the feasibility of a "limited nuclear war" in Europe.[8] One of the earliest statements of this type was Talensky's implication of escalation to a "total" war in the event of the use of tactical nuclear weapons in Europe:

> The present development of the means of atomic attack makes it possible to strike powerful blows across oceans as well. Consequently, the American atom-maniacs have no grounds for considering that if they precipitate atomic war, the territory of the United States will remain invulnerable. In a war against a strong adversary, it is impossible in our days to count on striking blows at the enemy without being subjected to his counter-blows, which might be even of greater impact.[9]

Thus the Soviets claimed that the United States could not escape some form of retaliatory blow against its territory in the event of U.S. first use of nuclear weapons, whether on a strategic scale or on a tactical scale. The likelihood was greater, however, given the comparatively poor Soviet delivery capabilities in 1955 vis-à-vis the United States, that the Soviets were more wary of the latter possibility's being chosen by the United States in the event of a war in Europe and so were hoping to create as much uncertainty in the minds of U.S. decision makers as possible.[10]

Soviet declaratory deterrence statements concerning the possible U.S. initiation of limited nuclear wars were often ambiguous, and deliberately so. For example, one military analyst contended that "there can be no guarantee that the use of 'tactical' atomic weapons will not lead to the use of 'strategic' nuclear weapons. On the contrary, use of 'tactical' nuclear weapons would *greatly increase* the likelihood of the use of 'strategic' nuclear weapons."[11] [Emphasis added.] It is interesting to note that while the author quite correctly claimed that one cannot guarantee that escalation from the tactical level use of nuclear weapons to the strategic level would not occur, he by no means was saying that such escalation was inevitable. Aside from the deterrence of U.S. limited nuclear wars against the "socialist camp," the Soviets would not have wanted the United States to know with any degree of certainty that it had a limited nuclear war option to exercise in the event of local Soviet aggression.[12]

The Soviet claims about the dangers of escalation to strategic nuclear war were also an attempt to dissuade the United States either from initiating limited wars for the suppression of so-called wars of national liberation or from preparing to defend against Soviet-initiated local wars.[13] By introducing such uncertainty into U.S. calculations about the possibility that a limited war might escalate to unacceptably dangerous levels, the Soviets were undoubtedly hoping to prevent the United States from engaging in such wars at all. On the other hand, the Soviets would not have wanted to state that such escalation to total war was absolutely inevitable. For if the Soviets closed off the option of limitations, the United States would be faced with the choice of either taking no action or immediately resorting to general war. Given U.S. discussions at the time about the merits of a preemptive strike and the known level of U.S. strategic capabilities,[14] the Soviets were probably willing to leave well enough alone. It was a direct reflection of the profoundly altered strategic balance in favor of the Soviet Union that Soviet pronouncements using the threat of escalation to strategic nuclear war were far less ambiguous in the early 1980s than they were during the mid-to-late 1950s.[15]

A variation on this theme was the assertion that the "coalitional" nature of local wars made their escalation into total war all the more likely. The reasoning was that since there existed several military blocs with binding treaty obligations, if any member of such a bloc should initiate a war, then it was possible to bring in the entire bloc to participate. Thus, it was claimed that "in this way an armed conflict can rapidly expand to dangerous size." [16] The falsity of this argument was in its implied contention that Western alliances were designed for an offensive war rather than as collective defense organizations. This was a case of distortion for the sake of propaganda, since the Soviets could not publicly attribute defensive intentions to any U.S.-supported military alliance without admitting the possibility that a "peace-loving" socialist state might start a war against such organizations.

The most prominent example of Soviet declaratory deterrence using the threat of uncontrolled escalation was Khrushchev's speech to the Supreme Soviet on January 14, 1960. By dismissing as "nonsense" limited wars, but not "wars of national liberation," Khrushchev sought to create the impression that any military involvement against the communist countries or their clients would develop into a world war:[17]

> If a war were to start now, hostilities would take a different course since the nations would have means of delivering their weapons to points thousands of kilometers away. It is first of all deep in the belligerent's territory that a war would start. Furthermore, there would not be a single capital, no large industrial or administrative center, and no strategic area left unattacked in the very first minutes let alone days, of the war. In other words, the war would start in a different manner, if at all, and would proceed in a different manner."[18]

Khrushchev seemed to have been placing primary emphasis on a posture of minimum deterrence, relying heavily upon the image, if not the reality, of Soviet retaliatory power as the basis for an aggressive political strategy. Khrushchev assumed that the U.S. reluctance to escalate was great enough that he could pursue an aggressive diplomatic strategy without worrying about his bluff being called. If it ever was, he apparently had confidence in his ability to control the ensuing risk of war. Khrushchev's error was in thinking that the Western "threshold of concession" was low enough that it could be overcome without producing situations that carried an unacceptable risk of escalation to all-out war.[19]

3. *The United States is using limited conventional wars as a preparation for unleashing a total nuclear war against the Soviet Union.*

This assertion was included along with otherwise quite valid observations such as U.S. use of limited wars against the "national liberation movement," contending that "the theory of 'local' war is a mask designed to conceal the preparations for total war and to justify the use of nuclear weapons in the struggle against the peoples who have unfurled the banner of national liberation." [20] In other words, the Soviets claimed that the concept of a limited war was camouflage designed to conceal preparation for a total nuclear war and that any so-called limited war that occurred was merely a potential pretext for escalation to all-out war. Although the Soviets realized that the lack of credibility of massive retaliation made limited war a safer means of enforcing the containment strategy for the United States, ideological constraints prevented the Soviets from making public speculation on this point. Indeed, given their assertion that the United States represented a social system that was immutably and inherently hostile and aggressive towards socialism, they could do little publicly other than assert that the U.S. limited war doctrine was really designed to conceal preparations for an all-out war.

It is noteworthy that Soviet analysts tended to qualify their statements regarding this theme with the phrase "should [or "if"] the aggressors succeed in unleashing war." This implied that there were restraining factors at work at the time that prevented the United States from following its "natural" inclination to initiate an all-out conflict against the socialist states. The development of the Soviet ICBM capability was identified as one of the main constraints on U.S. freedom of action, since contemporary war could now "bring fearful destruction to both sides." It was further asserted that "a thermonuclear blow can shatter the faith of a people in the economy, government, and national aim."[21] It is difficult to believe, however, that the Soviets actually meant these statements, given the fact that Soviet strategic capabilities were exceedingly limited with respect to the United States, even in 1958, when the Soviet ICBM was being deployed.

For comparison, the U.S. strategic force at that time possessed an estimated 2,150-plus strategic bombers capable of delivering megaton-range weapons to the Soviet Union. Of these, 250 were B-52s, with the remainder including 1,800 B-47s and less than 100 B-58s. The Soviets, on the other hand, had a force of slightly more than 1,000 Bison and Badger bombers with a capability of reaching the periphery of the United States only by one-way missions. Even by 1960, the United States had at least a 3-to-1 advantage in long-range bombers. The first Soviet operational ICBM was deployed in numbers that were virtually negligible (only 10 operational SS-6s by late 1959).[22]Nevertheless, it was argued by such Soviet analysts as Talensky that the United States and its allies could not easily resort to all-out war, despite their alleged wishes to do so:

> Such statements are fully justified, for Kissinger admits that thermo-nuclear war will lead to the collapse of the social system of Western Europe. This circumstance, plus the desire to conceal from the public, which is working for peace, the preparations for an all-out struggle for world dominion, explain the advocacy of the "local war" theory.

> But this cannot deceive anyone, because the strategy of "local war" serves also foreign policy aims connected with the struggle for world dominion. A head-on attack in this case is replaced by a system of [maneuvering] with "local" wars, behind which looms the shadow of nuclear war.[23]

It is indicative of the Soviets' real lack of confidence in their intercontinental capability that Talensky claimed that a thermonuclear war would be disastrous for Western Europe, but omitted mentioning the United States.

A similar argument was that the United States, restrained by "the forces of peace," had been successfully restricted to the use of limited wars. At the same time, because of the allegedly aggressive nature of imperialism, the United States was nevertheless continuing to make preparations for war, whether limited or total. This usually accompanied the accurate recognition of the United States' attempting to find a more realistic approach to its strategic deterrence/warfighting doctrine. The resulting line was that the supposedly aggressive nature of imperialism carried with it the perpetual threat of war.[24]

Aside from the propaganda value of this third theme, it had some strategic value as well. The only circumstances under which a limited war could not be possible were either if (1) the Soviets themselves launched an all-out thermonuclear attack (in which case the Soviets would already have decided against limitation of the conflict) or (2) the United States itself launched such an attack (in which case the United States would not have been serious about the idea of limitations anyway).[25] By contending that the United States was using limited war as a smokescreen to conceal preparations for a general war, the Soviets could thus argue that such limitations could not reasonably be expected to hold up in actual practice.

Even in such propagandistic statements, however, were indications that the Soviets were hedging in their public statements concerning U.S. use of limited war as a prelude to total war:

> The "limited" war concept has attracted the Pentagon directors because, in their view, it enables them to prepare for total war through a series of small wars, with *ample time for logistical preparation of a "major blow."*[26] [Emphasis added.]

These authors were clearly assuming a U.S. policy of *deliberate and controlled escalation*, rather than a surprise attack to initiate a total war. The passage further implied that the necessary logistical preparation would not be completed in advance of the conflict. This indicates that the Soviets were well aware that the U.S. would not be initiating local "aggression" in most cases, but rather it would be the Soviet Union sponsoring its clients in "wars of national liberation."

The most important point is that the Soviets publicly claimed that the United States would be controlled and deliberate in its preparations for unleashing a total war by means of limited wars, even though (as shown in the preceding chapter) the Soviets ascribed to U.S. strategic doctrine a similar appraisal of the value of surprise. Such being the case, if Soviet analysts assumed a U.S. policy of deliberate and controlled escalation as inherent in limited war strategy, *thus reducing the degree of surprise*, it would not have made sense to Soviet analysts for the United States to so negate surprise unless there were no U.S. intent to start a total war in the first place. This proves that this third theme of Soviet declaratory deterrence was propaganda, since it did not agree with their mirror-imaged view of U.S. strategic doctrine.

The Soviets obliquely admitted as much in the following passage from the August 1958 issue of *MEMO*. The author camouflaged his recognition that the United States had no intention to start a nuclear war by claiming that the United States had admitted the "impossibility" of destroying the Soviet Union in such a war:

> Thus, the doctrine of "limited war" originates from the calculations on the possibility of the successful conduct of "local wars" against the nations of the socialist camp. It is interesting that the starting point of this concept appears to be *the realistic recognition of the impossibility of destroying the camp of socialism with the aid of a total nuclear war.* Yet is in this case the doctrine of "limited war" realistic, which also has its own prerequisite suppositions about the "superiority" of the western nations over the USSR in military-technological relations? Today such calculations appear to be incorrect even among influential circles in the west.[27] [Emphasis added]

Soviet commentators still had to deal with the fact that the Korean conflict had not escalated as they had claimed it should have; indeed, the United States had taken pains to keep the war from going beyond the Korean peninsula by not attacking the Chinese mainland with U.S. airpower. Nor did the United States ever introduce tactical nuclear weapons into the battle, although Truman had briefly toyed with the idea. The Indochinese conflict was still at a comparatively low level of U.S. involvement, the French only recently having exited the scene following their debacle at Dien Bien Phu in 1954. In order to explain such conflicts, the standard Soviet line was that it had been "the forces of peace" that restrained the United States from escalating these wars into a total war. This claim was clearly false, since if the Soviets had really believed that these conflicts could have led to an all-out war with the United States, they would never have encouraged them:

> But aggressive tendencies are organically inherent in imperialism. Recent history has repeatedly borne out this Leninist precept. However, the objective possibilities of putting their aggressive plans into effect are slipping away from the imperialists owing to the new balance of forces. In 1950, for example, the imperialists were still able to keep up the aggression in Korea, but already unable to turn it into a world war in spite of the fact that America's atomic monopoly was then only just breached. Three or four years later the forces of peace were strong enough to compel the imperialists to accept a cease-fire in Korea and Indochina, and to give up their plan of involving new states and peoples in armed con flicts.[28]

Despite the especially great amount of propagandistic rhetoric and *desinformatsiya* that accompanied Soviet analyses and commentaries on the U.S. limited war concept, it is still possible to discern the actual Soviet perception of the limited war strategy by a variety of means.

The Actual Soviet View

One of the best means of checking the actual Soviet evaluation of limited war was the course of Soviet foreign policy during the years of the Khrushchev regime. The failure of the United States to make the Hungarian Revolution of 1956 a *casus belli* may have contributed heavily to Khrushchev's belief that the likelihood of U.S. initiation of nuclear war against the Soviet Union had greatly declined. There were also subsequent situations in which the Soviets "baited" the United States with missile threats. Examples were the Turkish-Syrian tensions in October 1957, the Quemoy Straits crisis from August to September 1958, the Soviet exertion of diplomatic pressure against Berlin from 1958 to 1961, and, of course, the Cuban missile crisis of October 1962.[29] After each of these provocations, with the exception of the Cuban missile crisis, the lack of an especially strong U.S. response undoubtedly helped to convince Khrushchev that he was operating within safe limits and that Soviet deterrence was effective against the possibility of threatening U.S. escalation. On the other hand, it should be noted that with the aforementioned exception of Indochina there were no overtly Soviet-sponsored "wars of national liberation," which would have put U.S. limited war doctrine to a decisive test.[30] In any event, Khrushchev was apparently not deterred from provocative actions, even if he was deterred from actual aggression, by either the massive retaliation or limited war doctrines of the United States.

During the entire span of Soviet analysis of the limited war concept, two predominant themes have emerged as the most consistent.

1. *The U.S. doctrine of limited war represents a U.S. search for a more credible strategic doctrine as a forced result of the qualitative shift in the strategic balance in favor of the Soviet Union. The United States hopes to avoid Soviet nuclear retaliation through the use of limited wars.*

One of the first Soviet analysts to discuss the U.S. rationale behind its limited war doctrine on a serious level was N. Inozemtsev, a political analyst for *MEMO* who was later to become the head of the Institute of World Economics and International Relations in July 1966.[31] In his March 1958 article in *MEMO*, he described the massive retaliation doctrine as essentially a "subjective idea; a relative conception of force based upon U.S. interpretation of its own superiority in the area of thermonuclear weapons." According to Inozemtsev, the growth of Soviet nuclear potential in combination with the improved capability of the Soviet Union to deliver such weapons had caused U.S. "ruling circles" not to dare "to unleash atomic war."[32] Given these circumstances, he described how U.S. leadership resolved the impasse:

> What was the way out? A rejection of the policy "from positions of strength" and "atomic diplomacy," of plans which had gone bankrupt, bound together by the groundless calculations of the "atomic superiority" of the USA? Nothing of the sort happened! The solution was merely a few variations and additions to the "massive retaliation" doctrine. This was done by means of setting forth in the years 1956-1957 the concepts of so-called "graduated restraint" ("graduated deterrence") and "local," "limited," wars.[33]

Inozemtsev did not claim that graduated deterrence was a fundamentally new departure in U.S. doctrine; he argued instead that it was simply a derivation of massive retaliation:

> The concept of "graduated restraint" is no less aggressive than all previous atomic concepts. It has the same basis as that of "massive retaliation": the rejection of the prohibition of thermonuclear weapons, the orientation towards atomic war. Kissinger admits this, declaring that "limited war" and the "gradual application of force" present themselves "not as an alternative, but a supplement to massive retaliation."[34]

In other words, the U.S. was attempting to increase its options by the expedient of changing its strategic doctrine to meet the needs of an altered power balance, or correlation of forces. It was natural, therefore, for the Soviets to have recognized this attempt and make use of declaratory deterrence statements in an effort to discredit the new concept.

One of the most controversial defense issues during the late 1950s was the publication of the Rockefeller and Gaither Reports (or at least, in the case of the classified Gaither report, the accepted version of the report that was leaked to the public). The Gaither and Rockefeller reports were the results of classified and unclassified studies, respectively, that were made in late 1957 concerning virtually every aspect of U.S. defense policy. Although initially appointed by Eisenhower for the purpose of investigating the future role of civil defense in U.S. defense policy, the Gaither Committee (which was to receive far more publicity than the unclassified and less pessimistic Rockefeller Report) carried its investigation further than had been originally envisioned. Although the report remained classified, leaks of the contents of the report from various persons led to the emergence of a widely accepted version of its findings over a period of several months.

The greatest single impact of the Gaither Report was on the missile debate. The committee claimed that SAC would be vulnerable to a major attack from a large projected Soviet ICBM force by the early 1960s. It called for additional military spending on missile sites once the U.S. developed an operational ICBM.[35]

The Rockefeller and Gaither reports were regarded as especially significant by the Soviets. In the July 1958 issue of *MEMO*, one analyst claimed that the United States was moving toward a more flexible strategic doctrine, because "inasmuch as the risk, connected with the delivery of an aggressive nuclear blow on the USSR has become too dangerous, the Rockefeller group is recommending using a more flexible strategy." This meant, therefore, that U.S. doctrine had actually changed under the primary impetus of the growth of Soviet strategic power.[36] This view was more explicitly stated by Konenenko in the July 1958 issue of *International Affairs*:

> It is not for nothing that American publications of all kinds are paying more attention to the idea of "limited," "local" and "little" wars, trying even to create the impression that a major world war can be replaced by a series of "little" wars, thus preventing military operations from touching American soil . . . The fear that the capitalist system would collapse as a result of a total nuclear war is the main reason for the interest in "little" wars. Henry A. Kissinger, the American military writer, writes in his *Nuclear Weapons and Foreign Policy* that "the fear that an all-out thermonuclear war might lead to the disintegration of the social structure offers an opportunity to set limits to both war and diplomacy."[37]

Konenenko reiterated this theme in the October 1958 issue of *MEMO*, claiming that "at the present time, political, military-economic and strategic centers on U.S. territory can come under retaliatory strikes of nuclear and rocket weapons of those nations which they are attacking in the event of American aggression."[38] This opinion was similar to one expressed in an earlier issue of *MEMO*, in which the authors asserted that "bourgeois ideologists" did not want to take into account the "new correlation of forces between the two systems" and therefore were making use of "limited" wars.[39] Both articles stressed the emergence of changes in the military balance that *had forced* the United States to consider changes in its strategic doctrine. The earlier article recognized, however, that the United States did not accept Soviet claims implying changes in the correlation of forces.

This theme was repeated during the 1960s as well.[40] The most authoritative source for this theme, however, was found in an article in the July 1969 issue of *Voennaia Mysl'*, in which the characteristics of limited wars were analyzed:

> The imperialists count mainly in these wars on the use of conventional means of destruction. True, in certain conditions they also permit the use of tactical nuclear weapons. However, before utilizing them, they must think a great deal about the possible consequences. In any case, the idea of achieving the goals in local wars by such means and methods which would not engender retaliatory nuclear strikes against the territory of the aggressor himself constitutes the most attractive idea for the monopolists.[41]

It is clear, therefore, that the Soviets were quite genuine in their perception of "limited" war as a forced accommodation by the United States to increased relative Soviet strategic power in addition to its being a "lower-risk" approach.

2. *The United States is employing limited war as a means of suppressing the "national-liberation movement," thereby attempting to enforce its overall strategy of containment.*

The accuracy of this Soviet theme of perception is based on the fact that it was merely a recognition of the defensively oriented "grand strategy" of the United States, given the name "containment" by George Kennan, former U.S. ambassador to the Soviet Union, in his well-known article outlining the containment strategy and its rationale in the July 1947 issue of *Foreign Affairs*.[42] One of the initial statements of this line was made in an October 1958 issue of *New Times*, in which the authors tacitly recognized limited war as an instrument of the overall strategy of containment:

> Believers in "limited" war suggest concentration on the achievement of partial aims, such as suppression of the national-liberation movement and bolstering of reactionary regimes, as a prelude to total war.[43]

Further corroboration was found in an October 1958 issue of *MEMO*. The author asserted that the U.S. espousal of a limited war doctrine meant that "they are attempting to galvanize the adventuristic policy 'from positions of strength,' consolidate the loosened system of colonialism, and to prolong the world support for the old discredited path of 'cold war.'"[44]

Soviet observers, therefore, did not perceive any U.S. willingness to restrain its own behavior, or even to accept such restraints once they had been placed on it. Once U.S. invulnerability had been lost with the development of Soviet intercontinental capability, it seemed logical to the Soviets that the United States would do everything it could to restore the credibility of U.S. strategic doctrine. Such was the view of one Soviet political analyst, who observed that the advocates of local war believed that "it restores the geographical factor-that it guarantees the United States invulnerability from without while keeping intact the possibility of waging war abroad, in Europe, Asia, and Africa."[45]

Similar to the other theme of Soviet perceptions on limited war, this notion of limited war as an instrument of the containment strategy was echoed in more authoritative Soviet journals in later years. And again, the premier example can be found in the July 1969 issue of the formerly classified Soviet general staff publication *Voennaia Mysl'*:

> [Local wars] are usually unleashed and conducted by the imperialist states for the purpose of suppressing the national-liberation movement of the peoples or overthrowing the governments in a particular country liberated from colonial

oppression which are unsuitable to the main imperialist powers, as well as seizing the important economic and strategic territories. [46]

Public Soviet statements were fully in consonance with that expressed above, charging that limited war was designed "as a means of gradually 'shattering' socialism, suppressing the national-liberation movement, and thereby shoring up the positions of capitalism."[47] Thus, it is clear that Soviet pronouncements were consistent and accurate in their recognition of the defensive objectives of the limited war concept, even though such recognition was camouflaged by a great amount of propagandistic rhetoric as part of the Soviet *desinformatsiya* strategy.

Conclusions

What effect did U.S. strategic doctrine have upon Soviet doctrine and policy development during the massive retaliation period (1954-1960)? When one looks at the content of Khrushchev's speech in January 1960 and the military programs that preceded and followed that speech, one would have to say that Khrushchev, at least, was impressed enough by the potential value of nuclear weapons for political leverage to have placed significant reliance on his own version of massive retaliation.

The demise of Khrushchev's minimum deterrence posture came with the denouement of the Cuban missile crisis in October 1962. The lesson of that publicly humiliating confrontation was forcefully driven home to the subsequent Soviet leadership under Brezhnev: In a confrontation situation, perceived strategic superiority in favor of one of the protagonists exerts a decisive influence on the outcome and enhances the use of other forms of military power to achieve political objectives. This explains the rapid strategic buildup following the accession of the Brezhnev regime to power in October 1964, in addition to an across-the-board increase in conventional, and especially naval, forces. Khrushchev's version of the Soviet nuclear warfighting doctrine had been discredited by the Cuban missile crisis; as will be seen in subsequent chapters, the U.S. doctrine of flexible response was to play its role in influencing Soviet doctrine and programs. The Soviet perspective concerning flexible response is examined next.

Notes

1. T. Wolfe, *Soviet Power and Europe, 1945-1970* (Baltimore: Johns Hopkins, 1970), 144-5.
2. See Joseph D. Douglass, Jr., *The Soviet Theater Nuclear Offensive* (Washington, D.C.: U.S. Air Force, 1975), 101-7. See also T. Aeppel, "East German Papers Yield War Scenario," *Wall Street Journal*, June 13, 1991, 13.

3. See Chapter 3.
4. Wolfe, *Soviet Power*, 195.
5. N. Talensky, "Atomic and Conventional Arms," *International Affairs* 1 (January 1955): 26.
6. Wolfe, *Soviet Power*, 160-84. See also F. Isayev, "The Small Atomic Weapons Myth," *New Times* 13 (March 1955): 7.
7. Isayev, "Weapons Myth," 7.
8. See issues of the *New York Times* in late November 1981 for documentation on the official Soviet reaction to President Reagan's remarks on the feasibility of limited nuclear war in Europe.
9. Talensky, "Atomic and Conventional Arms," 29.
10. Garthoff, *Soviet Strategy in the Nuclear Age*, 110.
11. Isayev, "Weapons Myth," 8.
12. Garthoff, *Soviet Strategy*, 110.
13. M. Mil'shtein and A. Slobodenko, "The Aggressive and Adventuristic Character of US Strategic Concepts," *MEMO* 3 (March 1957): 77. See also their book written at the end of the "massive retaliation" period, *O Burzhuaznoi Voennoi Nauke* (Concerning Bourgeois Military Science) (Moscow: Voennoe Izdatelstvo, 1961), 303-20. See also Garthoff, *Soviet Strategy*, 111.
14. See chapter 2.
15. See n. 8.
16. V. Mochalov and V. Dashichev, "The Smoke Screen of the American Imperialists," *Krasnaya Zvezda*, December 17, 1957. Trans. in L. Goure, *Soviet Commentary on the Doctrine of Limited Nuclear Wars* (Santa Monica, Calif.: RAND, T-82, 5 March 1958), p. 8.
17. See the analysis of Khrushchev's speech by H.S. Dinerstein in *Soviet Strategic Ideas: January 1960* (Santa Monica, Calif.: RAND, RM-2532, February 19, 1960), 27-28.
18. See H.F. Scott, *Soviet Military Doctrine: Its Continuity, 1960-1970* (Menlo Park, Calif.: Stanford Research Institute, SSC-TN-8974-28, 17 June 1971), 78, for a translation of Khrushchev's speech.
19. Bonds, *Soviet War Machine*, 206. See also Wolfe, *Soviet Power*, 89; Horelick and Rush, *Strategic Power and Soviet Foreign Policy* (Chicago: University of Chicago Press, 1966), 115.
20. N. Talensky, "Military Strategy and Foreign Policy," *International Affairs* 3 (March 1958): 28.
21. Ibid., 29.
22. Bottome, *Missile Gap*, 223-4. See also Bonds, *Soviet War Machine* 207, 212; Bonds, *US War Machine* (New York: Crown, 1978), 60, for the estimated number of operational B-58s; 0. Penkovskiy, *The Penkovskiy Papers*, trans. by P. Deriabin (New York: Doubleday, 1965), 320-35; Wolfe, *Soviet Power*, 180.
23. Talensky, "Military Strategy," 29.
24. L. Dikin, "Problems of US Military Policy and Strategy in the Reports of the Rockefeller and Gaither Committees," *MEMO* 7 (July 1958): 100-1.
25. Garthoff, *Soviet Strategy*, 111.
26. M. Mil'shtein and A. Slobodenko, "'Limited War': Weapon of Unlimited Aggression," *New Times* 40 (October 1958): 14.
27. O. Bogdanov, "Nuclear Weapons and the Problem of World Security," *MEMO* 8 (August 1958): 9.

28. L. Fyodorov, "International Relations and the Battle of Ideologies," *International Affairs* 3 (March 1960): 9-10.
29. Wolfe, *Soviet Power*, 88-89. See also Horelick and Rush, *Strategic Power*, 105-41.
30. Wolfe, *Soviet Power*, 88-89.
31. *Directory of Soviet Officials, Volume 1: National Organizations* (Washington, D.C.: National Foreign Assessment Center, CR 78-14025, 1978), 381.
32. N. Inozemtsev, "US 'Atomic Diplomacy': Plans and Activities," *MEMO* 3 (March 1958): 38. See also V. Korzun, "Strategy of Aggression," *KVS* 3 (February 1967): 91, for a later corroboration.
33. Inozemtsev, "Atomic Diplomacy," 38.
34. Ibid., 39.
35. See Bottome, *Missile Gap*, 44-48.
36. Dikin, "Rockefeller and Gaither," *MEMO* 7 (July 1958), 97.
37. A. Konenenko, "Present U.S. Military Thinking and the Arms Drive," *International Affairs* 7 (July 1958): 35.
38. A. Konenenko, "'Local Wars' in the Policy and Strategy of the USA," *MEMO* 10 (October 1958): 17-18.
39. M. Mil'shtein and A. Slobodenko, "The Problem of the Correlation of Policy and War in Contemporary Imperialist Ideology," *MEMO* 9 (September 1958): 73.
40. The following references all offer the same corroboration of this theme: Y. Oleshchuk, "Small Wars and the Aggression in Vietnam," *International Affairs* 5 (May 1966): 35-36; V. Matsulenko, "The Small War Theory at the Service of the Imperialists," *Soviet Military Review* 4 (April 1966): 53; P. Zhilin and Y. Rybkin, "Militarism and Contemporary International Relations," *International Affairs* 10 (October 1973) 27; T. Kondratkov, "Limited War-Instrument of Imperialist Aggression," *KVS* 8 (April 1967): 25; B. Teplinsky, " U.S. Military Programme," *International Affairs* 8 (August 1967): 47; V. D. Sokolovskiy, *Soviet Military Strategy*, trans. and ed. by H. F. Scott (New York: Crane, Russak, 1975), 64.
41. V. Zemskov, "Characteristic Features of Modern Wars and Possible Methods of Conducting Them," *Voennaia Mysl'* 7 (July 1969), trans. in FBIS No. 0022/70, April 6, 1970, 25.
42. See [George Kennan], "The Sources of Soviet Conduct," *Foreign Affairs* 2 ʲ, 4, (July 1947), 566-82. See also Dikin, "Rockefeller and Gaither," 97.
43. Mil'shtein and Slobodenko, "Limited War," 14.
44. Konenenko, "Local Wars," 17-18. See also N. Talensky, "On the Character of Modern Warfare," *International Affairs* 10 (October 1960): 26; Bogdanov, "Nuclear Weapons," 10.
45. I. Yermashov, "The Doctrine of 'Acceptable War': Illusions and Reality," *International Affairs* 11 (November 1960): 17.
46. Zemskov, "Modern Wars," 25. See also S. Malyanchikov, "On the Nature of Armed Struggle in Local Wars," *Voennaia Mysl'* 11 (November 1965), trans. in FBIS, No. 953, March 8, 1966, 12-24.
47. V. Mochalov, "What Lies Behind the Theory of 'Limited Wars'?", *Soviet Military Review* 8 (August 1969): 54. See also note 40.

Part III

FLEXIBLE RESPONSE PERIOD
(1961-1968)

5

Flexible Response and Soviet Reaction

Did U.S. strategic doctrine ever exert an influence on Soviet military behavior and programs? Until the fall of Khrushchev in 1964, one could not really answer in the affirmative with any solid evidence. Once the Brezhnev-Kosygin regime was firmly entrenched, however, Soviet military programs sharply increased over the entire spectrum of nuclear and conventional capability. The Soviet perception of flexible response had much to do with the decisions regarding military buildup, as well as with the gradual increase in scale of the Soviet use of military power in support of foreign policy objectives during the latter half of the 1960s.

Three main conclusions can be drawn about the Soviet perception and reaction to the new U.S. strategic doctrine of flexible response. These perceptions were reflected in Soviet foreign policy behavior and in Soviet military programs during this period. First of all, the Soviets continued to project their own strategic concepts onto U.S. doctrine during this period. This projection was a carry-over from massive retaliation; it manifested itself primarily in Soviet analyses claiming that the United States was emphasizing surprise and the possibility of delivering a successful preemptive strike on the Soviet Union at the outset of a future war. Second, the Soviets continued to perceive the evolution of U.S. strategic doctrine as the result of a forced response to the growth of Soviet strategic power. Following the development of the Soviet ICBM, the United States was compelled to come up with a doctrine that would restore the credibility of U.S. deterrence to its former predominance, without having to rely principally on the massive U.S. nuclear capability. Moreover, the U.S. abandonment of the flexible response doctrine in 1969 (when the realistic deterrence doctrine was outlined by President Nixon), although due in part to the U.S. failure in Vietnam, was also seen as having been caused by the Soviet attainment of strategic parity with the United States in 1969. This meant, in conjunction with the Soviet development of its capabilities for power projection into more distant areas during this period, that the Soviets felt they now had more freedom to support "national liberation movements" in Third World countries.

Finally, the Soviets were increasingly recognizing the likelihood of waging both nuclear and conventional limited wars without an undue risk of escalation to strategic nuclear war. This was conceded in such publications as *Voennaia Mysl'* and, though less directly, in publications intended for foreign audiences. The U.S. flexible response doctrine undoubtedly impressed the Soviet leadership with its use of "nuclear superiority" to enhance the use of U.S. conventional forces in opposing the Communist insurgency in Vietnam, and it also convinced them that a similar range of capabilities was desirable for the Soviet Union in order to support its more aggressive foreign policy goals. This view was substantiated by the shape of Soviet military programs after the accession of the Brezhnev-Kosygin regime to power in 1964, particularly the major efforts devoted to augmenting Soviet airlift and sealift capabilities.

More specifically, the great increase in Soviet naval power and sealift capability improved the Soviet ability to support "national- liberation movements" in more distant areas, or to lend logistical support to its allies, such as North Vietnam.[1] The Soviets increased their capabilities for amphibious landings by adding helicopter and landing ships and by boosting the size of Soviet marine forces from 6,000 to 12,000 men by 1969.[2]

Soviet airlift capacity was also significantly enlarged, as evidenced by its successful resupply of then Egyptian president Gamal Nasser's forces after the 1967 Arab-Israeli war, followed by smaller-scale airlifts to Yemen later in 1967 and 1968. The trend toward the development of air-landing and assault techniques, already in evidence during the Khrushchev period, was even more pronounced under Brezhnev.[3]

The most dramatic increases, however, came in the area of strategic deployments of land-based intercontinental ballistic missiles and submarine-launched ballistic missiles. Assuming a lead time of about 18 months, the decision to accelerate the construction and deployment of ICBMs and SLBMs was probably made shortly after Brezhnev and Kosygin came to power. By October 1966 the number of land-based ICBMs reached 340, and a year later the total stood at 720. Soviet ICBM levels surpassed the U.S. total of 1,054 by September 1968.[4] By 1970, the number of operational Soviet ICBMs had reached 1,300.[5] The number of long-range SLBMs rose dramatically with the deployment of Soviet Y-class submarines, comparable to the U.S. Polaris, in 1968. By 1970, these missiles numbered roughly 300.[6]

The Soviet policy of peaceful coexistence (later "detente"), as it emerged under the Brezhnev-Kosygin regime, reaffirmed the Soviet intent to avoid thermonuclear war with the United States but nevertheless to unremittingly support "national-liberation movements" in the Third World.[7] This increased scale of the use of military power in support of Soviet foreign policy objectives was reflected in the presence of Soviet "advisers" in such places as

Indonesia and Cuba in 1962, the Middle East during the late 1960s and early 1970s, and in Vietnam during the same period.[8] Although Soviet ground forces were not committed in a direct intervention during the 1960s except for Czechoslovakia (where the Soviets acted in accordance with their subsequently declared "Brezhnev Doctrine," which basically stipulated that the Soviet Union would intervene in any socialist nation that it believed was threatened by "counterrevolutionary" forces), the Soviets undoubtedly believed that the risk of confrontation with the United States was being reduced enough to justify their increased support of national liberation movements in a more direct way. This behavior stemmed from their perception and evaluation of the U.S. doctrine of flexible response.

The Soviet Propaganda Line

In keeping with the Soviet strategy of *desinformatsiya* through use of declaratory deterrence, many Soviet statements regarding flexible response were highly propagandistic in nature. While some were the same as those used against the massive retaliation doctrine back in the 1950s, other statements were tailored for use against flexible response.

1. *The ultimate goal of flexible response still remains the unleashing of total nuclear war against the Soviet Union. Flexible response envisions the use of limited wars as a preparation for unleashing such a war.*

Even by the early 1960s, this assertion had become a standard theme of Soviet propaganda. A statement typical of this kind was in an article by Colonel General N. Lomov, author of several books and articles on Soviet military doctrine. Writing in *KVS* in May 1962, Lomov claimed that the "contemporary military doctrine of the United States of America" was "an expression of the imperialist policy 'from positions of strength,'" and that "the course of imperialism had not changed."[9] Reflecting Soviet strategic thinking concerning the value of surprise, he argued that the basis of U.S. strategy was "the striving for the establishment of world domination, for the unleashing of a world nuclear rocket war *by means of a surprise attack* on the Soviet Union and the other nations of the socialist camp."[10] [Emphasis added.]

Commenting on the limited war aspect of the flexible response doctrine, Lomov quoted Khrushchev's contention that "small imperialist wars may escalate into a world nuclear war." Lomov maintained that since the United States saw that "a world war may result in the complete collapse of capitalism," the imperialists would attempt to achieve "their aggressive and reactionary goals by means of waging not only world, but also 'limited,' 'local' wars." Thus, he concluded that "a new world war may arise as a result either of a surprise attack on the part of an aggressive bloc, or the escalation of a local war."

Lomov's assertion, however, was contradictory, because starting a strategic nuclear war by escalation from a limited war would have sacrificed the element of surprise, something Soviet analysts thought was as important to U.S. planners as it was to them. This same thinking was reflected in the following passage from the first edition of Sokolovskiy's *Voennaia Strategia*, published in April 1962:

> They are afraid to take the initiative in unleashing a nuclear war, since this would be disadvantageous from a political standpoint and extremely dangerous from a military standpoint. The whole point of their plans in this regard is to use nuclear weapons in the course of expanding local conflicts, particularly at critical moments, in order to alter the situation (locally) in their favor. They expect to be able to limit the employment of nuclear weapons to their satellites and to defend their own territory, at least at the beginning of the war, from a crushing nuclear blow. This is the essence of their aggressive plans to initiate a new world war, using local wars and conflicts.[11]

The implication of the above was that the United States planned to use limited wars as a disguise for unleashing a nuclear war against the Soviet Union, since an outright nuclear strike was supposedly too dangerous for the United States itself. This made little sense, however, since the Soviets could still launch a retaliatory strike, regardless of whether it was preceded by a limited war. Also, this statement contradicted the Soviets' earlier perception that the United States placed great emphasis on surprise. Proof of this was Sokolovskiy's discussion within *Voennaia Strategia* of alleged U.S. preparation for a preventive war by means of a "preemptive strike."

The editors of *Voennaia Strategia* also implied that the United States did not intend to refrain from escalation unless the circumstances were unfavorable. This was a nonfalsifiable argument; when the United States failed to escalate a local war by using nuclear weapons, as Soviet propaganda claimed it would, this did not mean that the United States had somehow become more "responsible," but that "the forces of peace" had stopped the United States from further escalation. Soviet military commentators found this line especially useful, since it was a ready-made rationalization for "maintaining vigilance" and for further strengthening Soviet military power. This call for maximum military preparedness is illustrated in the following passage:

> Only the fear of a powerful retaliatory strike will stop the imperialists. Therefore the Soviet Union and all the socialist countries are compelled to have in readiness the necessary forces and weapons for instantaneous retaliation to aggression.[12]

As implied in the above passage, the emphasis of Soviet strategy was still based on a nuclear strike, although the preemptive aspect of such a strike was not directly stated. The reason for this emphasis was that Soviet missile deployment was still slow, not being accelerated appreciably until 1966. The stress was therefore on deterrence of U.S. strategic power through such declaratory statements.

2. *It is not possible to establish "rules of the game" for waging limited wars using nuclear or conventional weapons. Every limited war may therefore escalate into a total war.*

This was a continuation of the first theme; namely, that since the United States allegedly intended to unleash a total nuclear war using limited wars, there was constant danger that such wars would escalate into total wars. An example of this was an article in the August 1964 issue of *KVS*:

> All discussions concerning small, limited, and local wars only mask preparation for a total, global war. In the same regard, where is the guarantee that a small war does not escalate into a big one? To the point, the military ideologists of imperialism see such a guarantee in the capacity of the warring states to conduct "limited" along with "unlimited" war . . . Consequently, the discussions about a "local" war are being used as a cloak for the preparation for a large thermonuclear war.

> Any war, if the imperialists unleash it, has a tendency to escalate into an unlimited war.[13]

An integral part of this propaganda theme was the alleged impossibility of distinguishing neatly between military targets and populated areas in the employment of tactical nuclear weapons, whether in a European war, a strategic exchange, or a local war in the Third World. Nor would Soviet commentators have wanted to admit publicly that both sides would find it advantageous, or even be able, to restrict themselves to the means and areas designated for a limited nuclear war:

> War has its own laws. Its logic forces each side to defeat the other completely. Now the losing side is unlikely to abide by some restrictions. Similarly, the victorious side will try to finish the war as soon as possible. Can . . . the Pentagon guarantee that the U.S. generals will, in the heat of the battle, judiciously identify each object as a military or civil target?[14]

In understanding the logic behind this propaganda, one should remember that it was (and still is) a uniquely American strategic concept that increased civilian damage is a primary consideration in determining the escalation of a war. The Soviets realized this and used it in their arguments against U.S. doctrine in an effort to make their statements appear more credible to a Western audience. For their own part, the Soviets never adopted this concept. Instead, it was the political goals of the war in question that determined the level of military force to be employed. Furthermore, such statements were a contradiction of the Soviets' own historical experience in conducting wars with limited political objectives. The Soviets had had such experience against Finland in 1939-40 and against the Japanese in Manchuria in 1945, and in Afghanistan from 1979-1989. In each of these conflicts, the limited nature of the political objectives the Soviets sought imposed its own restraints on the level of military force necessary to achieve their political objectives.

3. *The nature of flexible response is essentially no different from that of massive retaliation.*

The claim being made in this instance was that flexible response was merely a continuation of the "positions of strength" policy, but using different military means. This was a public distortion of the actual Soviet recognition that flexible response represented a U.S. attempt to increase its range of available options to deter the widest possible range of Soviet threats. Elements of this view are illustrated in the following passage from the November 1965 issue of *Soviet Military Review*:

> One feature has been common to all the post-war phases in the evolution of the U.S. military doctrine: a steady expansion of the arsenal of American militarism. Every "new" prevalent conception of war and every new twist in the development of the armed forces have, in accordance with the aggressive "policy of strength," had the purpose of providing such ways and means of prosecuting a war that, in the opinion of the U.S. leaders, would bring imperialism victory over socialism and over the national-liberation and revolutionary movement of the peoples.[15]

4. *The use of military force by the United States is an inappropriate response to the "national-liberation movements" in the Third World.*

This theme was used most often by Soviet commentators in reference to the U.S. intervention in Vietnam. This was correctly perceived by the Soviets as the premier example of flexible response in practice, but one that neither posed a direct threat to the Soviet Union itself or threatened nuclear escalation.[16] But rather than admit such a thing publicly or concede the potential effectiveness of flexible response, they instead claimed that "the doctrine overestimates the U.S. potential and underestimates the strength of the world socialist system and the international Communist, labour, and national-liberation movement."[17]

Moreover, U.S. efforts at counterinsurgency were derided as "absurd" because they ignored "the deep social and economic roots of national-liberation movements. The local wars strategy, therefore, and the operations being mounted on its principles are doomed to failure because the U.S. ruling classes are incapable of correctly assessing the role of these factors supporting the national-liberation struggle, and unable to understand the nature and socio-political substance of the struggle."[18]

In view of the failure the Soviets later experienced trying to bring the guerrillas in Afghanistan under complete control, one wonders how the author of this statement would have applied his reasoning to that conflict.

The standard Soviet line concerning U.S. involvement in Vietnam was that the United States was using sheer military power to crush what essentially was a guerrilla movement (one supported quite heavily by North Vietnamese regular forces and supplied by the Soviet Union and China). No matter what level of force called for by flexible response was used, the Soviets maintained, it would do no good because armed intervention was an inappropriate response to a national-liberation war. In reality, however, the Soviet leadership was well aware that sufficient military power could suppress any national-liberation movement, and in its recent experience had used such power to crush so-called counterrevolutions in Hungary and Czechoslovakia.

The first three themes discussed above were basically carried over from the massive retaliation period; in contrast, the fourth theme was applied specifically to U.S. involvement in Vietnam. This last theme, however, was additionally intended to deter all U.S. efforts to oppose national-liberation movements with armed intervention.

The Real Soviet View

The overall pattern of the actual Soviet evaluation of flexible response revealed a generally realistic recognition of its nature and purpose. As with massive retaliation, however, Soviet analysts continued to interpret the precepts of U.S. doctrine within the context of their own strategic mindset.

1. *Flexible response was designed to increase the ability of the United States to suppress the "national-liberation movement." This required a broad buildup of conventional as well as nuclear capabilities, which signified that the United States was becoming more active in opposing the establishment of new Communist regimes.*

One of the initial expressions of this notion was in a Soviet radio broadcast in English to Europe in July 1961:

> The aims of the new program in foreign policy announced by Kennedy have nothing in common with the talk about protection of the "freedom" of West Berlin, which nobody has been or is threatening. Washington simply needed a pretext for aggravating general international tension, for trying to enhance its role as the gendarme of the "free" world. This is factually supported by the *New York Times*, which points out that the new plan is primarily aimed not at the defense of the former German capital, but at increasing the ability of the Western allies to wage any kind of war in any part of the world.

> Active opposition to the national liberation movement in Africa, Asia, and Latin America is of course what is chiefly meant [i.e., local wars]. Only this can explain the words of the President about the need for creating a "sea and airlift capable of moving forces quickly and in large numbers to any part of the world."[19]

The broadcast also claimed that the military program announced by Kennedy in his speech "was outlined a long time ago" (possibly in reference to the proposals made by Maxwell Taylor in his book *The Uncertain Trumpet*, although the commentator was not specific), and that the "long-term buildup" of U.S. strength "has been underway since January" of 1961. This illustrates that the Soviets were aware of a fundamental shift in the U.S. doctrinal stance at this time, even though no formal pronouncement acknowledging the shift had yet been made.

The Soviets also recognized early that the United States was building up its conventional capability to cope with Soviet-supported insurgency movements in Third World countries. This was commented on in *Izvestia* on May 24, 1962.

> The "grand strategy" primarily means a further stepping up of the arms race. It is openly stated in Washington that it envisages reinforcement of naval and air transport facilities, formation of nuclear units in the army which could be swiftly transferred to any area where in the opinion of the American military the possibility arises for triggering military gambles. The masterminds of this "strategy" loudly declare that it would be wise for the United States to organize for so-called special warfare. This means armed punitive action against peoples fighting for or defending their national independence.[20]

The Soviet recognition of the defensive nature of flexible response could be found even in statements that were otherwise propagandistic. One such statement claimed that "when the USA has built up its forces to wage limited wars, it will not stop at armed intervention in the internal affairs of any country whose Government pursues a policy the US imperialists do not like." [21] Stripped of its rhetoric, the statement simply meant that the United States might become more willing in the future to oppose the establishment of new Communist regimes. The statement is also of interest in that it argues that "power tempts policy," a theme that has been in vogue with certain U.S. analysts as well as Soviet. Briefly, the argument runs, given increased capability and power to carry out certain actions, the United States would therefore be tempted to intervene in instances in which it would not otherwise have considered doing so. However, even though power might "tempt" policy to some degree, it is self-evident that policy cannot be carried out without power. The argument is therefore simplistic, since it ignores the objectives and purposes of such intervention.[22]

The verity of this particular Soviet perception is reflected in the fact that it was restated in official declarations of Soviet military doctrine such as the three editions of Sokolovskiy's *Voennaia Strategia*,[23] as well as in publications written after the end of the flexible response period. An example of such confirmation in retrospect was *Scientific-Technical Progress and the Revolution in Military Affairs*, a book in the Soviet Officer's Library series. The author stated that the flexible response strategy "was also aimed at preventing the transition of the peoples in the young developing nations to a path of non-capitalist development, and at restoring the capitalist system in the socialist nations without involving the United States in a catastrophic thermonuclear war."[24] This amounted to a tacit recognition of the inherently defensive nature of flexible response as a means of enforcing the overall grand strategy of containment perceived by the Soviets.

   2. *Changes in the strategic balance in favor of the Soviet Union forced the United States to modify its strategic doctrine. The United States was trying to expand its range of options to deal locally with Soviet direct or indirect expansion.*

   This theme of Soviet perception was a carryover from the massive retaliation period. One analyst, writing in the July 1962 issue of *International Affairs*, saw flexible response as a hybrid strategy combining elements of massive retaliation and limited war:

> The doctrine put forth by Taylor and others who think as he does is a kind of cross-pollination between Massive Retaliation and the theories of limited wars, and is an attempt to strike a balance in the effort to develop all types of armed forces and especially to increase appropriations for ground forces without re-laxing attention to rocket, air and naval forces . . . The description of the "new" doctrine shows that it lays claim to being a synthesis of all earlier Western theories of modern warfare, and proceeds on the false premise that the political and social problems arising in the world today can be solved in favour of imperialism by military methods.[25]

The same analyst also noted that the limited wars aspect of flexible response had been regarded in the United States as a forced expedient for the period in which the United States perceived a mutual "balance of terror" to have existed between the superpowers. Flexible response was "rooted in the change in the relation of forces [a mistranslation; "relation" should instead read "correlation"] and is in effect designed to serve through the period until that balance becomes 'favourable' for U.S. imperialism."[26] The United States then, according to Soviet analysis, not only had been forced to reconsider its doctrine, but had also recognized, if reluctantly, the factors responsible for forcing this change. One of the most authoritative early analyses of flexible response along this line was made by a regular observer of U.S. doctrinal developments, Major General M. Mil'shtein, in the August 1962 issue of *MEMO*:

> The onset of the third stage of the overall crisis of capitalism showed the funda-mental change in the correlation of forces in the world arena, which was accom-panied by a sharp weakening of the economic and political positions of Ameri-can imperialism. The former military-strategic concepts of the United States suffered

failure, and American military policy as a whole reached a crisis. Under these conditions, not wishing to come to terms with the objective laws of history, the ruling circles of the United States are taking a decisive stand on the further acceleration of the arms race and new military-strategic concepts, trying in this manner to "modernize" nothing more than the method of realizing all of that more than once bankrupted policy, "from a position of strength." [27]

Mil'shtein also recognized U.S. efforts to increase its conventional warfare capabilities "as concrete means for realizing one of the basic principles" of the flexible response doctrine, that of "'raising the threshold' for the conduct of war with the use of conventional means of destruction." He argued that the reason for the "threshold" concept was "the maximum widening of the sphere and possibilities of waging such wars in which the United States could get by without the use of nuclear weapons."[28] He therefore clearly recognized that the United States was trying to make its doctrine more usable for carrying out the aims of U.S. foreign policy, and that the United States was matching its military capability to the requirements of its doctrine. He also saw that the United States was trying to restore the inviolability of U.S. territory and preserve a sense of invulnerability.[29]

This theme was confirmed in the August 1967 issue of *Voennaia Mysl'*. The author's main argument was that the United States was periodically compelled to modify its strategic doctrine to adjust better to changing international conditions:

> The main thing that worries the U.S. imperialists is the alignment of political forces in the world arena: the growing power and prestige of the Soviet Union and the other socialist countries, the increase in the number of states taking the path of socialist development, the shrinking of the system of imperialism, and the active struggle of peoples against colonialism and imperialism. Therefore, the world gendarme which has military bases on every continent of the world and is conducting a struggle for its world supremacy, has to periodically change and modernize its aggressive strategic concept, adapting it to the concrete conditions of the international situation.[30]

This statement confirmed the validity of the viewpoints expressed in the open Soviet press during this period about the development and nature of U.S. strategic doctrine. The tone of the article concerning the "struggle" of the United States for its "world supremacy" suggested that the Soviets recognized that the U.S. objective was not the destruction of the Soviet Union, but rather the containment of Soviet expansionistic efforts. And the Soviets, of course, gave credit to "objective" changes in the overall balance of forces (i.e, changes over which the United States had no volitional control) for producing a situation that, in their view, was lessening the danger of a strategic nuclear war.[31]

The main "objective factor" responsible for forcing change in U.S. strategic doctrine, particularly in compelling the United States to reconsider its flexible response doctrine, was the attainment of strategic parity with the United States in land-based ICBMs in 1969. Such were the words of Major General R. Simonyan, a prominent Soviet military analyst, in the January 1969 issue of *Soviet Military Review:*

> Although these military plans remain unchanged, the US ruling circles are compelled to modify their military-strategic concepts. From the military-technical point of view, these changes have been and still are decisively influenced by the growing defence potential of the countries belonging to the socialist community, above all the Soviet Union, its indomitable nuclear-missile might, which has basically changed the balance of strategic forces between the United States and the Soviet Union.[32]

3. *The Soviets continued to project their own strategic mindset onto U.S. doctrine.*

Mil'shtein was again the earliest authoritative Soviet analyst to show this mirror-imaging tendency; he evaluated the U.S. discussion of "atomic survival" as the precursor of a nuclear war. This strategy was embodied, according to Mil'shtein, in "the famous pronouncement of Kennedy concerning the 'initiative of the United States in an atomic conflict with the Soviet Union.'" (Kennedy's statement was taken out of context; the reference was probably to an interview in the *Saturday Evening Post* of March 31, 1962, in which President Kennedy implied the threat of a U.S. first strike "under certain circumstances" in which the United States would have "to seize the initiative.")[33]

Even the most prominent Soviet military analysts and writers were not immune to the mirror-imaging tendency, as demonstrated in this passage from Sokolovskiy's *Military Strategy:*

> In accordance with the above military strategy of the United States and NATO [i.e., flexible response], there has been vast preparation of the imperialist camp, primarily the United States, for various wars against the countries of the socialist camp, primarily for a general nuclear war. Since such a war would entail the tremendous danger of mutual annihilation, the American aggressors exert all effort to assure victory in the event of the unleashing of a war, with the least losses and destruction. They see the possibility of such an outcome of a war and in achieving surprise in the creation of strong and the most combatready forces which technically would be considerably superior to the armed forces of the enemy.[34]

The best proof of Soviet mirror imaging however, was in a December 1962 issue of *KVS*, the Soviet military theory journal published by the Main Political Administration, the organization through which the CPSU maintained control over the Soviet Armed Forces.[35] The author perceived the United States as striving to fulfill the requirements for a nuclear warfighting doctrine and outlined the alleged U.S. "projections" concerning the nature of a future war. Upon careful examination, these projections are virtually identical to a similar Soviet discussion of a future war in Sokolovskiy's *Voennaia Strategia*:[36]

- There will be no essential differences between front and rear areas.
- The first few days of the war will be the period of maximum military activity, and hence of the greatest destruction.
- The war will be intercontinental as well as being waged on several continents.
- It will be necessary to have forces in peacetime prepared for such a war.
- Plans for a future war will be based on the primary employment of forces deployed at the start of the war.[37]

4. The U.S. buildup of its strategic forces provided a "nuclear umbrella" for the waging of local conflicts.

This appraisal accurately described the deterrence purposes of U.S. strategic nuclear forces and undoubtedly had a decisive influence, in combination with the results of the Cuban missile crisis, on the Soviet decision to accelerate the buildup of its strategic nuclear forces after 1964. One such analysis along this line was by V. Larionov, a member of the Sokolovskiy study group, in the July 1963 issue of *International Affairs*, not long after the Cuban missile crisis. Noting statements by U.S. generals to the effect that the United States still intended to devote its major efforts to improving its strategic nuclear arsenal, he undoubtedly had the Cuban missile crisis on his mind when he concluded that:

> The U.S. nuclear potential continues to be regarded as an instrument of political blackmail and a means of ensuring freedom of action in a limited war. Even after the "flexible response" doctrine had been approved, the essential aims of U.S. policy in no way changed. The new doctrine merely takes into account the need to act cautiously in the changed conditions, to appraise every foreign policy action in the light of the possibilities of U.S. military strategy and to take a "flexible initiative" in unleashing either a full-scale nuclear war or limited wars.[38]

Soviet commentators did not picture the United States as being effectively restrained from using military power across the entire spectrum of conflict. Although the Soviets correctly understood that the United States was deterred from initiating an all-out nuclear war, they were much less sanguine about their capacity to dissuade the United States from taking action against Soviet supported national-liberation movements. The three editions of Sokolovskiy's *Voennaia Strategia* (in 1962, 1963, and 1968) portrayed a United States with a powerful and still growing military capability. This respect was especially reflected in their description of the U.S. strategic arsenal.[39] From the Soviet perspective, it was this superior strategic arsenal that enabled the United States to use its conventional military power without fear of the Soviet threat of uncontrolled escalation.[40]

5. *The Soviets increasingly recognized, both publicly and privately, the likelihood of limited wars being waged with both nuclear and conventional weapons without escalation to strategic nuclear war.*

As early as the mid-1960s, the Soviets were admitting the possibility of having to conduct limited wars, even with the use of nuclear weapons, without escalation. One such reference was made in *Nedelia* in April of 1965 by a Soviet military analyst. Contending that "the development of the military might of the USSR and the socialist camp has influenced the evolution of the military doctrine of the imperialist countries, particularly the United States," he further argued:

> This is why not only principles of military doctrine more flexible in form and contents have emerged in Washington-principles such as the "strategy of flexible reaction" and the "counterforce strategy"- but there are more and more frequent references to a war without nuclear weapons or in which only tactical nuclear means will be used within the framework of "local" and "limited" wars. *Soviet military doctrine does not exclude such wars,* but we are against the use of any nuclear weapons in general and in the talk of the imperialist militarists about tactical nuclear weapons we see only a trick intended somehow to help motivate and help legalize the use of the atom against mankind.[41] [Emphasis added]

This was corroborated in part by Sokolovskiy in the April 1965 issue of *Soviet Military Review;* he contended that "the possibility of a relatively protracted war cannot be excluded, particularly a war involving no nuclear weapons, for instance, a local war." Although Sokolovskiy did not speak directly of the possibility of a limited nuclear war, he was at least admitting that a conventional local war could be waged without escalation. The prolonged U.S. involvement in Vietnam, just then coming into greater prominence with the commitment of significant numbers of ground troops, was a clear demonstration of this. Furthermore, Sokolovskiy stated that "preparations for a relatively protracted war should not be neglected."[42] This was an apparent call for the Soviet Union to develop a more flexible military capability similar to what the United States already had.[43]

The most definitive proof, however, could be found (or, rather, not found) in the third edition of Sokolovskiy's *Voennaia Strategia,* published in 1968, in which there was a significant omission. The part left out discussed the difficulties involved in keeping a limited war from escalating to strategic nuclear war. This discussion, which had been included in the 1962 and 1963 editions, was much in keeping with Khrushchev's practice at the time of denying the possibility of conducting a limited war. Its omission in the 1968 edition seems to have reflected the Brezhnev regime's acceptance of limited war without escalation, coupled with the idea that it was necessary to develop a similar military capability.[44] This was confirmed by an article in the October 1968 issue of *Voennaia Mysl'* by Sokolovskiy and Major General M. Cherednichenko, in which they discussed various problems of military strategy, including that of being able to conduct a *limited nuclear war.*

> Along with this the possibility is not excluded of wars occurring with the use of conventional weapons, *as well as the limited use of nuclear means in one or several theaters of operations,* or of a relatively protracted nuclear war with the use of capabilities of all types of armed forces. To maintain in peacetime massive armed forces for conventional war, and in the case of escalation, nuclear war, is impossible, and inexpedient primarily for economic reasons. Therefore, it is necessary to develop appropriate plans for mobilization deployment.[45] [Emphasis added.]

Thus, even though Soviet commentators would continue to stress that there could be no such thing as a limited nuclear war in their public declaratory deterrence statements, the above passage demonstrates that the Soviets in fact did not believe their own propaganda.

6. *The collapse of the flexible response doctrine was caused by the failure of the United States to achieve decisive results in Vietnam, in combination with the Soviet attainment of strategic parity with the United States.*

When President Nixon proclaimed the Nixon Doctrine shortly after he took office in 1969, the Soviets quickly recognized that U.S. strategic doctrine was undergoing another change. Since Nixon had publicly acknowledged the attainment by the Soviets of strategic nuclear parity with the United States, Soviet analysts were all the more eager to proclaim it as having been a decisive factor:

> US imperialism is finding it more difficult and dangerous to place all its hopes on world nuclear war. The US strategists realise that a head-on armed clash with the USSR would be suicidal for the USA. Understandably enough, all US doctrines for the 1970s are based on the so-called "nuclear balance" which, they say, exists today in US-Soviet relations.[46]

This notion was reaffirmed more explicitly by G. Trofimenko, a prominent Soviet analyst of U.S. strategic doctrine, in an article in *International Affairs* written well after the demise of flexible response (October 1975):

> To sum it up, the balance of world forces had further shifted in socialism's favour by the early 1970s as evidenced, for example, by the attainment of Soviet-American nuclear and missile parity and the awareness by the USA of its limited possibilities to influence diverse events in the world by means of military forces. This made the US ruling class start a "reappraisal of values" and acknowledge the need to reconcile the reality of competition between the two systems with the imperative of coexistence.[47]

Although the Soviets also called the war in Vietnam a major factor in the demise of flexible response, it was not given the repeated emphasis that the attainment of strategic nuclear parity was given, which was an accurate indicator of what the Soviets thought was the stronger influence on U.S. doctrinal development. G. Arbatov, a prominent observer of U.S. doctrinal developments, claimed that "the war in Vietnam showed that military might alone can no longer bring the United States victory not only in the struggle against the "main" enemy, but also on the periphery."[48]

The Effect of Flexible Response

The Soviet response to the U.S. doctrine of flexible response during this period unmistakably reflected a strong Soviet conviction that qualitative and quantitative improvements in Soviet strategic power yielded substantial political returns. This belief was directly reflected in Soviet usage of military power during the latter half of the 1960s, the period when Soviet ICBM levels were increasing the fastest. Whereas the Soviet leadership under Khrushchev in the 1950s and early 1960s felt sufficiently restrained by U.S. strategic superiority to have used only threats and military maneuvers for the most part, the scale of Soviet military support gradually increased during the 1960s to include logistical efforts in support of her Vietnamese and Arab allies. The greater degree of freedom for the United States to use its military power under cover of its nuclear umbrella was an object lesson that was not lost on either the Soviet military or the political leadership.

Despite the Soviet perception that the restraints on the use of her own military power were being steadily weakened, Soviet analysts were always wary of new U.S. strategic concepts, examining them from the standpoint of their usefulness in a warfighting strategy. Soviet analysts read their own thinking into all such concepts, even though certain concepts such as assured destruction were obviously not designed for warfighting from the U.S. viewpoint. The Soviet perception of the ideas set forth by McNamara in the 1960s had important implications for future U.S. doctrine.

Notes

1. T. Wolfe, *Soviet Power and Europe,* 442-7.
2. Ibid., 450.
3. Ibid., 448-9.
4. Ibid., 432-3.
5. Bonds, *The Soviet War Machine,* 210.
6. Wolfe, *Soviet Power,* 434.
7. F.D. Kohler, *Soviet Strategy for the Seventies,* 76-78.
8. Wolfe, *Soviet Power,* 449.

9. N. Lomov, "On Soviet Military Doctrine," *KVS* 10 (May 1962): 14.

10. Ibid., pp. 16, 19.

11. Cited in translation by H. Dinerstein, L. Goure, and T. Wolfe, *Soviet Military Strategy* (Santa Monica, Calif.: RAND, R-416-PR, April 1963), 396-7. See also Y. Oleshchuk, "Small Wars and the Aggression in Vietnam," *International Affairs* 5 (May 1966): 36.

12. Dinerstein, Goure, and Wolfe, *Soviet Military Strategy*, 397.

13. N. Ponomarev, "Crisis of Bourgeois Theories of War and Peace," *KVS* 16 (August 1964): 13.

14. V. Mochalov, "Concerning the Theory of Limited Wars," *Soviet Military Review* 2 (February 1965): 41.

15. V. Glazov, "The Evolution of US Military Doctrine," *Soviet Military Review* 11 (November 1965): 57.

16. V. Zavyalov, "Flexible Response Strategy: Theory and Practice," *Soviet Military Review* 5 (May 1965): 36-38. See also S. Malyanchikov, "On the Nature of Armed Struggle in Local Wars," *Voennaia Mysl'* 11 (November 1965), trans. in FBIS, FPD, No. 953, March 8, 1966, 12-24; See also K. Bochkarev, "On the Character and Types of Wars of the Contemporary Epoch," *KVS* 11, (June 1965): 8-17.

17. Glazov, "US Military Doctrine," 57.

18. Oleshchuk, "Small Wars," 36. See also Y. Melnikov, "U.S. Foreign Policy: A Threat to Peace," *International Affairs* 1 (January 1967): 64-70.

19. Radio broadcast by Moscow TASS in English to Europe, 26 July 1961, trans in FBIS, *USSR and Eastern Europe*, 27 July 1961, BB6.

20. Radio broadcast by Moscow TASS in English to Europe, 24 May 1962, trans. in FBIS, *USSR and Eastern Europe*, 25 May 1962, BB4. See also Glazov, "US Military Doctrine," 57.

21. V. Pechorkin, "Crisis of Imperialism's Military Doctrines," *International Affairs* 7 (July 1962): 33. See also V. Larionov, "The Doctrine of 'Flexible' Aggression," *International Affairs* 7 (July 1963): 46-51.

22. R.A. Aliano argued this thesis in relation to the decision to intervene in Vietnam in *American Defense Policy from Eisenhower to Kennedy: The Politics of Changing Military Requirements, 1957-1961* (Athens: Ohio University Press, 1975). See also N. Prokopyev, "Problems of War and Peace in Our Age," *International Affairs* 12 (December 1967): 59; R. Simonyan, "Doctrine of the American Aggressors," *Soviet Military Review*, 1 (January 1969): 50.

23. Cited in translation of Sokolovskiy in H.F. Scott, *Soviet Military Strategy*, 66.

24. Lomov, *Scientific-Technical Progress*, 254. See also B. Teplinsky, "US 'Grand Strategy,'" *International Affairs* 2 (February 1964): 25.

25. Pechorkin, "Crisis of Imperialism's Military Doctrines," 33.

26. Ibid., 33-34. See also the Russian-language version in *Mezhdunarodnaya Zhizn* 7 (July 1962): 44.

27. M. Mil'shtein, "Certain Strategic Military Concepts of American Imperialism," *MEMO* 8 (August 1962): 85.

28. Ibid., 94.

29. See S. Konstantinov, "The Military Doctrine of American Imperialism," *KVS* 23 (December 1962): 83.

30. Kh. Dzhelnaukov, "The Evolution of U.S. Military Doctrine," *Voennaia Mysl'* 9 (September 1967) trans. in FBIS, No. 0132/68, September 5, 1968, 94.

31. Ibid., 97-98. See also Wolfe, *Soviet Power*, 452-3.

32. Simonyan, "Doctrine of the American Aggressors," 50. See also Lomov, *Scientific-Technical Progress*, 253.
33. Mil'shtein, "American Imperialism," 87. Kennedy's remarks were taken out of context. See Stewart Alsop, "Kennedy's Grand Strategy," *The Saturday Evening Post*, March 31, 1962, 11, 13. Quoted in Dinerstein, Goure, and Wolfe, Soviet Military Strategy, 166.
34. Cited in Scott, *Soviet Military Strategy*, 117. See also Simonyan, "American Aggressors," 52.
35. J. Dziak, *Soviet Perceptions of Military Power: The Interaction of Theory and Practice* (New York: Crane, Russak, 1981), 9-10.
36. Scott, *Soviet Military Strategy*, 201-11.
37. Konstantinov, "American Imperialism," 80.
38. Larionov, "'Flexible' Aggression,'" 46.
39. Scott, *Soviet Military Strategy*, 74-100.
40. This is alluded to in Lomov, *Scientific-Technical Progress*, 254.
41. S.M. Shtemenko, "The Queen of the Battlefield Yields Her Crown," trans. and quoted in W. Kintner and H.F. Scott, *The Nuclear Revolution in Soviet Military Affairs* (Norman: University of Oklahoma Press, 1968), 55.
42. V.D Sokolovskiy, "On the Soviet Military Doctrine," *Soviet Military Review* 4 (April 1965): 8.
43. R. Kolkowicz, "Strategic Parity and Beyond," *World Politics* 23 (April 1971): 439. See also W.F. Scott and H.F. Scott, *Armed Forces*, 54-56. See also Wolfe, *Soviet Power*, 451-2.
44. Scott, *Soviet Military Strategy*, 378-379. See also B. Teplinsky, "U.S. 'Grand Strategy,'" *International Affairs* 2 (February 1964): 25; idem, "U.S. Military Programmes," *International Affairs* 8 (August 1967): 49.
45. V.D. Sokolovskiy and M. Cherednichenko, "Military Strategy and Its Problems," *Voennaia Mysl'* 10 (October 1968): trans. in FBIS, No. 0084/69, September 4, 1969, 37.
46. A. Baryshev, "New US Doctrines: Same Old Aims," *International Affairs* 12 (December 1969): 12-13. See also Lomov, *Scientific-Technical Progress*, 254; G.A. Trofimenko, "Some Aspects of US Military and Political Strategy," *SShA: Ekonomika, Politika, Ideologia* 10 (October 1970), trans. in JPRS No. 51895, December 1, 1970, 19.
47. G. Trofimenko, "From Confrontation to Coexistence," *International Affairs* 10 (October 1975): 38. See also the Russian version of Trofimenko's article in *Mezhdunarodnaya Zhizn* 9 (September 1975): 42.
48. G.A. Arbatov, "American Foreign Policy at the Threshold of the 1970's," *SShA: Ekonomika, Politika, Ideologia* 1 (January 1970), trans. in JPRS No. 49934, February 26, 1970, 19.

6

Soviet Reaction to the McNamara Concepts

The public Soviet reaction to the concepts of counterforce, damage limitation, and assured destruction have just as much relevance to the discussions of nuclear strategy in recent years, much as they did at the time when then Secretary of Defense Robert McNamara first enunciated them in 1962. This is so because, although the concept of damage limitation was dropped not too long after its inception (largely because of McNamara's reasoning that it would be more cost-effective to carry out an assured destruction strategy than one based on damage limitation), the concepts of counterforce, damage limitation, and assured destruction still dominate much of the dialogue in nuclear strategy today, although the concepts often have gone under different names. In addition, it was during this same period of time that Herman Kahn, in his book *On Escalation: Metaphors and Scenarios*, introduced the 44-step escalation ladder that was to dominate U.S. strategic thinking until recently. The Soviet response to this notion, although it proved erroneous, foreshadowed their reactions to later developments in U.S. strategic doctrine.

Most of the public Soviet response to the so-called McNamara concepts focused on the notion of counterforce. Counterforce, in its simplest terms, is merely targeting of enemy nuclear forces during nuclear war to reduce his ability to massively damage either U.S. nuclear forces or cities. Soviet observers tended to read into the counterforce concept their own notions of nuclear warfighting based on a preemptive strike; in fact, as will be seen later in this chapter, they did the same thing with the assured-destruction concept, even though it was intended more to support arms control than a nuclear warfighting doctrine. Since the Soviets tended to interpret counterforce as indicative of a U.S. attempt to move towards a strategic doctrine similar to their own, they directed the majority of their *desinformatsiya* statements towards discrediting counterforce.

The Soviet Propaganda Line

This section addresses five major themes of the Soviet declaratory deterrence strategy, four of which deal with counterforce. The fifth theme covers the predominant Soviet line regarding the escalation concept.

1. *The Soviets implied a high readiness to "launch on warning" or "launch under attack," a capability that nullified the effectiveness of counterforce.*

One Soviet analysis in *International Affairs* implied that upon receiving word via radar and other sources that an attack was in progress, they would immediately launch the vulnerable portion of their strategic forces (bombers and ICBMS) rather than wait for the missiles to strike and then retaliate with the undestroyed part of their forces:

> The element of surprise, rather important in past wars, now has a different character. Even such weapons as instant-action rockets, launched at any time of day or night and in any weather, can be detected in the first section of their flight path by ever vigilant radars and other instruments. In this age of radioelectronics and targeted ready-to-fire rockets, a counterstrike will follow the first strike in a matter of minutes. The first rockets and bombers of the side on the defensive would take off even before the aggressor's first rockets, to say nothing of his bombers, reached their targets.[1] [Emphasis in original.]

The authors also recognized the fact that even to achieve a modicum of surprise, an attacker "would have to use in his very first salvo a small but most efficient part of his means of attack." In response to such a move, they said that "after the aggressor's strike the attacked [sic] could discount the element of surprise and would use all his counterstrike means set in motion before the first explosions on his territory or remaining intact after the start of the enemy's nuclear bombardment."[2]

It is important to note, however, that the U.S. concept of launch on warning describes a high state of readiness of strategic forces. In the case of the Soviets, their strategic forces in the 1960s were not in such a high state of readiness, particularly at the time the above statement was made (November 1963). Consequently, much of what was said in the early and mid-1960s was largely academic, and indicated a Soviet reliance on early warning and preemption rather than on the concepts of launch on warning or launch under attack. An example of this kind of indirect statement was in an article in the April 1965 issue of *Soviet Military Review* by Sokolovskiy, which implied such a preemptive strategy:

> Imperialist atom-mongers [sic] pin their hopes on a surprise attack and here lies the main danger. Consequently, the important, the primary mission of the Soviet Armed Forces is to be ready to *nip in the bud any attempts* by aggressors

at launching a surprise attack against the USSR and other socialist countries.[3] [Emphasis added.]

2. *Since a U.S. counterforce strike cannot guarantee the destruction of all Soviet missiles, it is ineffective. Relative superiority in missiles is therefore meaningless, since the Soviet Union possesses an assured capacity for "crushing" retaliation.*

This theme was an obvious Soviet attempt to reduce the deterrent value of U.S. strategic nuclear superiority by publicly declaring that nuclear superiority had no real meaning, not even if a counterforce strategy was employed. In the April 1962 issue of *International Affairs*, less than two months before McNamara actually announced the counterforce strategy and six months before the onset of the Cuban missile crisis, Talensky was the first to argue that a successful surprise attack could not possibly knock out all of a major power's means of nuclear delivery. This was supposedly due to the high level of nuclear saturation that then existed.[4] This was obvious propaganda on Talensky's part, since Soviet strategic forces in 1962 were still quite small in absolute numbers, as well as being numerically inferior relative to those of the United States.[5] Talensky repeated his argument in a later issue of *International Affairs* on the eve of the Cuban missile crisis:

> To unleash war with the use of such weapons clearly implies suicide, for no one can ever guarantee the aggressor from a retaliatory blow with similar weapons. Western military theoreticians, the apologists of "preventive war," seek to prove the advantages of this type of war by claiming that a preemptive attack would greatly lessen the effect of the retaliatory blow from the attacked side. A surprise attack naturally would inflict greater losses and destruction on the target state but it would not save the aggressor from a retaliatory blow. *At the present day there is as yet practically no possibility of preventing a retaliatory blow or of diminishing its power to any considerable extent.*[6] [Emphasis in original.]

Talensky was trying to make two propaganda points: (1) it is not possible to carry out an effective counterforce attack, and (2) the United States might be able to make such an attack successfully and must therefore be told that it cannot hope to do so. Talensky conveniently did not mention Soviet antiballistic missile (ABM) development efforts during this time, since this would have detracted from his arguments against the likelihood of limiting damage. Much of the remainder of his article was devoted to pointing out the technical difficulties involved in carrying out a counterforce attack, such as accuracy and the uncertainty of strategic intelligence.[7] The overall impression one gets from Talensky's statements is that they were principally for their propaganda value, and used weak arguments for lack of better ones.

What must be remembered above all else, though, is that at the time this statement was made, Soviet strategic forces were greatly inferior with respect to the numbers of nuclear weapons and delivery systems available. This kind of "mutual vulnerability" argument was natural coming from a power that was inferior in the above respects. The obvious aim of these statements was to negate the value of U.S. nuclear superiority as an effective instrument of political leverage. Soviet behavior during the Cuban missile crisis, however, proved that the Soviet leadership did perceive more actual U.S. political leverage than they were willing to admit; they also acknowledged their self-perceived need to make up for their lack of intercontinental capability by trying to move their intermediate-range ballistic missiles (IRBMS) forward into Cuba, thus gaining "counterleverage" against the U.S.

The editors of *Voennaia Strategia* also tried to discredit the counterforce strategy by using a combination of "strategic bluffing" with the "all-or-nothing" argument that if you could not destroy all of an opponent's missiles, the strategy was ineffective:

> The ruling circles of the imperialist states, especially of the United States, recognize that, in conditions where the *Soviet Union has superiority in strategic missiles*, a surprise nuclear strike would be even more dangerous, since it would not obviate a crushing retaliatory missile-nuclear strike from the Soviet Union.[8] [Emphasis added.]

The point of the editors' argument against counterforce was that since the United States (allegedly) was not capable of executing a counterforce strike with any reasonable hope of success, the Soviet Union automatically possessed the ability to retaliate in kind. This made any attempts to establish nuclear superiority meaningless. This line of propaganda, however, did not square with the statements of Soviet military spokesmen concerning the necessity for preparing to fight a nuclear war with the idea of attaining victory. It was an attempt by Soviet propagandists to use American arguments as a means of making Soviet declaratory deterrence statements more believable to U.S. observers. This kind of argument was typified in the May 1966 issue of *International Affairs*:

> Superiority has become a concept which has no bearing on war. No superiority can save the aggressor from retribution. Any efforts of an aggressor to achieve *relative* nuclear superiority are neutralized in advance by the fact that the other side possesses *absolute* power which guarantees the destruction of the aggressor. For the same reason, the aggressor can gain nothing from a nuclear war or even from nuclear blackmail . . . Although these conclusions logically follow from recognition of the impossibility of victory in a nuclear war and from arguments about a guaranteed destruction potential, Washington sacrifices logic to military considerations.[9] [Emphasis in original.]

One does well to be skeptical of this kind of statement asserting the uselessness of superiority and the impossibility of attaining victory in a nuclear war. These arguments were simply a carbon copy of similar statements being made in the United States concerning the "nonutility" of nuclear superiority. The aim was to create in the minds of U.S. analysts a picture of a Soviet Union whose strategic outlook was similar to that of the United States. When you also consider the fact that the Soviet strategic buildup was rapidly accelerating at the time of this article, it is clear that it was designed to persuade U.S. observers and analysts that the Soviets were not trying to attain nuclear superiority, but would cease building once numerical equality was attained. This aspect of Soviet declaratory deterrence worked quite well.

3. *It is not possible to establish "rules of conduct" for a nuclear war by making arbitrary distinctions between civilian and military targets, as implied by counterforce.*

The corollary of this assertion was that it was not possible to separate military targets from civilian targets reliably because of the great destructive power of nuclear weapons. An early example of this line was given in an article by Talensky in *International Affairs.* He doubted McNamara's contention that "in a nuclear-missile war blows would be struck primarily at military targets and not at cities and industrial areas," arguing that historical experience with very powerful weapons tended to prove that one could not reasonably expect to exclude cities from nuclear attack.[10]

Another Soviet commentator, writing in a January 1963 issue of *New Times,* maintained that making a distinction between purely military as opposed to civilian targets would be very difficult, and that McNamara was not considering the effects of radioactive fallout:

> But how is he [McNamara] going to distinguish between military and non-military targets? And what does he intend to do about the lethal radioactive fallout which, originating from an attack on a military objective would doom every living being for miles around?[11]

It should be pointed out that the Soviets were already hard at work trying to solve this problem with their civil defense efforts.[12] A similar argument was made on a more sophisticated level in the November 1963 issue of *International Affairs.* The authors emphasized the difficulty of hitting a relatively small military target with a weapon designed to devastate a much larger area (a reference to the question of yield versus accuracy) without resulting in heavy collateral damage among the civilian populace:

> It is self-evident that any belligerent, if only to reduce his own losses, will first strive to knock out the enemy's military targets, especially his nuclear strike means. This does not at all mean that in the massive use of nuclear weapons cities and their inhabitants would be able to escape without huge losses. How can a multi-megaton bomb strike be limited to selected military targets when their area usually runs to no more than two figures, and the area directly hit by the bomb blast, to four or five figures? Besides, many important military objec-

tives are located in cities or in their vicinity, and in heavily populated areas. [This is an exercise in sophistry; it depends upon where the weapons that constitute military targets are located. The Soviets always made up for poor accuracy with large yields.] All this quite apart from the spread of radioactive fallout, fire storms, and the disruption of supply systems and medical services.[13]

The authors further argued that "to accept the Western doctrine of limiting the use of nuclear weapons to geographical areas, specified targets, or size of warheads would be to recognise as lawful the annihilation of millions of people through the use of dozens or hundreds of 'small' nuclear missiles or rockets." Moreover, they contended that any effort to set any sort of rules of the game for nuclear war was unrealistic, "because nuclear war differs in principle from all previous wars in that it *cannot be limited*." [emphasis in original].[14] The deterrence value of this assertion should not be ignored, since it was in the Soviet interest to weaken the credibility of U.S. deterrence, especially with regard to the conduct of a limited nuclear war in defense of NATO, by creating as much uncertainty as possible in the minds of U.S. planners as to the willingness of the Soviet Union to resort to a strategic nuclear strike against the United States in the event of a confrontation in Europe in which the U.S. resorted to a limited use of nuclear weapons.

The Soviets were therefore claiming that counterforce was unworkable on the grounds that it was impossible to make the necessary fine distinctions between civilian and military targets. This, however, was a false argument. For one thing, Soviet missile deployment was such that Soviet ICBMs, the likely targets of a counterforce strike, were not near large population centers.[15] Furthermore, even if strikes against military targets caused limited civilian damage, this by itself would not justify making a retaliatory strike against the enemy's cities. In fact, Soviet targeting doctrine did not target cities per se.[16] Missiles and submarines would be the targets for counterforce attacks, and since these targets are not located in cities, this Soviet argument was based on a false assumption. As stated by Soviet analysts themselves, the problem was a matter of defining what constituted a military target.

4. *Counterforce is merely another name for a preemptive strike, and merely conceals preparations for a preventive war by the United States.*

This propaganda line was a carryover from the late 1950s. It was given notoriety by such commentators as Talensky. The likely reason that the Soviets made such prominent use of Talensky in their declaratory deterrence strategy is that he was known in the West as a former editor of *Voennaia Mysl'*. As such, his statements would therefore carry more credibility than most other commentators of lesser reputation. His basic argument was that the idea of a counterforce strategy was inseparable from that of a preventive war, and that the United States was actively planning for this contingency.[17] As shown in chapter 4, the Soviets had long since been aware of the difference between a preemptive strike, as implied by the counterforce concept, and a preventive war. Soviet commentators were claiming that the latter notion was the real intent of counterforce, while American analysts such as Bernard Brodie, whom the Soviets were citing to support their claims, were vigorously denying it.[18]

The theme of U.S. preparation for preventive war by means of the counterforce strategy was reiterated in *Voennaia Strategia* as well:

> The strategy of "counterforce" primarily stems from the necessity for preventive war and the achievement of surprise. A strategy which contemplates attaining victory through the destruction of the armed forces cannot stem from the idea of a "retaliatory blow"; it stems from preventive actions.[19]

Although the distortion of the terms "preemptive strike" and "preventive war" is fairly obvious, this passage also reflects a substantial degree of Soviet projection of their own thinking on nuclear war onto U.S. doctrine and intentions. This is evidenced in the Soviet attribution to U.S. planners of the goal of victory in a nuclear war and the emphasis on surprise.

Larionov asserted that attempts to wage war according to "agreed rules" was "contradictory to the principle of excluding war as a means of deciding international questions."[20] He further contended that the counterforce strategy, "from the political point of view, bears an openly aggressive character, because it may be considered to be operational only under conditions of a preventive strike."[21] But Larionov had little cause to doubt the nature of Soviet strategic doctrine, which advocated a preemptive strike.[22] While Soviet commentators complained about the U.S. strategy of counterforce, they omitted mentioning that they had a similar doctrine. The fact that demonstrates the falsity of this propaganda theme is that, since this particular article was written in June 1966, the author by this time was well aware of the unilateral U.S. freeze on further strategic buildup.

5. *The escalation concept is a means for the United States to unleash a total nuclear war.*

The main theme of Soviet propaganda regarding the concept of "escalation" was that the United States was planning to unleash a total nuclear war by means of escalation of local conflicts up the 44 rungs of Herman Kahn's escalation ladder. This, of course, assumed that Kahn's escalation theory had actually been adopted as a tenet of the U.S. doctrine of flexible response, which in fact it had not, although Kahn's ideas influenced U.S. thinking on nuclear strategy considerably.

Soviet commentators claimed to find evidence that Kahn's escalation theory was being put into practice in the U.S. conduct of the Vietnam war. A prime example of this was in the April 1967 issue of *Soviet Military Review*, when the U.S. involvement in Vietnam was approaching its peak. The author attempted to demonstrate that "the US war in Indo-China is the most typical example of how imperialism is broadening out aggression in the spirit of the escalation theory." The author then matched up the events in the chronology of initial U.S. involvement in Vietnam with the steps in the escalation ladder.[23] He then claimed that the United States was continuing to climb the escalation ladder not only by increasing the scale of violence in Vietnam, but also by initiating conflicts in other areas so as to further exacerbate the situation:

> Recklessly climbing the escalation ladder, the US imperialists are drawing their military bloc partners into adventure. They are seeking to provoke other conflicts in South-East Asia and elsewhere. It is considered that the unleashing of new conflicts when those already started are in the stage of aggravation is a key proposition of the theory of escalation . . . The aggressive theories of the US military theoreticians thus conform with the aggressive objectives of imperialism. This is freshly borne out by the escalation theory.[24]

In retrospect, however, there was little real evidence that the United States was attempting to spread the conflict throughout Southeast Asia, unless the author was referring to U.S. air actions in Laos or the limited actions at that time on the Cambodian border. The argument that the escalation theory was inherently aggressive because it conformed to the inherently aggressive tendencies in imperialism has long been a standard part of the Soviet declaratory deterrence strategy against all previous U.S. strategic doctrinal concepts. It should therefore be considered accordingly.

Although Soviet analysts were able to make connections between the stages of U.S. involvement in Vietnam and the steps in Kahn's escalation ladder, Soviet observers failed to realize that the escalation ladder was *descriptive* rather than *prescriptive* in its intentions regarding potential crises. Although the editors of *Voennaia Strategia* did not go so far as to attribute Kahn's theory as being part of U.S. strategic doctrine, it is clear that they also had difficulty in telling the difference between mere academic discussion and analysis of real doctrine; they tended to assume that all such theoretical analyses reflected doctrine to some extent. The propaganda line against escalation can easily be dismissed if one considers it in conjunction with the growing Soviet admission of the likelihood and necessity of having to wage limited conflicts of both nuclear and conventional types. Given also the Soviet emphasis on surprise and their tendency to assume the same for U.S. doctrine, it is not at all likely that they seriously believed the United States to be preparing to unleash a total nuclear war through escalation of limited conflicts, since this would negate the chances of surprise. This argument was similar to that used against the strategy of limited war. It foreshadowed the argument that would later be used against James Schlesinger's proposed strategy of limited nuclear options.

The Real Soviet View

Continuing the practice from the 1950s, Soviet analysts projected their own nuclear warfighting mindset onto U.S. doctrine in analyzing the intent and rationale behind the McNamara concepts, as well as Herman Kahn's theory of escalation. Two of the following four themes pertain to the concepts of McNamara's nuclear strategy, while the latter two deal with the Soviet perception of escalation.

1. *The Soviets initially perceived the United States as attempting to adopt a nuclear warfighting doctrine as embodied in the concepts of counterforce and damage limitation.*

As first illustrated in Chapter 4, Soviet analysts viewed U.S. strategic doctrine within the context of their own nuclear warfighting doctrine. This tendency did not change with U.S. doctrine.[25] This was proven in the first serious academic analysis of the new concepts by Mil'shtein in the August 1962 issue of MEMO. (However, Soviet commentators had made reference to the McNamara concepts in statements predating this article, even though the depth of analysis was lacking.)[26] Mil'shtein argued that the phraseology of U.S. strategists regarding "the enemy's attack" or "the retaliatory blow" was merely camouflage "by which the accelerated formation of the [so-called] 'second strike force' is justified."[27] Considered with the following passage, Mil'shtein apparently believed the U.S. counterforce strategy to be based on carrying out a first strike. As can also be seen, though, he recognized its retaliatory aspects as well:

> First of all, the American military command, under the pretense of creating a "counterforce" and "second strike force," is in fact creating at a forced rate and is holding in a high state of readiness the necessary means for inflicting not the second but the first strike.

> The second conclusion: American strategists admit that as the result of a *counterblow* [i.e., a preemptive strike] on the part of the Soviet Union, many means of atomic attack of the United States, especially those which require fixed installations, will either be fully destroyed or so badly damaged that they cannot be used in the future. Therefore, they hope to preserve mobile weapons of such types as nuclear missile-launching submarines, Minuteman missiles on mobile launchers [!], a part of their strategic aviation, etc., and thereby attain, *in the course of war*, atomic superiority over the Soviet Union. Such are their hopes.[28] [Emphasis added]

Although Mil'shtein tried to prove that the United States was in fact contemplating a first-strike and not a second-strike capability, he contradicted himself almost immediately. He recognized that the U.S. was trying to deny success to a Soviet preemptive strike by emphasizing the survivability of its strategic forces, which would not have been an important consideration if the United States was really committed to a first-strike strategy. Mil'shtein's own nuclear warfighting orientation was reflected in his contention that the U.S. sought to gain, "in the course of war, atomic superiority over the Soviet Union" by means of increasing the survivability of its strategic forces.

Mil'shtein also took note of the debate within the U.S. military regarding the objectives to be emphasized in a nuclear attack. According to Mil'shtein, "Adherents of one point of view, primarily representatives of the Army and Navy, consider that the primary objectives should be the 'key centers' or large cities."[29] In other words, this was an argument in favor of deterrence by the threat of a countervalue attack, a consideration unrelated to a warfighting strategy. On the other hand, the counterforce advocates "consider that they should be primarily military objectives, more precisely, the enemy's atomic means: rocket bases, launching sites, airports, storage sites for atomic ammunition, etc."[30] What is interesting about this latter statement is that it is identical to the *Soviet* targeting priorities later given in Sokolovskiy's *Voennaia Strategia*.[31]

As an "answer" to the U.S. counterforce strategy, Mil'shtein strongly implied the use of a Soviet preemptive strike.[32] In this sense, Mil'shtein used the same formula as Sokolovskiy did later for the determination of a Soviet "counterblow": Soviet "retaliatory" strikes are to destroy enemy strategic forces *before* they are launched.

Another military analyst, writing only a few months after Mil'shtein in *KVS*, reflected the mirror-imaging tendency as well, emphasizing U.S. discussions of the necessity to attain surprise in order to support his propagandistic assertion that the United States intended to undertake a preventive war against the Soviet Union.[33]

Soviet analysts also recognized the difficulties inherent in a counterforce strategy. In the second edition of Sokolovskiy's *Voennaia Strategia*, which appeared in December 1963,[34] the authors discussed the difficulty of attempting to destroy well-dispersed and hardened forces. In addition, it was pointed out that a decision about what type of objectives should be attacked was dependent to a great extent on the type and accuracy of the weapons involved:

> The launching of nuclear strikes against enemy strategic weapons is a more difficult task in comparison with the launching of strikes against large cities. These difficulties are caused primarily by the fact that, first of all, there are significant numbers of such weapons, and, secondly, by the fact that the majority of them, especially rocket weapons, in modern conditions are an *absolute* weapon [This phrase was incorrectly translated by the editor. Taken in the context of the passage, a better translation would have been "the *perfect* weapon."], located in

underground bases of low vulnerability, on submarines, etc. In this connection, there is a growing tendency toward the increase of their invulnerability.

The decision as to which objectives should be the ones against which nuclear strikes are launched-against strategic weapons or cities-depends to a considerable degree on the weapons system on hand and on its quantity. If the weapon is so inaccurate that it cannot be used to destroy small-dimension targets such as ballistic missile launching pads or airports, and there is not enough room for them, it can only be used against large objectives, for example, cities.[35] [Emphasis added]

The Soviets at this time did not seem to anticipate (nor, for that matter, did the United States) the great improvements that would be made in missile accuracy by both themselves and the U.S., thus increasing the vulnerability of the land-based ICBM.[36] Soviet analysts correctly doubted the effectiveness of a counterforce strategy at the time these statements were made in the early 1960s. The number of U.S. land-based ICBMs, though at the time much more numerous than what the Soviets had, were still too few in absolute terms to pose a genuine threat to destroy Soviet nuclear forces with a high degree of reliability. This was because these ICBMs were still highly inaccurate compared with those of later years.[37] Just because the Soviets recognized this fact, though, does not mean that they did not appreciate the warfighting aspects of counterforce; it did mean that their line that the United States was planning a first strike as a prelude to a "preventive war" was sheer propaganda, since they had little confirmation of this from U.S. strategic capabilities. A considerable amount of mirror-imaging went into these propaganda claims, as demonstrated in the following passage from an article in the March 1965 issue of *International Affairs*:

But from the standpoint of warfare it was valid only in case the United States was to start war first. Indeed, the aggressor is above all interested in knocking weapons out of the hands of his victim and in this way saving himself from a retaliatory blow. *The counterforce strategy is unsuitable for defense.* [But it is apparently suitable for preemption.] What is the sense in destroying the launching pads if the missiles are already heading for their targets? Counterforce is only another name for the selfsame idea of the first strike.[38] [Emphasis added.]

2. *The Soviets interpreted the later abandonment of counterforce and damage limitation as a U.S. move away from a warfighting doctrine towards a deterrence-oriented strategy.*

Since the concept of damage limitation was abandoned rather quickly by the United States in favor of assured destruction shortly after its enunciation by McNamara in 1963, the Soviets made very little mention of it in their writings, with the exception of the third edition of Sokolovskiy's *Voennaia Strategia*.[39] Soviet analysts were apparently confused by the assured destruction concept at first, mainly because they viewed it as part of the requirements for a warfighting strategy instead of perceiving its true nature as an arms-control requirement. This was demonstrated by the following passage from an analysis in *KVS*:

> US Defense Secretary McNamara set forth the notorious "counterforce strategy," the basic thinking of which amounts to the use of nuclear weapons in a future war only on the main groupings of armed forces, but not on the industrial-economic centers and civilian population. . . Indeed, McNamara himself repeatedly declared that the United States of America "through necessity" uses nuclear weapons on the "military-industrial complex" of any opponent and that the essence of the "strategy of counterforce" is to have a few American rockets for the "assured destruction" of each Soviet rocket.[40]

The author had definitely misread the assured destruction concept, in that he implied that it applied only to Soviet strategic forces, rather than to the ability specified by McNamara of being able to inflict unacceptable damage on the Soviet population and industry. Counterforce and assured destruction were not compatible with each other as part of a warfighting strategy. The former notion was correctly interpreted as a possible move towards a nuclear warfighting strategy. Assured destruction, however, was actually an arms-control assessment of the requirements for credible deterrence.[41]

Conversely, the Soviets realized that the United States was actually moving more in the direction of a deterrence posture because of the growing U.S. emphasis on the assured-destruction concept, coupled with the decline of counterforce and damage limitation in U.S. strategic doctrine. Even in the third edition of Sokolovskiy's *Voennaia Strategia*, however, the Soviets still tended to attribute warfighting goals to U.S. nuclear planners:

> Thus, the strategic concepts of "assured destruction" and "damage limitation," considered together, suppose the delivery by the strategic strike forces of the U.S. and their allies of massive nuclear strikes on a whole complex of objectives *that make up the military-economic potential of the enemy* [a projection of Soviet targeting doctrine], and at the same time an active and passive defense of the U.S. so as to limit to a maximum degree the damage from a decisive retaliatory strike by the enemy. The realization of these strategic concepts, according to the military-political leadership of the USA, *requires a balanced combination of strategic offensive forces, defensive forces, and means of passive defense* [This was really the *Soviet* view of what was logically required from strategic doctrine.]. This fact is characteristically acknowledged in the West, that an all-out nuclear rocket war, no matter how it is unleashed, will be destructive for both sides.[42]Emphasis in original.

Found within the same work was an interesting new passage on the alleged intent behind the notion of assured destruction:

> The military circles of the USA openly admit that the basic principle of the American strategy is the achievement of victory in a war by means of destroying the industrial potential and undermining the morale of the civilian population of the enemy . . . the aim of the US strategic nuclear forces is said to be the assurance of the "guaranteed destruction" of the enemy. It is also flatly stated how many millions of the population of the socialist countries can be annihilated, as well as what percentage of the industrial potential can be destroyed.[43] [Emphasis added.]

It is interesting that Soviet military analysts attempted to find analogous ideas of attaining victory in a nuclear war in U.S. strategic thinking. They apparently did not understand initially that the notion of assured destruction was primarily designed as a means of achieving war *avoidance* as opposed to attaining a warfighting objective. Instead, they perceived it as a postulation of military goals in the event of an actual nuclear war.

It should be remembered, however, that the third edition of *Voennaia Strategia* was not set in type until November 1966.[44] The Soviets by this time were well aware of the freeze on further U.S. strategic buildup and the virtual abandonment of a national civil defense program. This recognition of the real nature of the shift in emphasis of U.S. strategic concepts was more explicitly recognized almost a year later in the August 1967 issue of *Voennaia Mysl'*. Although the subject of the article dealt with the evolution of U.S. military doctrine in general, the author's comments on the intent behind the counter-force strategy and the reasons for its subsequent decline are revealing:

> And here we see the striving of the U.S. militarists to represent their aggressive strategy as defensive, although in reality, counting on the supposedly invincible forces of the "retaliatory strike," American strategists intend to *blackmail their enemies and impose their will upon them within the limits of a limited nuclear war* . . . As a result of the evaluation of the nuclear capabilities of the Soviet Union and criticism inside the country, the concept of "counterforce" gradually lost its significance as a new position of U.S. military doctrine. The strategy of "flexible response" . . . received further recognition as the leading strategic concept.[45] [Emphasis added.]

Three main points should be gleaned from the above passage. First, the author implied that it was indeed possible to conduct a limited nuclear war. Second, he projects Soviet estimations of the political utility of nuclear weapons and of "victory" in the context of a nuclear war, whether limited or not, onto U.S. doctrine. Third, and most important, he states that one of the factors responsible for the demise of counterforce was the U.S. recognition of the growing nuclear capabilities of the Soviet Union. It is difficult to believe that the Soviets would not have known of the discussions in the United States regarding the limitations of U.S. strategic forces for counterforce strikes, particularly the U.S. problem with Circular Error Probable (CEP) margins that were still too large for an effective counterforce strategy. CEP is the measure of the accuracy of land- and sea-based ballistic missiles. It represents the area of impact within which there is a 50% probability of a hit by a given missile. If 20 missiles with a CEP of 0.2 miles each are fired at a target, then it is expected that 10 of these missiles will land within a radius of 0.2 miles from the target, with the remainder landing outside this radius at varying distances.[46] Because of the limited capability of U.S. ICBMs and SLBMs to destroy Soviet missiles in their silos, the United States continued to move in the direction of a pure retaliatory concept, which made counterforce less desirable from the standpoint of arms-control advocates.

Soviet analysts therefore seemed inclined to take the "best-case" analysis, so to speak, in explaining why the U.S. was emphasizing assured destruction over the concept of counterforce. Their conclusion was that the United States was abandoning the counterforce strategy only because it was compelled to do so by the growth of Soviet strategic power as the chief factor among those that made up the correlation of forces.[47]

3. *The Soviets interpreted the escalation concept as an actual part of U.S. strategic doctrine.*

On some occasions Soviet analysts had difficulty making a proper distinction between academic discussions of strategic concepts never officially or completely adopted as doctrine, and those that were eventually adopted (such as Maxwell Taylor's arguments for the flexible response doctrine in *The Uncertain Trumpet*). The premier example of this kind of error was the overemphasis given to Herman Kahn's escalation concept, interpreted by the Soviets as the logical extension of flexible response. It is no surprise, then, that the Soviets would pay a lot of attention to the writings of its chief exponent, Herman Kahn. His writings first drew attention in *Voennaia Mysl'*. In the September 1965 issue, two Soviet officers analyzed the escalation concept, giving particular weight to the model of the escalation ladder with its 44 rungs of conflict intensity. They first quoted Kahn as to the precise definition of "escalation":

> A consistent, gradual increase of threats and military efforts in carrying out the strategy of "flexible response" should be, in the opinion of US military theoreticians, the basis of carrying on "protracted conflict." This has been more clearly formulated in the so-called theory of "escalation," which is applied both to the hot and cold war. As H. Kahn says, escalation is a consistent increase of the scale of threats and military pressures in a limited conflict under conditions where it not possible for the opposing side, at each given moment, to counter with even greater pressure. In other words, escalation is "competition in risk to be taken by one's own side."[48]

As one might expect, the Soviets looked for evidence that escalation was actually being applied. According to the authors of the above-quoted article,

"Escalation finds application primarily in conditions of international military-political crises and military intervention in the affairs of underdeveloped countries. A typical example of putting this theory into practice is the U.S. intervention in Vietnam."[49] From the Soviet perspective then, the U.S. involvement in Vietnam was the prime example and definitive proof that the escalation concept was being put to a practical test.

In more open Soviet publications, Soviet treatment of escalation was more general, stressing mainly the application of strategy in Vietnam. Although such references were almost always couched in propagandistic rhetoric, the implication was still that "the 'strategy of flexible response' has been put to a practical test in Vietnam in the form of the escalation strategy, where the American brasshats are constantly extending the scale of their aggression."[50]

4. *The Soviets saw the escalation concept as evidence that the United States might not be deterred from the increased use of force by the Soviets' implied threat of uncontrolled escalation.*

In an extensive public analysis by Larionov in the June 1966 issue of *MEMO*, he stated that the principles of the escalation ladder were those that guided the U.S. intervention in Vietnam, as well as continuing U.S. efforts to "escalate" the conflict.[51] The other conclusions drawn by Larionov about the nature of the escalation theory were as follows:

1. The 44-step escalation ladder made the process of unleashing a nuclear war "smoother."
2. The intent of the escalation ladder was to disarm world public opinion and to paralyze those who opposed universal nuclear war.
3. The escalation theory served to "open the door to the unleashing of war with the use of nuclear weapons."
4. The concept of escalation, along with the concepts of graduated deterrence and the nuclear threshold, were a logical continuation of the flexible response doctrine.[52]

These conclusions agreed with those expressed in *Voennaia Mysl'* and confirmed that Soviet analysts placed considerably more emphasis on Kahn's escalation ladder than was justified. This is really not surprising, since the implication of escalation, like the later concept of limited nuclear options as enunciated by Schlesinger, was that the United States may not be deterred from the use of force by the Soviet implied threat of uncontrolled escalation. This was quite a disturbing prospect for Soviet analysts, as illustrated by the tone of the following passage from an article in the April 1967 issue of *Soviet Military Review*:

> Even a cursory examination of the Kahn theory allows one to draw at least two fundamental conclusions. The first is that the purpose of this theory is not to *avert* but to *kindle* another world war. The second is that it tries to prove that today a world war cannot break out without a preliminary and gradual development of a conflict. The aggressors thereby plan to dull the peoples' vigilance by making believe that the danger of the hotbeds of tension created and fanned by US militarism in various parts of the world is not very great. There is hardly any need to dwell on the deadliness of this camouflage.[53] [Emphasis in original.]

Although the second "conclusion" could be dismissed as propaganda, the first conclusion reflected the Soviet fear of the possibility of a United States undeterred by the threat of uncontrolled escalation. The author of the above passage, commenting on the "step" of officially declaring nuclear war with one or two atomic bombs, objected to such a step with the assertion that "no person is naive enough to believe that the Pentagon seriously intends to announce nuclear strikes beforehand. It is well known that the surprise factor does not by any means figure last in the aggressive plans of the top US brass."[54] (Yet this type of warning by the U.S. is included as part of the later Schlesinger doctrine involving limited nuclear options.) As in all earlier cases, the author once again projected Soviet thinking regarding the value of surprise onto U.S. military plans. Later Soviet analysis, however, conceded the possibility of a limited strategic exchange.[55]

An analysis in the August 1967 issue of *International Affairs* contradicted the Soviets' own propaganda line regarding the escalation strategy. Instead of asserting that the United States was planning to unleash a global nuclear conflict at a propitious moment by escalating local conflicts, the author contended that the so-called strategy had the more limited objective of exhausting the national-liberation movement:

> The US imperialists think that a long, strenuous struggle carried on through small, "limited," local wars and conflicts will sap the material resources and demoralise the peoples [of the Third World involved in national-liberation movements]. They want to achieve their aims by the old "strategy of attrition," extending on a global scale over decades.[56]

In other words, the United States was not "recklessly" climbing the escalation ladder ostensibly for the purpose of unleashing global nuclear war. Rather, the argument went, the U.S. sought the suppression of the national liberation movement by means of localized armed intervention.

Surprisingly, there is practically no reference to Kahn's escalation ladder in the third edition of Sokolovskiy's *Voennaia Strategia.* This could be partially explained by the fact that the third edition was not set in type until November 1966, perhaps not allowing the editors enough time to formulate an official pronouncement. A more likely explanation, however, is that they saw the Kahn theory as just that, a theory, and little more. Their uncertainty over how to treat such theories was reflected in their statement that many military theories "often . . . reflect the opinion of the individual military theoreticians and practitioners. However, in these opinions, there is probably also some reflection of official doctrine."[57] From the above statements, it is clear that the Soviets saw far more of the Kahn escalation theory being reflected in U.S. strategic doctrine and practice than the available evidence supported.

Conclusion

Whereas we were able to say with some certainty in the last chapter that U.S. doctrine had a definite influence on Soviet military planning and programs, it is not as clear in determining the influence of the McNamara concepts on Soviet doctrine or programs, or both. Certainly the Soviets never adopted anything resembling the assured-destruction concept, because this would have meant denying the political utility of nuclear weapons. If the Soviets had really believed that nuclear superiority carried no political leverage advantages, they would never have embarked on such an extensive strategic buildup past the point of parity with the U.S. to the verge of strategic superiority in the early 1980s. This was the fatal error of the arms control theorists and advocates in the United States- in order for arms control to have a chance to succeed, both sides would have to have similar strategic outlooks and foreign policy goals that were intended to preserve the international status quo. And if this situation were indeed the case, then arms control would never have become an issue, since neither side would either have felt threatened or have desired to take advantage of the other's passivity to expand its influence and power at the expense of the other. In other words, in order for arms control to have succeeded between the United States and the Soviet Union, both sides would have to have been basically peace-loving and nonexpansionistic, which would have removed the problem all by itself.

As far as counterforce was concerned, the Soviets already had their own equivalent of it in their own doctrine; that is, if you interpret counterforce in its strictest military application as a preemptive strike against the enemy's warmaking capability, particularly his strategic nuclear forces, then the Soviets had a counterforce concept. It is also clear, judging from the Soviet civil defense program that was extensive even during this period, that the Soviets had their own notions of how to achieve damage limitation (see note 13).

Overall, then, it cannot be said that the McNamara concepts had any appreciable effect on Soviet doctrine, military programs, or even on Soviet uses of military power in support of its expansionist foreign policy objectives. The reasons for this are quite clear. Soviet strategic doctrine had been almost exclusively formulated and carried out by professional military men operating in complicity with the political objectives of the Communist Party of the Soviet Union. As such, military considerations such as nuclear warfighting, war survival, and the attainment of victory in the traditional Clausewitzian sense of having the ability "to compel the opponent to fulfill your will" were predominant. On the other hand, U.S. nuclear strategy during the 1960s was formulated by a man whose primary concern was cost effectiveness, a distinctly managerial consideration that was anathema to the essence of grand strategy. The available means and resources should not have determined the objectives of U.S. strategic doctrine; rather, it should have been the objective that determined the means to be obtained for achieving it with available resources. This may seem like a mere word game, but it accurately describes the backwards logic of the managerial school of strategic thought.

Many military programs that would have contributed significantly to the U.S. ability to defend against a nuclear attack as part of a war survival strategy were not considered cost-effective by McNamara, e.g., programs such as civil defense and a large-scale antiballistic missile system. To McNamara's way of strategic thinking, offensive systems were cheaper and easier to develop than defensive systems and could be produced in greater numbers for the same amount of resources assigned to them. Therefore, a strategic doctrine based on an ability to inflict assured destruction on the Soviet Union, at a level that McNamara considered would be unacceptable to them, was the most cost-effective way to deter nuclear war. Unfortunately, McNamara assumed a like strategic mindset on the part of both Soviet as well as U.S. strategic planners. The Soviets, for their part, saw the advantages that could be attained by convincing the U.S. that they too did not perceive any political leverage in the possession of nuclear superiority. Their declaratory deterrence strategy during this period was designed to create this impression in the minds of unwary U.S. strategic analysts who were inclined to interpret all public Soviet statements at face value without considering them in the context of other factors. Ironically then, the asymmetry between U.S. and Soviet strategic thinking helped to stimulate the very kind of arms buildup that U.S. strategic doctrine under McNamara had hoped to prevent.

Moreover, as the Soviets increasingly admitted the likelihood of more limited conflicts occurring, along with their perception of the U.S. move away from the warfighting-oriented concepts of counterforce and damage limitation towards the deterrence-oriented concept of assured destruction, they reached an important conclusion. They reasoned that this change in the nature of U.S. strategic doctrine was mainly due to the growth of Soviet strategic power, which served as a self-sustaining motivation for a continued Soviet military buildup of both strategic as well as conventional capabilities of all kinds.

Following this reasoning, the more strategic nuclear power that the Soviets possessed, the more that U.S. strategic doctrine would have to change in order to accommodate itself to an unfavorably altered strategic balance. This would insure greater freedom for the Soviets' own use of military power to support their objectives, a freedom that the Soviets had perceived the U.S. as having when it had possessed a large margin of nuclear superiority. As can be seen from Appendix B, the Soviet use of military power had increased in scale during the 1960s as a direct result of this Soviet perception of increased restraints on U.S. freedom of action.

Finally, the Soviets saw a decreased risk of escalation involved in the limited use of force by either side. The exception to this was the Soviet misreading of the escalation concept as espoused by Herman Kahn. Mistaking it as having been part of U.S. strategic doctrine, they were disturbed by the prospect of the United States being undeterred by the implied Soviet threat of uncontrolled escalation. This point is important because it foreshadowed the later Soviet response to the proposed Schlesinger doctrine of limited nuclear options, which would irritate the Soviets even more.

By the end of 1968, the Soviets were fast approaching a state of strategic parity vis-à-vis the United States. The attainment of nuclear parity, from the Soviet view, was one of the fundamental shifts in the overall world correlation of forces in favor of socialism and the Soviet Union. Ironically, then President Lyndon Johnson had reached an agreement with the Soviet leadership to begin the first round of the Strategic Arms Limitation Talks (SALT), which would actually take place after President Nixon took office in 1969. Nixon would also bring with him a new U.S. strategic doctrine that would eventually come to be known as realistic deterrence. The advent of SALT and the realistic deterrence doctrine would have a significant and lasting impact on the Soviet perception of U.S. doctrinal intentions and development.

Notes

1. I. Glagolev and V. Larionov, "Soviet Defense Might and Peaceful Coexistence." *International Affairs* 11 (November 1963): 32.
2. Ibid.
3. V.D. Sokolovskiy, "On the Soviet Military Doctrine," *Soviet Military Review* 4 (April 1965): 8. See also H.F. Scott, *Soviet Military Strategy*, 210.
4. N. Talensky, "The 'Absolute Weapon' and the Problem of Security," *International Affairs* 4 (April 1962): 25. See also Glagolev and Larionov, "Soviet Defense," 32.
5. For ICBM figures see Bonds, *The Soviet War Machine*, 210.
6. N. Talensky, "'Preventive War'-Nuclear Suicide," *International Affairs* 9 (September 1962): 14.
7. Ibid.

8. Sokolovskiy, *Soviet Military Strategy*, trans. and ed. H.S. Dinerstein, L. Goure, and T. Wolfe (Santa Monica, Calif.: RAND, R-416-PR, April 1963), 395. See also Glagolev and Larionov, "Soviet Defense," 33.

9. G. Gerasimov, "Pentagonia, 1966," *International Affairs* 3 (May 1966): 28. See also V. Pechorkin, "About 'Acceptable' War," *International Affairs* 3 (March 1963): 20-23.

10. Talensky, "Preventive War," pp. 14-15.

11. V. Zorin, "The Three McNamara Doctrines," *New Times* 3 (January 1963): 13.

12. For an accounting and description of Soviet civil defense efforts during the sixties, see L. Goure, *Civil Defense in the Soviet Union* (Berkeley: University of California Press, 1962). For a later analysis coupled with a discussion of its place in Soviet warfighting/war survival doctrine, see Goure, *War Survival in Soviet Strategy* (Coral Gables, Fla.: Center for Advanced International Studies, 1976).

13. Glagolev and Larionov, "Soviet Defense," 31.

14. Ibid.

15. For Soviet ICBM deployment see Collins, *Military Trends*, 90.

16. Scott, *Soviet Military Strategy*, 210.

17. Talensky, "Preventive War," 14.

18. See Brodie, *Strategy in the Missile Age*, 229-41, for a complete discussion.

19. Scott, *Soviet Military Strategy*, 61.

20. Larionov, "The Development of the Armed Means and Strategic Concepts of the USA," *MEMO* 6 (June 1966): 78.

21. Ibid., 78-79.

22. Scott, *Soviet Military Strategy*, 210.

23. V. Glazov, "Strategic Concept of the Aggressors," *Soviet Military Review* 4 (April 1967): 49-50.

24. Ibid.

25. G.A. Trofimenko, *SShA: Politika, Voina, Ideologia* (Moscow: Izdatelstvo "Mysl," 1976), 234-44.

26. See, for example, the Izvestia article by Matveyev broadcast by the Moscow Domestic Service in Russian, June 25, 1962, trans. in FBIS, *USSR and Eastern Europe*, June 26, 1962, BB3-5.

27. M. Mil'shtein, "On Certain Military Strategic Concepts of American Imperialism," *MEMO* 9 (August 1962): 91.

28. Ibid., 91-92.

29. Ibid., 92.

30. Ibid.

31. Scott, *Soviet Military Strategy*, 288.

32. Mil'shtein, "Military-Strategic Concepts," 91-92. See also N. Krylov, "The Nuclear Missile Shield of the Soviet State," *Voennaia Mysl'* 11 (November 1967) trans. in FBIS, FPD No. 0157/68, 13-21.

33. S. Konstantinov, "The Military Doctrines of American Imperialism," *KVS* 23 (December 1962): 84.

34. Scott, *Soviet Military Strategy*, xvi.

35. Ibid., 59.

36. As an example of such argumentation against the case for the likelihood of a successful first counterforce strike, see J. Fallows, "Muscle-Bound Superpower: The State of America's Defense," *The Atlantic* (September 1979): 66-72. For a counterpoint, see Collins, *Military Trends*, 75-154.

37. Collins, *Military Trends*, pp. 88-96.

38. G. Gerasimov, "The First Strike Theory," *International Affairs* 3 (March 1965): 41. See also Larionov, "Armed Means," 78-79.

39. Scott, *Soviet Military Strategy*, 62-63.

40. V. Shmuratov, "Doctrines of Aggression and Piracy," *KVS* 15, (August 1965): 78.

41. This was recognized later in Trofimenko, *SShA*, 245-248. See also Scott, *Soviet Military Strategy*, p. 63.

42. Scott, *Soviet Military Strategy*, 63.

43. Ibid., p. 277.

44. Ibid., p. xvi.

45. Kh. Dzhelaukhov, "The Evolution of U.S. Military Doctrine," *Voennaia Mysl'* 9 (September 1967), trans. in FBIS, FPD No. 0132/68, 97. See also Scott, *Soviet Military Strategy*, 63.

46. Bonds, *The US War Machine*, 1978, 65. See also Collins, *Military Trends*, 93-94, for a comparison of the CEPs of U.S. and Soviet missiles.

47. R. Simonyan, "Doctrine of the American Aggressors," *Soviet Military Review* 1, (January 1969), 50.

48. A. Kvitnitskiy and Ym. Nepodayev, "The Theory of the Escalation of War," *Voennaia Mysl'* 9 (September 1965): trans. in FBIS, FPD No. 952, March 2, 1966, 16-17.

49. Ibid., 17.

50. V. Glazov, "The Evolution of U.S. Military Doctrine," *Soviet Military Review* 11, (November 1965): 57.

51. Larionov, "Armed Means," 79.

52. Ibid.

53. Glazov, "Strategic Concept," 48.

54. Ibid., 48-49.

55. S. Ivanov, "Soviet Military Doctrine and Strategy," *Voennaia Mysl'* 5 (May 1969) trans. in FBIS, FPD No. 0116/68, December 18, 1969, 47.

56. B. Teplinsky, "U.S. Military Programmes," *International Affairs* 8 (August 1967): 51.

57. Scott, *Soviet Military Strategy*, 279.

Part IV

REALISTIC DETERRENCE
PERIOD
(1969-1982)

7

The Crisis of Capitalism: Soviet Views of the Nixon Doctrine

Shortly after his inauguration in January 1969, President Richard Nixon outlined the tenets of a new U.S. strategic doctrine that was to become known as the Nixon Doctrine. At the foundation of the Nixon Doctrine was the concept of realistic deterrence, which Defense Secretary Melvin Laird explained in a report to the House Armed Services Committee on March 9, 1971. Laird specified that the realistic deterrence strategy rested on the fulfillment of three important criteria:

1. Preservation by the United States of a sufficient strategic nuclear capability as the cornerstone of the Free World's nuclear deterrent.
2. Development and/or continued maintenance of Free World forces that are effective, and minimize the likelihood of requiring the employment of strategic nuclear forces should deterrence fail.
3. An international security assistance program that will enhance effective self-defense capabilities throughout the Free World, and, when coupled with diplomatic and other actions, will encourage regional security agreements among our friends and allies.[1]

Although similar points of this strategy had been implied in earlier statements during the Nixon administration, the Soviets had recognized the retreat in the U.S. doctrinal stance as early as 1969. But although Soviet analysts accurately saw the true nature of the Nixon Doctrine and realistic deterrence as a U.S. retreat from a higher level of military commitment abroad, they still showed a marked tendency to look for nuclear warfighting trends in U.S. strategic doctrine. Since the United States was clearly moving not in the direction of a warfighting doctrine, but in the direction of a pure deterrence strategy as symbolized by the notion of mutual assured destruction, Soviet analysts publicly concluded that the main cause was the growth of Soviet military power, particularly the attainment of strategic parity with the United States in 1969.

Given this kind of perception, the Soviets could not have been expected to restrain their own military buildup, particularly in the area of strategic nuclear weapons; the stature that they had already attained as early as 1969 had produced such obvious benefits as a change in U.S. strategic doctrine, which was accommodating their foreign policy objectives, and a U.S. willingness to engage in arms-control talks. This was a signal to the Soviets, however unintentional on the part of the United States, that their military buildup had wrung these concessions from an otherwise unwilling and "aggressive" adversary. It was difficult for the Soviets to conclude otherwise, since the U.S. was at the height of its involvement in Vietnam at that time. Logically, from the Soviet perspective, if the military buildup that they had already completed could produce such a U.S. willingness to make concessions, then further military buildup, even while the Soviets ostensibly were engaging in arms-control limitation talks, would reap even greater benefits. Viewed within this context, SALT was therefore not a means for achieving and maintaining strategic stability, but was merely another weapon in the Soviet military-political arsenal for the attainment of its expansionist goals.

The Soviets well understood, however, that it was still necessary to project an attitude similar to that of the United States toward nuclear weapons and their political utility. This became the focal point of the Soviet declaratory deterrence strategy during this period. It was expressed in their foreign policy declarations through the vehicle of detente. While many Americans hailed the concept of detente as signaling a new era in Soviet-American relations and an end to the days of the Cold War, there were few who bothered to take a serious look at the nature of the Soviet statements concerning detente.[2] What we called "detente" in the United States was still "cold war" as far as the Soviets were concerned; the only difference was that there was now a greatly reduced danger of strategic nuclear war as seen by the Soviets.

In their evaluations and pronouncements on the various aspects of the Nixon Doctrine, Soviet analysts saw elements of continuity between it and previous U.S. doctrine. This tendency to look for continuity and consistency was in part a reflection of these same features that the Soviets saw within their own doctrine; that is, U.S. objectives remained the same, but the strategy to achieve them changed depending upon the correlation of forces. One should remember, then, that the Soviets had consistently attributed far more rationality and purposefulness to U.S. strategic doctrine and its development than some might think justified. This is an error on the conservative side; when one is not sure of an adversary's intentions, the safest thing to do is to assume that he knows what he is doing, and not that he is aimlessly blundering along. U.S. analysts, of course, had been assuming the same thing with regard to Soviet strategic doctrine.

The body of Soviet views on the nature of the Nixon Doctrine and realistic deterrence was strongly reflected in their military programs and foreign policy behavior during the period from 1969 to 1982. The use of threats and military maneuvers, as employed during the 1973 Yom Kippur War, was a carryover from the massive retaliation period. Likewise, the use of Soviet sea and airlift capability to mount logistical operations during the flexible response period to Egypt and North Vietnam was still very much in evidence during the realistic deterrence period. But the single greatest escalation in the Soviet use of military power in its aggressive foreign policy strategy was the introduction of the use of proxy troops to do the actual fighting, thus taking the onus of physical intervention off Moscow. First the Cubans, and later the Ethiopians, Yemenis, and East Germans, were to be employed in this role, supported by Soviet logistical efforts.

The singular exception to this trend was in December 1979 when Soviet troops invaded Afghanistan to prop up a tottering pro-Soviet regime. But unlike the earlier Soviet interventions in Hungary and Czechoslovakia, the Afghanistan invasion represented yet another important escalation in the Soviet use of military power, since it took place outside her recognized sphere of influence in Eastern Europe. This increase in scale of the use of military power matches up very closely with what one could expect from the Soviet perception of U.S. strategic doctrine during these years and demonstrates that the Soviet leadership was indeed influenced by, and acted upon, these perceptions.

Even though this perception was being communicated in public Soviet sources, the Soviet leadership still had to mask its real views as much as possible so as not to alarm U.S. observers. Therefore, the aim of Soviet declaratory deterrence statements during this period was to portray the United States in the most aggressive light possible vis-à-vis the Soviet Union in addition to undermining the credibility of realistic deterrence. This propaganda campaign had the beneficial (for the Soviets) effect of drawing attention away from the Soviet military buildup and toward U.S. efforts merely to stay close.

The Soviet Propaganda Line

1. *United States military power is not usable for the attainment of its political goals.*

G.A. Trofimenko, an analyst for the Institution for the Study of the U.S.A. and Canada, was a prominent spokesman for this line. When considered within the context of Soviet military doctrine, however, his statements clearly referred to a hoped-for "reality" rather than the real situation:

> Understanding that the possibilities for the United States' direct utilization of military force in today's world are seriously limited . . . the U.S. leadership ap-

parently cannot and is not prepared to renounce the traditional philosophy which believes the accumulation of "military hardware" to be the chief means of "insuring security."[3]

Other Soviet analysts claimed that the United States had taken on commitments that were beyond its real capacity to fulfill. This was obviously not entirely sincere, since the Soviets would not have wished to acknowledge publicly the political utility of U.S. military power.[4] Soviet English-language publications, such as *Soviet Military Review, New Times*, and *International Affairs*, all stressed this theme heavily. These English-language periodicals often used arguments that had their origins in the American press in order to make their statements seem more plausible to Western readers.

Even though the Soviets had recognized that they had achieved strategic parity with the United States, and that the U.S. apparently was not undertaking any massive strategic buildup in response, Soviet commentators such as Trofimenko nevertheless maintained that the United States still intended to attempt to gain advantages over the Soviet Union regardless of how defensive its new strategic doctrine seemed:

> Finally, proceeding from the formal recognition of the strategic equality an parity of the United States and the USSR, this strategy nonetheless does not want to come to terms with the fact of this equality and is aimed at searching for crafty, devious ways to nonetheless achieve for the United States some military advantages compared with the USSR.[5]

The real proof that this was not a genuine Soviet perception, however, was that it did not coincide with the Soviets' own behavior and attitudes toward military power and its support of national-liberation movements in the Third World.[6] The Soviet use of military power definitely increased in scale during a period when Soviet commentators were asserting that military power allegedly was not a viable instrument for the attainment of foreign policy objectives.

2. *The U.S. failure in Vietnam showed that flexible response was not a reliable doctrine because of its emphasis on military force. In addition, this failure in Vietnam was the main reason for the lowering of the U.S. conventional force requirement from "two-and-a- half wars" to "one-and-a-half wars."*

This was a more subtle theme of Soviet declaratory deterrence, since it contained elements of truth mixed with distortion. G.A. Arbatov was one of the first to argue this theme in the first issue of *SShA: Ekonomika, Politika, Ideologia* in January 1970:

> The basis of this strategy [flexible response] always was reliance on military force. The war in Vietnam showed that military might alone can no longer bring the United States victory not only in the struggle against the "main" enemy, but also on the periphery . . . It became clear that even the tremendous military

power created by the United States has its limits, in which respect these limits are much narrower than required by the political plans of Washington.[7]

Arbatov also claimed to perceive ostensible contradictory behavior in U.S. military allocations in that "on the one hand, it is proceeding towards some reductions in the current military budget, and on the other, it is making a decision on building new, expensive weapons systems."[8] Such behavior was not contradictory, however, in the context of U.S. deterrence strategy and posture;[9] rather, it was contradictory in Soviet eyes to the way they would have wanted the United States to behave.

In an article in *MEMO* in August 1971, Mil'shtein observed that the concept of one-and-a-half wars was a step back from the previous requirements of being able to wage two-and-a-half wars; he was not specific about why the United States had stepped back from the requirements.[10] The apparent explanation given was that "the government and military commands of the USA calculated the 'Vietnam conflict' only as a 'half war' . . . Yet after some time the complete baselessness of such calculations became evident."[11] The miscalculation of the probable scale of the war in Vietnam was so great, according to Mil'shtein, that it was the main factor responsible for the demise of the two-and-a-half-wars concept.[12]

It is unlikely, however, that Mil'shtein actually believed the explanation that he offered. The clear implication of the U.S. deterrence strategy and posture was that the United States did not expect the Soviet Union and the People's Republic of China (PRC) to ally with each other against the United States in the event of a major conflict in Europe or Asia.[13] Given that the political split between the Soviet Union and the PRC was quite unmistakable by this time, the two nations having had border clashes along the Ussuri River as recently as 1969, and that President Nixon at the time of this article (August 1971) was effectively exploiting the rift with overtures to China, the Soviets were not about to acknowledge the fact in their analyses of U.S. doctrine. Instead, they openly rationalized the U.S. lowering of its force requirements by claiming that it was a forced development resulting from Vietnam:

> The fiasco in Vietnam served as a powerful catalyst for Washington's reassessment of the strategic situation because: (a) it fostered the coming to power in the U.S. government of a different party, the Republicans, and the logic of the interparty struggle was obligated to a certain "change of landmarks" and (b) it forced new people in a new government to make a critical analysis of the weaknesses and shortcomings of the Kennedy-Johnson strategy of "flexible response," the unsoundness of which had been revealed in Vietnam.[14]

3. *The realistic deterrence concept of "sufficiency" was no different from the previous flexible response concept of assured destruction. It is such an open-*

ended concept that it can be used to justify a continued arms race and other attempts to gain "one-sided advantages."

This third major theme of the Soviet declaratory deterrence strategy had previously been directed towards U.S. strategic doctrine in general and was now a very prominent theme in Soviet discussions of SALT. When the Soviets did discuss SALT, however, it was as a separate entity. It was almost never mentioned in Soviet military writings and very rarely was discussed at any length in conjunction with Soviet analyses of U.S. strategic doctrine. That the Soviets would compartmentalize their analysis in such a fashion demonstrated their perception of SALT as an offensive propaganda weapon, rather than a serious alternative as a foreign policy objective. Soviet propagandists still wished to portray the United States as inherently aggressive, even though their actual perception (to be discussed later) was that the United States was retreating from its previously higher level of military commitment while trying to enforce its containment strategy.

Soviet commentators and analysts alike concentrated on the notion of sufficiency in trying to prove that U.S. "aggressive intentions" still had not changed. Trofimenko noted the seemingly deliberate open-endedness of sufficiency, citing American military leaders in support of his claim that the United States was still striving for superiority.[15] Another analyst asserted that sufficiency was little different from the McNamara concept of assured destruction. He claimed that "the new aggressive concept opens the way for the utilization of strategic nuclear weapons not only on targets of a global scale, but also for the attainment of advantage in periods of local crisis situations."[16] Mil'shtein made a similar argument, saying that sufficiency "in fact proceeds from the necessity of creating superiority in the strategic nuclear forces and keeping them in such a state of preparedness, which would have allowed the USA to continually threaten the world with the prospect of a nuclear blow on a global scale."[17]

In reality, however, the Soviet emphasis on the vagueness of the sufficiency concept was more an attempt to paint the United States as the instigator of the arms race than a real indicator of Soviet belief. For one thing, Soviet observers were well aware of the large body of opinion in the United States that was against trying to keep a clear-cut superiority in nuclear weapons, which was restricting U.S. freedom of action to maintain the levels of spending on strategic forces necessary to maintain superior numbers.[18] Another point is that they had already recognized the fact that the United States was cutting back on the level of forces it was willing to commit or support. Given that the Soviets believed the United States to be relying more on its allies, they would not believe at the same time that the United States was embarking on another massive buildup recalling the early 1960s. A variation on this was that the United States was striving for "qualitative" superiority. The argument was that while realistic deterrence rejected "the thesis of absolute military superiority, it nevertheless stressed the significance of technical military superiority."[19] And, of course, the Soviet leadership emphasized the need for the Soviet Union to attain and maintain "military-technical supremacy" over the United States.[20]

The Real Soviet View

1. *The Soviets saw realistic deterrence as a retreat from the flexible response doctrine, seeing the new doctrine as signifying a lower level of U.S. military commitment. Nevertheless, Soviet analysts saw much more similarity between realistic deterrence and flexible response than between flexible response and massive retaliation.*

Soviet analysts, even in publications primarily directed at Western audiences, did not fail to make the point that they considered the Nixon Doctrine to have been a retreat from previous periods:

> The military-political activity of the Nixon Administration since it was installed has outlined with sufficient clarity the conception which, it may be assumed, is to shape US foreign policy and military strategy over the immediate period ahead. It is a buildup of the armoury and the maintenance and strengthening of military commitments and greater wariness over participation in local conflicts.[21]

When compared with Defense Secretary Laird's statements at the beginning of this chapter, one can see that this was an accurate assessment. The same analyst also recognized the defensive nature of the new doctrine and its implied retreat from the previous doctrine of flexible response. He observed that the new doctrine "envisages primarily suppression of the national liberation movement and the mounting of local wars," and that it was by such means that "US strategists hope to change the world balance of strength in favor of the USA and to fortify the positions of imperialism as a whole."[22] Such a statement contrasts with earlier pronouncements during the massive retaliation and flexible response periods that pictured the United States in a much more aggressive foreign posture.

This theme was more explicitly stated by Arbatov in the February 1971 issue of *SSHA: Ekonomika, Politika, Ideologia*:

> But in the 1960's it was revealed that even the limited wars undertaken within the framework of the doctrine of "flexible reaction" can prove to be very difficult for the United States, and can prove to be such that the United States, in essence, is incapable of winning any kind of decisive victory. These lessons were becoming more and more obvious and had to find some kind of reflection in the doctrines that were formulated by the new administration.[23]

An even more incisive analysis was found in the May 1971 issue of the same publication. The author recognized the new strategic situation that necessitated the change in U.S. domestic constraints, such as increasing public American protests against the war, which were forcing change upon U.S. leadership:

> The Nixon Doctrine, as we can see, by no means signifies U.S. abandonment of those positions which it has seized abroad. It is only a change in the method of retaining them dictated by the altered situation. Remarking that "over 25 years the American people have become tired of the international burden," the message's authors openly declare that the Nixon Doctrine is intended "to satisfy the demands within the country concerning the manifestation of restraint in our international role without sacrificing our interests abroad."[24]

Soviet analysts saw the primary change in U.S. strategic doctrine as being a reduced U.S. willingness to commit its own military forces to enforce its grand strategy of containment. This was a clear signal to the Soviet leadership that an increase in the scale of Soviet military power employment in support of its foreign policy would not be met directly by U.S. military opposition, particularly in the Third World.

The Soviets saw far less difference in the specifics of the realistic deterrence strategy in comparison with flexible response. One of the few distinguishing features was the change in force level requirement from two-and-a-half wars to one-and-a-half wars.[25] Under the concept of one-and-a-half wars, according to one Soviet analyst:

> The United States must be ready to simultaneously wage an aggressive war against the socialist countries in Europe or Asia and to resolve an 'emergency situation in any other place.' What is meant by the latter case is the suppression of the national liberation movement in different regions of the world.[26]

It was also contended that the new strategic doctrine of realistic deterrence was merely an updated version of flexible response:

> What has been set out . . . leads to the conclusion that the "realistic restraint" strategy does not in fact reject the "flexible response" doctrine, as some leading Washington figures say. It only brings it up to date. The anti-communist trend-the basis for all American military-political concepts-is fully preserved in this strategy. It is essentially distinguished from its predecessor in that it relies on a broader military-technical and military-organizational base, and this endows it with a character which is still more dangerous for the cause of peace.[27]

Culling out the rhetoric in the above passage regarding the "dangerous character" of realistic deterrence, Soviet observers saw little change in the broader aspects of U.S. doctrine. This was further corroborated by Mil'shtein in the August 1971 issue of *MEMO:*

The difference of the strategy of "realistic deterrence" from the strategy of "flexible response" consists mainly in the means and methods of attaining objectives. Beyond these limits "realistic deterrence" and "flexible response" are in fact identical. The new strategy is called the strategy of "realistic deterrence," yet the English word "deterrence" may also have another meaning, for example, "intimidation." [Note: the Soviets do not have an exact word for "deterrence" in the Russian language!] Therefore the new strategy is sometimes called the strategy of "realistic intimidation," that perhaps better reflects its actual direction.[28]

It is interesting that Mil'shtein leaned toward "intimidation" as more descriptive of the intent behind the notion of deterrence. The Russian word *sderzhivania*, meaning literally a "holding in check," implied a more defensive connotation than the Russian word *ustrashenia*, which could best be translated as "intimidation." Mil'shtein may have been trying to make a propaganda point by ascribing a more aggressive intent to the idea of deterrence. In any event, Mil'shtein's point, propaganda or not, was contradicted in the November 1971 issue of *SShA: Ekonomika, Polilika, Ideologia* by Larionov. Larionov stated that "much of what the United States believed feasible (even if only speculatively so) a few years ago is now discarded by Washington as impractical."[29] Larionov, therefore, confirmed the overall Soviet perception of realistic deterrence as basically defensive. Since the U.S. withdrawal program from Vietnam was well underway by this time, there was ample corroboration for this perception in U.S. behavior, not to mention U.S. willingness to participate in SALT negotiations.

2. *The United States was adapting itself to the growth of Soviet strategic power.*

This theme was stated across the board in English-language Soviet publications as well as in Soviet military and academic journals. For example, in the September 1971 issue of *Soviet Military Review*, the authors accurately observed that realistic deterrence was simply an attempt to increase the utility of U.S. military power in a situation of nuclear parity, as opposed to the previous condition of nuclear "superiority":

> This above all explains Washington's attention to the "realistic deterrence strategy." Carried out in the framework of the "flexible response" concept, it has as its aim to consolidate the leading position of the USA in the capitalist world, galvanise NATO and other military blocs, make the "allies" shoulder an additional burden of militarisation, and extend the scale of their participation in US imperialism's aggressive ventures . . . In short, the "realistic deterrence strategy" is another attempt to find more effective means for solving military-political tasks from "positions of strength" in the situation when the new world balance of forces is no longer favorable for imperialism.[30]

Trofimenko, author of several books and articles on U.S. and NATO doctrine, was one of the most prominent spokesmen for this theme. He characterized the central problem of postwar U.S. foreign policy as the resolution of the dilemma between "seeking ways to retain war as an instrument for implementing U.S. imperialism's foreign policy aims, on the one hand, and to utilize military force in such a way that its application does not threaten the United States' very existence on the other."[31] He claimed to see a great deal of continuity in the evolution of U.S. strategic doctrine, asserting that "each subsequent strategy has emerged not in a vacuum but has been organically linked with the preceding one."[32] In explaining the shift by the U.S. from flexible response to realistic deterrence, Trofimenko named what he believed were the main factors in the shifting correlation of forces, among them the growth of Soviet military power:

> The U.S. defeat in Vietnam- a defeat which has called the fundamental post-ulates of the "flexible response" strategy into question- the new correlation of forces in the world- a correlation linked with the intensification of the Soviet Union's economic and military might and with the further development of the world revolutionary process, on the one hand, and the Peking leaders' definite about-face in foreign policy on the other- all made the latest revision of U.S. military-political strategy inevitable.[33]

Soviet analysts recognized that the Nixon Doctrine was "a modification of various elements of the policy of 'containment' in a new situation, with a correction for those reduced capabilities that the United States has at its disposal today."[34] By "reduced capabilities" the Soviets did not actually mean that the United States had declined in the level of its *absolute* military power, but that its relative position of superiority with respect to the Soviet Union had been eliminated, and therefore greater restraints were now placed on the use of U.S. military power. This, according to Arbatov, was one of the main factors compelling the United States to reappraise its strategic doctrine:

> To a greater degree than his predecessors, Nixon has been forced to adapt American foreign policy to the changing ratio of forces in the world, to the new conditions that have been created as a result of the further weakening of the military-political and economic positions of the United States, on the one hand, and the increase in the might of the Soviet Union and the entire socialist community with their increasing influence upon the course of world events, on the other . . . The admission that the United States is incapable of fulfilling the role of world policeman in all conflicts and critical situations is not a voluntary course, but a forced line governing the conduct of the American ruling circles.[35]

Other analyses were still more blunt, arguing that the Soviet attainment of strategic parity with the United States had been primarily responsible for the change. Furthermore, Trofimenko argued that it was the possession of such nuclear parity that was effectively restraining the United States from first use of its nuclear weapons against the Soviet Union:

But since, in reality, it was a question all these years not of restraining the USSR from attacking the United States but, on the contrary, of the USSR restraining U.S. imperialism from unleashing a big thermonuclear war, the U.S. concept of "deterrence" signifies, in fact, a recognition that the Soviet Union possesses such strategic strength which effectively restrains the United States from direct use of its nuclear missile arsenal against the USSR. This is how the situation of the well-known nuclear balance between the USSR and the United States arose, which is characterized by the second part of the formula of the new strategy, that is, by the word "deterrence."[36]

Trofimenko showed good insight into the real nature of U.S. doctrine, noting that realistic deterrence "officially proceeds from U.S. reluctance to be the initiator of unleashing such a conflict and stipulates only the U.S. right and resolve to inflict a counterstrike in the event of an attack on itself."[37] Examining its conventional aspects, he contended that "by expanding military partnership and promoting U.S. allies as the main and, according to the optimum variation, the only suppliers for waging 'local wars,' the Washington leaders are trying to create freedom of action for themselves in critical situations."[38]

In other words, an ongoing struggle was perceived in U.S. strategic planning between the weakening power positions of the United States relative to the Soviet Union on the one hand, and U.S. efforts to counter such a trend by modifying its strategic doctrine to meet the needs of a changing situation on the other. This was spoken of as "the contradiction between the desire to preserve war as a political means and imperialism's ever narrowing opportunities for waging a successful war which brings results."[39] Such a statement should be viewed with some skepticism, however. Although the relative power position of the United States had indeed declined, and though Vietnam-style interventions had proven to be counterproductive, the utility of U.S. military power had not declined to the extent ostensibly believed by Trofimenko, who claimed that realistic deterrence was "a futile search for ways and means of waging war which are without danger for the United States."[40] In a state of strategic parity, the use of military power by the Soviets would have been as risky for them as they said it was for the U.S. But since the Soviets themselves had increased the scale of their use of military power, then it was still possible logically for the United States to use its military power in similar fashion without undue risk of escalation to a strategic exchange.

Another analysis by Trofimenko, while criticizing the use of the word "deterrence" as mere camouflage, nevertheless conceded that the statement by Secretary Laird to Congress (March 9, 1971) projecting the U.S. military posture for 1972-1976 "can be viewed as a very frank description of the forms of and conditions for U.S. participation in future military conflicts provoked by the forces of imperialism."[41] One of the main differences noted between flexible response and realistic deterrence was that the latter implied that the level of military response made by the United States would not necessarily match that used by an adversary, either in kind or degree:

> Generalizing, it can be said that while under Kennedy and Johnson "flexibility" consisted in creating a capability for using American armed forces in a broad range of variations of force with inflexibility in the military obligations taken on by the USA, under Nixon the "flexibility" is interpreted primarily as preserving great freedom for the USA to decide whether it will or will not become involved in a particular military conflict, with greater rigidity in the use of military force if the USA all the same decides to use it.[42]

By changing the meaning of "flexibility," therefore, the United States was trying to resolve "the dilemma of how to keep war as an instrument of U.S. foreign policy and at the same time do it in such a way that if the war does break out, it is not a catastrophe for the USA itself." It must be emphasized that the Soviets saw the Nixon Doctrine and realistic deterrence as forced developments, not as a manifestation of any basic pacifism in the nature of U.S. society. Their rationale was that because of "the sharp qualitative improvement and the quantitative growth in the nuclear missile arsenals of the main rivals, and the improvement in the strategic arsenals of other nuclear powers, the current leaders in Washington have been forced to develop their military concepts with due regard for current realities."[43]

The culmination of U.S. reassessment of its strategic doctrine was said to have taken place in the May 1972 summit meeting between President Nixon and Party Secretary Leonid Brezhnev in Moscow. This development was stressed in the October 1973 issue of *International Affairs*, which stated that "the recognition by the US ruling circles of the nuclear parity between the Soviet Union and the United States was recorded in the documents signed during the May 1972 summit meeting in Moscow."[44] The most important conclusion the Soviets drew from this series of events was that the growth of its own strategic power was a decisive factor in the global "correlation of world forces," which was asserted by Trofimenko in the October 1975 issue of *International Affairs*:

> To sum it up, the balance of world forces had further shifted in socialism's favour by the early 1970's as evidenced, for example, by the attainment of Soviet-American nuclear and missile parity and the awareness by the USA of its limited possibilities to influence diverse events in the world by means of military forces. This made the US ruling class start a "reappraisal of values" and acknowledge the need "to reconcile the reality of competition between the two systems with the imperative of coexistence."[45]

3. *The United States, despite the adaptation of its strategic doctrine to the growing strategic nuclear power of the Soviet Union, still is attempting to incorporate a nuclear warfighting strategy into its doctrine.*

Notwithstanding the general accuracy of the Soviet appraisal of U.S. doctrinal developments during this period, there was nevertheless a marked inclination by Soviet analysts to look for warfighting characteristics in the realistic deterrence strategy. A U.S. move toward such a doctrine would be the very kind of "reactionary reversal" in U.S. strategic doctrine that the Soviets feared most. Such fears would later be heightened by the proposal of the limited nuclear options strategy by Defense Secretary James Schlesinger and confirmed by the declaration of SDI under Ronald Reagan. Because this mirror-imaging tendency has been noted and documented extensively in previous chapters, only a few representative examples are presented.

One example of Soviet mirror-imaging was in an article by Soviet military analyst Major General R. Simonyan. He claimed that realistic deterrence, "like its predecessor, stems from the need to prepare and wage wars of different scales: from local wars to all-out nuclear war."[46] The reasons for such mirror-imaging are not as strange as we might think, since the Soviets believed that there existed certain "laws" governing military science and strategy. Since these laws supposedly hold true regardless of the circumstances surrounding a potential conflict, it would be foolish from the Soviet perspective for an adversary to knowingly violate them.[47] Since the Soviets consistently credited U.S. actions with a certain degree of rationality, it follows that Soviet analysts would expect U.S. planners to adopt a strategy the Soviets considered rational.

Even with the Soviet recognition of a U.S. retreat in its doctrine, they continued to look for warfighting orientations. Simonyan, writing for *New Times* in March 1977, claimed that "Pentagon and NATO strategists see in surprise attack the best way to start a general nuclear war, since this could substantially weaken retaliatory strikes, give the strategic initiative to the attacker and sharply shift the balance in his favor."[48] One might be tempted at first to dismiss such statements as pure propaganda designed to portray the United States in the most aggressive light possible. When considered within the context of Soviet strategic doctrine, which emphasized surprise and the notion of a preemptive strike, however, it becomes merely another instance of Soviet mirror-imaging of their own strategy onto U.S. doctrine. If the Soviets themselves considered a preemptive strike an optimum strategy to adopt, then they would have considered it optimum for the United States as well. This is why Soviet declaratory deterrence statements were designed to convince the United States that such a strategy could not possibly work. The last thing the Soviets wanted was for the United States to adopt a nuclear warfighting doctrine similar to their own; this would have negated much of the benefit that the Soviets were getting from the U.S. deterrence posture in terms of freedom to use their own military power in support of their objectives.

In the April 1977 issue of *Voenno-Istoricheskii Zhurnal* an article appeared that analyzed the development of U.S. strategic doctrine in the postwar period. As illustrated by the following passage, much of the thinking attributed to U.S. planners conceming a future nuclear war could just as easily have been taken from Soviet statements concerning their own doctrine:

> In accordance with present actual military doctrine, the basis on which the strategy of "realistic deterrence"[ustrashenia, meaning "intimidation" in the literal sense] is composed, the USA should be prepared for the waging of total, as well as limited nuclear war. The doctrine considers total nuclear war as a war between two opposing social systems, capitalist and socialist. It is considered, that a future war will be coalitional, short and decisive, with the mass use of nuclear-rocket weapons. A total nuclear war may be unleashed by two means: by a surprise nuclear attack or gradual engagement in war, by the escalation of a local war into a total, nuclear war.[49]

The words regarding the "clash between two opposing social systems," with emphasis on the "coalitional, short and decisive," nature of a nuclear conflict, is reminiscent of some of the characteristics of Soviet military doctrine as it was originally stated by Khrushchev and Malinovskiy in 1960, and as it remained almost until the collapse of the Soviet Union itself in 1991.

Conclusion

On the whole, the Soviet analyses of the Nixon Doctrine and realistic deterrence were quite accurate. By 1969 the strategic balance had changed (see Appendix A), and opposition to the Vietnam war was mounting in the United States. Clearly the United States was no longer able to engage in Vietnam types of containment actions, and now sought a new formula whereby the other countries would take the responsibility of defending themselves and the United States would be more selective in its intervention. The Nixon Doctrine played a part in the eventual move to the 1972 detente. It signaled an important retrenchment in U.S. policy and obviously a greater readiness on the part of the United States to seek some form of cooperation with the Soviet Union. Of course, certain propagandistic themes such as the aggressive nature of capitalism, U.S. reliance on military power and responsibility for the arms race, the danger of a reactionary reversal in U.S. policy, and fundamental U.S. "anti-Sovietism" remained constant themes of Soviet declaratory deterrence strategy. But the Soviets, for the most part, saw the Nixon Doctrine and realistic deterrence as a retreat, as indeed they were.

In 1974, however, there would be a proposal in U.S. strategic doctrine set forth by Defense Secretary James Schlesinger that would produce a surprisingly worried reaction from Soviet commentators, who saw certain elements of his proposed limited nuclear options strategy as the very kind of "dangerous reversal" in U.S. strategy that they had feared. These particular elements, and the Soviet reaction to the proposed doctrine in general, are the focus of the next chapter.

Notes

1. See Melvin Laird, *Statement of Secretary of Defense Melvin R. Laird before the House Armed Services Committee on the Fiscal Year 1972-1976 Defense Program and the 1972 Defense Budget* (Washington, D.C.: U.S. Government Printing Office, March 1, 1971), 15.
2. An examination of the Soviet view of detente in their foreign policy strategy is found in F. Kohler, *Soviet Strategy for the Seventies: From Cold War to Peaceful Coexistence*, 87.
3. G.A. Trofimenko, "Some Aspects of US Military and Political Strategy," *SShA: Ekonomika, Politika, Ideologia* 10 (October 1970), trans. in JPRS No. 51895, December 1, 1970, 30. See. also A. Baryshev, "New US Doctrines, Same Old Aim," *International Affairs* 12 (December 1969): 12.
4. G.A. Arbatov, et al., "The Nixon Doctrine: Declarations and Realities," *SShA: Ekonomika, Politika, Ideologia* 2 (February 1971), trans. in FBIS, *USSR Daily Report*, March 5, 1971, A34.
5. Trofimenko, *SShA: Ekonomika, Politika, Ideologia* 12 (December 1971), trans. in JPRS No. 54971, January 19, 1972, 15.
6. Kohler, *Soviet Strategy for the Seventies*, 76-78. See also ibid., 83-88 for Soviet commentary on the need for continued military buildup.
7. G.A. Arbatov, "American Foreign Policy at the Threshold of the 1970's," *SShA: Ekonomika, Politika, Ideologia* 1 (January 1970), trans. in JPRS No. 49934, February 26, 1970, 16, 19.
8. Ibid., 24.
9. Endicott and Stafford, *American Defense Policy*, 80-81.
10. M. Mil'shtein, "American Military Doctrine: Continuity and Modifications," *MEMO* 8 (August 1971): 34-35.
11. Ibid., 35.
12. Ibid., 36.
13. Endicott and Stafford, *American Defense Policy*, 81.
14. G.A Trofimenko, "Military-Strategic Aspects of the Nixon Doctrine," *Doktrina Niksona*, ed. by Y. Davydov, (Moscow: Izdatelstvo Nauka, 1972), trans. in JPRS No. 58317, February 26, 1973, 49.
15. Trofimenko, "US Military and Political Strategy," 19. See also Trofimenko, "Nixon Doctrine," 54.
16. 0. Bykov, "Concerning Some Features of the Foreign Policy Strategy of the USA," *MEMO* 4 (April 1971): 57.
17. Mil'shtein, "American Military Doctrine," 33. See also V. Larionov, "The Transformation of the 'Strategic Sufficiency' Concept," *SShA: Ekonomika, Politika, Ideologia* 11, (November 1971), trans. in JPRS No. 54676, December 10, 1971, 38. See also 39-40 of the latter article for the Soviet definition of the U.S. concept of "sufficiency."
18. Mil'shtein, "American Military Doctrine," 35-37.

19. V.F. Petrovskiy, "The Evolution of the 'National Security' Doctrine," *SShA: Ekonomika, Politika, Ideologia* 11 (November 1978), trans. in FBIS, *USSR Daily Report Annex*, November 17, 1978, 5.
20. Kohler, *Soviet Strategy*, 86-89.
21. B. Teplinsky, "Some Aspects of US Global Strategy," *International Affairs* 5 (May 1970): 70. See also G.A. Trofimenko, "Anti-Communism and Imperialism's Foreign Policy," *International Affairs* 1 (January 1971): 53. See Soviet admission of limited war possibility in Editorial, "ON Guard for peace and the Building of Socialism," *Voennaia Mysl'* 12 (December 1971), trans. in FBIS FPD No. 0003/74, January 17, 1974, 12.
22. Teplinsky, "US Global Strategy," 70.
23. Arbatov, "Nixon Doctrine," A3. See also Trofimenko, *SShA: Ekonomika, Politika, Ideologia* 12 (December 1971) trans. in JPRS No. 54971, January 19, 1972, 3.
24. D.Z. Khoskin, "Labyrinth of Contradictions," *SShA: Ekonomika, Politika, Ideologia,* 5 (May 1971), trans. in JPRS No. 53268, June 2, 1971, 80. See also A. Migolat'yev, "The Aggressive Essence of the Military-Political Strategy of American Imperialism," *KVS* 10 (May 1971): 84; P. Zhilin and Y. Rybkin, "Militarism and Contemporary International Relations," *International Affairs* 10 (October 1973): 28.
25. J. Collins, *American and Soviet Military Trends since the Cuban Missile Crisis* (Washington, D.C.: Center for Strategic and International Studies, 1978), 157-8.
26. R. Simonyan, "A Strategy Doomed to Failure," *Pravda,* August 14, 1971, 4, trans. in FBIS, *USSR Daily Report,* August 25, 1971, A5.
27. Ibid., A6.
28. Mil'shtein, "American Military Doctrine," 40-41. See also Trofimenko, "Nixon Doctrine," 60.
29. Larionov, "Strategic Sufficiency," 33.
30. V. Perfilov, "New Doctrine-Old Aims," *Soviet Military Review* 9, (September 1971): 57. See also B. Dmitriev, "Policy of Detente," *New Times* 43 (October 1971): 7.
31. Trofimenko, "US Military and Political Strategy," 15.
32. Ibid., 18.
33. Ibid., 19. See also I. Potapov, "The Evolution of the Strategic Concepts of Imperialism in the Post-War Period," *Voenno-Istoricheskii Zhurnal* 5 (May 1971): 44-49, passim.
34. Arbatov, "Nixon Doctrine," A7.
35. Ibid.
36. Trofimenko, *SShA: Ekonomika, Politika, Ideologia* 12 (December 1971): 8, 14. See also similar statements by Brezhnev and Grechko quoted in L. Goure, F. Kohler, and M. Harvey, *The Role of Nuclear Forces in Current Soviet Strategy* (Coral Gables, Fla.: Center for Advanced International Studies, 1975), 49.
37. Trofimenko, *SShA: Ekonomika, Politika, Ideologia* 12 (December 1971): 14.
38. Ibid., 10.
39. Ibid., 13.
40. Ibid., 14-15. See also Trofimenko, "Nixon Doctrine," 47-49.
41. Trofimenko, "Nixon Doctrine," 55.
42. Ibid., 60.
43. Ibid., 68. See also Petrovskiy, "National Security Doctrine," 3.
44. A. Gromyko and A. Kokoshin, "US Foreign Policy Strategy for the 1970's," *International Affairs* 10 (October 1973): 69.

45. G. Trofimenko, "From Confrontation to Coexistence," *International Affairs* 10 (October 1975): 38. See also P. Sergeyev and V. Trusenkov, "Evolution of the US Military Doctrine," *Soviet Military Review* 11 (November 1976): 52.
46. Simonyan, "Doomed to Failure," A6.
47. For an example of Soviet commentary regarding the laws of armed conflict, see *The Philosophical Heritage of V.I. Lenin and Problems of Contemporary War* (Moscow: Voennoe Izdatelstvo, 1972), trans. by U.S. Air Force (Washington, D.C.: U.S. Government Printing Office, 1972), 95-116. See also Sergeyev and Trusenkov, " US Military Doctrine," 52.
48. R. Simonyan, "'Realistic Deterrence': The Real Implications," *New Times* 10 (March 1977): 18. See also Simonyan, "The Pentagon's Nuclear Strategy," *New Times* 35 (August 1977): 22-24.
49. N. Nikitin, "The Evolution of the Military Doctrine and Strategic Concepts of the USA after the Second World War," *Voenno-Istoricheskii Zhurnal* 4 (April 1977): 66.

8

Dangerous Reversal: Soviet Reaction to the Limited Nuclear Options Strategy

Why the Soviet Reaction Was Important

Soviet analysts were clearly disturbed by the announcement of the strategy of limited nuclear options (LNO) as an important part of the proposed Schlesinger doctrine, because it signaled the possibility of the very kind of "dangerous reversal" in U.S. strategic doctrine that the Soviets had long feared might take place. They expressed this fear even though they were claiming at the same time that the likelihood of strategic nuclear war had been greatly reduced, largely because they perceived the United States as restrained in its ability to threaten escalation by the growth of Soviet strategic power.

The timing of the LNO strategy was especially distressing since it came in January 1974, a time when the United States had just about extricated itself from the quagmire of Indochina. U.S. willingness to commit its military power in support of anything was at an all-time low, particularly because of the domestic turmoil being stirred up by the Watergate affair. The Soviets were at the stage of considering the use of proxy troops in more overt fashion to support their supposed national liberation movements in Third World countries. It is not surprising then that the Soviets would have been nervous over the possibility that the United States might actually respond to an increased use of Soviet military power with a limited strategic strike on Soviet territory using only one or a few nuclear weapons.

The reasons behind this kind of Soviet reaction can be understood if we look at the logic behind the Soviet *desinformatsiya* strategy of the previous periods. Soviet reaction in the past to any declared U.S. attempts to limit conflict on either a conventional or a nuclear scale had always consisted of statements designed to give the impression that such attempts might lead to uncontrolled escalation to strategic nuclear war. Despite the public Soviet use of this threat, other analyses from both public and private Soviet sources increasingly admitted the likelihood and necessity of having to wage a limited, localized conflict *without* escalating to strategic nuclear war. By the use of their declaratory deterrence strategy, however, the Soviets were hoping to encourage the United States to remain in its purely retaliatory posture based on mutual assured destruction and to believe that any attempts to use its nuclear weaponry for any other purposes were too dangerous.

But with the LNO strategy, the United States was threatening to wipe out the entire basis for the Soviet declaratory deterrence strategy in one stroke. The earlier Soviet reaction to Herman Kahn's escalation ladder provides the reason why. Both public and private Soviet evaluations of Kahn's escalation concept indicate that the Soviets were highly disturbed by the apparent U.S. willingness to escalate in complete disregard of Soviet implied threats of further escalation to dangerous levels. The Soviets were counting on the United States remaining in its defensive retaliatory posture so that the Soviets might have more freedom to use military power to aid in the attainment of their political and strategic objectives. A United States that apparently was willing to disregard the dangers involved in escalation was a great restraint on Soviet freedom of action, from their point of view, because the Soviets themselves were afraid of the consequences of such escalation. Although it is true that the nuclear balance was more in favor of the Soviets at the time of the LNO strategy as compared to the mid-1960s (see Appendix A), there were enough similarities in the Soviet response to escalation and LNO to suggest that the actual adoption of an LNO strategy might have improved the U.S. ability to discourage Soviet use of her military power during the 1970s.

This point, however, cannot be proven or disproven. Since the Schlesinger doctrine was never wholly adopted, Schlesinger having been fired by President Ford in 1976, the LNO strategy fell by the wayside. Some features, though, such as increased targeting flexibility and accuracy, were picked up later and incorporated into U.S. strategic planning. In fact, they were to show up in the U.S. "countervailing strategy" announced during the Carter administration. Since the LNO strategy never became an operational part of U.S. strategic doctrine, it is not practical to compare Soviet foreign policy behavior with their stated views on LNO. The reason for this is that the doctrine actually in force during this brief period (1974-1976) was at best an attenuated version of the Nixon Doctrine. Examining the Soviet perception of the LNO strategy is still useful, nevertheless, since the nature of the Soviet response provides important clues to what the Soviets would find deterring or restraining to them. The Soviets reacted most strongly to those features of the LNO strategy that looked like moves towards a nuclear warfighting doctrine similar to what the Soviets themselves adhered.

The Soviet Propaganda Line

As was the case with previous U.S. strategic doctrines, the primary purpose of the Soviet declaratory deterrence strategy was to discredit the feasibility of limited nuclear options. Soviet commentators used basically these three lines of argument:

1. *The use of limited strategic strikes against military targets in the Soviet Union carried the danger of uncontrolled escalation to total nuclear war. Such a limited strike would not be conducted according to the rules of the game envisioned by Schlesinger and would not remain confined for long to limited exchanges.*

Even before the LNO strategy had been set forth in January 1974, at least one Soviet military analyst foresaw the possibility of a limited strategic exchange for purposes of political intimidation. Army General S. Ivanov, in the May 1969 issue of *Voennaia Mysl'*, pointed out this possibility even while saying that such an exchange could not characterize the entire war:

> Of course, theoretically it can be assumed that for the purpose of scaring one another the belligerents will limit themselves to inflicting some selected nuclear attacks on secondary objectives, but will not dare to expand the nuclear conflict any further. But such an exchange of individual nuclear attacks, even if it should take place, cannot characterize the war in entirety.[1]

This assertion reflected the warfighting mindset of the Soviet military, which was not inclined to think of nuclear attacks as a means of political "signaling" or incremental coercion, even if they were on a limited scale.

Soviet propagandists once again borrowed from the Western press in their selection of arguments that would appear most credible to unwary Western readers. For example, then Lieutenant General M. Mil'shtein and Colonel L. Semeyko, in the November 1974 issue of *SShA: Ekonomika, Politika, Ideologia*, claimed that "even having begun by inflicting strikes on several selected military targets, such a conflict will not develop in accordance with the 'rules of the game' now being drawn up in Pentagon offices but will most likely develop into a general war which does not lend itself to 'flexible response.'"[2] In other words, regardless of U.S. efforts to impose limits on the kind of targets that were to be attacked, there was no guarantee that the war would not escalate further. What Soviet commentators were careful not to say, though, was that there was also no guarantee that the war *would* escalate.

Arbatov reiterated this Soviet propaganda theme in *Soviet Military Review*, arguing that it is "hard to assume that nuclear war, once it begins, will remain within the artificial 'rules' and not grow into a universal war."[3] Notice that the Soviets never tried to provide any solid argumentative evidence that an LNO strategy would lead to strategic nuclear war; they asserted it flatly and without elaboration, as if it were an unchallengeable tenet of faith. Also, Schlesinger never said that war would not escalate, but he did say that the president should have the option to initiate a U.S. response at various levels of intensity.

2. *The United States is striving to derive unilateral advantages from the LNO strategy through a lowering of the nuclear threshold.*

The Soviets tried to argue that any lowering of the so-called nuclear threshold was destabilizing. Such was the case in the May 1975 issue of *Mezhdunarodnaya Zhizn*, the Russian-language version of *International Affairs*:

> In substantiating the need for the strategy of "retargeting," the US military theoreticians assert that the United States' possession of the ability to wage "limited" nuclear wars intensifies the "deterrent" effect and strengthens international stability. But in reality, this theory, which preaches the permissibility of the use of nuclear weapons, leads to an erosion of the differences between conventional and nuclear wars and creates an illusion of the legitimacy of a war in which nuclear missile means are used. Therefore the US researcher Barry Carter is profoundly correct when he writes that the concept of "retargeting" in fact contains a "tendency to overcome arguments against the use of nuclear arms- in essence a tendency toward lowering the nuclear threshold."[4]

Of course, what the Soviets did not say was the fact that the ability of the *defender* to "lower the nuclear threshold" by means of an LNO strategy was highly destabilizing for Soviet planning. It introduced still more uncertainty into the calculations of Soviet strategic planners by confronting the Soviets with the hitherto excluded possibility (at least in public discussions) of a series of nuclear strikes on Soviet territory that were limited in scope and number; that is, a low-level counterforce war. By increasing the range of possible U.S. responses in this way, Soviet planners would have had to exercise more caution in their evaluation of the US intent in the event of a confrontation.

The author of the above article also argued that the LNO strategy represented an "arbitrary convention" between "nuclear wars of various degrees of intensity," and thus was "extremely unstable and mobile." He argues further that:

> once used, nuclear missile weapons set off a chain reaction which, taking into consideration the distinctive features of modern military equipment and the military-ideological doctrines of the United States which envisage the direct participation of strategic forces in the implementation of the tasks of a 'limited war,' could prove to be totally uncontrolled and extremely rapid."[5]

This was a presumptuous statement on the author's part, since there has never been a military conflict in which nuclear weapons have been used on anything resembling a large scale, nor one in which nuclear weapons were possessed by more than one side. So it is difficult to take seriously a statement that baldly asserts that the use of nuclear weapons will in fact set off a chain reaction.

It was Arbatov who put forth one of the most refined propaganda arguments against LNO in a July issue of *New Times*. In the following passage, he basically argued that neither side could be expected to restrain itself during a crisis to highly circumscribed rules of the game that were arbitrarily defined by the United States:

> For example, even if one were to suppose that a situation emerged in which the threat of the escalation of a nuclear conflict right up to a massive ("spasmodic," to use Schlesinger's term) strike against cities did not prevent the hypothetical "enemy" from carrying out a "limited attack," then the enemy would be deterred still less by the threat of a "selective retaliatory strike." On the contrary, it would create the impression that such actions are less risky and more acceptable. Furthermore, if we were to suppose that a "limited nuclear war" had nevertheless started, the other side could not be requested to hold its missiles meant for a retaliatory strike (including a strike against cities) "in reserve" in the silos-after all, these missiles, according to Schlesinger's ideas, are in fact the main target of a "limited" (essentially, disarming) strike by the foe's nuclear forces.[6]

The problem with Arbatov's argument was that LNO was not intended to have included a "disarming" strike, but was designed to be a means of incremental coercion to persuade the opponent to end the war quickly at minimum loss to the United States and its allies. If one looked at the LNO strategy in terms of its usefulness in an actual nuclear warfighting doctrine, then it made little sense. If a nation adopts a warfighting strategy, then it follows that it must have conditions or objectives that define "victory." On the other hand, if the national objective (as in the case of the United States) was the avoidance of nuclear war in the first place or the early termination of the war at minimum loss should deterrence fail, then it was not necessary to define victory. Since the Soviet strategic culture was dominated by nuclear warfighting concepts, the Soviets saw the LNO strategy as evidence that the United States was trying to break out of its strategic impasse, which had been imposed by the growth of Soviet military power:

> Since the strengthening of the USSR's defense put an end to hopes that a nuclear war was possible and safe for the United States, the military-industrial complex and its patrons in the United States have repeatedly tried to break out of the deadlock that had developed. They created increasingly refined strategic concepts. Of course, this did not reduce the threat of general war.[7]

3. *No nuclear conflict can be limited because of the very nature of the weapons involved.*

Typical of this kind of propaganda is the following excerpt from a Radio Moscow commentary. Since this theme was the simplest, it was used most often and most widely by Soviet commentators:

> It is always said that it wouldn't be a total strike but rather a selective one with small nuclear warheads, as though that changes anything. A nuclear war is a nuclear war, with all its horrors and untold suffering, especially when it is started against a country in possession of equal means to make a return strike.[8]

A variation of this argument was that the destructive power of nuclear weapons was so great that it was not possible to use them against isolated military targets without causing heavy casualties among the civilian population. This allegedly made it impossible to have a limited nuclear war. The following passage from an article by Simonyan in a March 1979 issue of *New Times* was typical:

> Actually, as the U.S. press has noted, the location of military installations is such that nuclear strikes at them, however "selective," would inevitably cause enormous loss of life among the civilian population. For instance, Pentagon experts have estimated that a nuclear strike at the Whiteman air base in Missouri could take a toll of 10.3 million lives. The consequences of "limited" nuclear warfare would be still more disastrous if massive strikes with scores or perhaps hundreds of warheads in the megaton class were used against military targets.[9]

This was a false argument, since the Soviets deliberately omitted the fact that the United States had the technology to produce low-yield warheads and to deliver them with sufficient accuracy to minimize the collateral damage inflicted. The implication that LNO would involve a "massive strike" with "hundreds of warheads" was also false, since the strategy was originally intended to provide a number of lesser options short of such a massive strike.[10] This kind of argument was really little more than a word game, since its validity rested on the basis of the Soviets' having defined nuclear weapons beforehand as unlimited by their very nature.

The Real Soviet View

The period of the most active Soviet response to the strategy of limited nuclear options dated from November 1974 to the end of 1976, by which time it had become fairly obvious to the Soviets that the Schlesinger doctrine with its attendant strategy of LNO was not going to be adopted as part of U.S. strategic doctrine. Between the time of Schlesinger's initial statements on LNO in January 1974[11] and the first comprehensive response to LNO in the Soviet press in November 1974, there was an unusually long pause, during which there was little real attempt at serious public analysis of LNO. The

Soviets were undoubtedly using this time to analyze its implications before going public with their preferred line. However, there was a considerable amount of discussion of LNO in the East European press during the early part of 1974, the very period when the Soviets themselves were silent on the subject for the most part.[12]

1. *Soviet analysts saw LNO as a move towards a nuclear warfighting doctrine similar in some respects to their own, equating it with the counterforce strategy formerly espoused by McNamara. The Soviets further believed that this strategy was an abandonment of a pure retaliatory posture in favor of a possible U.S. first use of nuclear weapons.*

The Soviet preference for viewing U.S. strategic doctrine through the prism of their own nuclear warfighting strategy was still fully evident during this period, even in some of the most authoritative and comprehensive analyses. For example, Mil'shtein, in the first major analysis of LNO, in the November 1974 issue of *SShA: Ekonomika, Politika, Ideologia*, showed this mirror-imaging tendency even while making the propagandistic assertion that possession of strategic power had little political utility:

> If we sum up the results of the period from the end of the forties through the sixties, the main point which emerges is that, during that period, the focus of American military-political thinking and of official military-strategic aims was by no means the problem of the impossibility of nuclear war, despite the many loud statements made about the horrors such a war would entail, but, on the contrary, the problem of seeking ways of using that power *and seeking out forms and methods of waging war which would enable the United States to survive and win in a nuclear clash.* [This is a virtual mirror-image of the thinking in the Soviet Union during the late forties and up through the early sixties.] Emphasis was placed on this despite the growing awareness of the fact that attempts by the United States to use all or even part of its nuclear potential could have suicidal consequences. *It took a fundamental change in the Soviet-American strategic nuclear balance and in the correlation of forces in the world as a whole for the political realism which enabled the agreement on the prevention of nuclear war to be signed with the USSR in 1973 to begin to gain the upper hand in the United States.*[13] [Emphasis added]

Soviet military publications disregarded the political signaling aspects of the LNO strategy, looking instead at its warfighting applications. For example, in the July 8, 1975, issue of *Krasnaya Zvezda*, two military officers looked at the possible application of the Schlesinger LNO strategy to the NATO alliance, particularly in regard to limited nuclear war in Europe. As can be seen in the following passage, the authors emphasized the warfighting applications of Schlesinger's ideas:

> The Atlantic strategists are not only looking at "limited nuclear war" on the theoretical plane. They are engaging in direct preparations for waging such a

war. Its prospects were discussed at the recent meeting of the NATO Nuclear Planning Group. That meeting decided on a fundamental modernization of American tactical nuclear weapons in Europe. In addition, the United States promised to allocate additional Poseidon missiles . . . to strengthen the bloc's nuclear might.[14]

But if the Soviets were indeed projecting their own notions of nuclear warfighting onto the LNO strategy, then they probably found that it was very awkward as a nuclear warfighting doctrine. The LNO strategy was never designed to support a nuclear warfighting posture; this was because the U.S. lacked the strategic defenses in the form of civil defense and an ABM system that would have given the United States the credible war survival/recovery capability necessary for such a warfighting doctrine. Instead, the goal of LNO was to strengthen the credibility of U.S. deterrence, with the goal of "early war termination" should deterrence fail, instead of pressing for any sort of victory. It should also be noted that early war termination is not a recognized military objective; instead, it is a political objective that does not fall under the jurisdiction of military operations. It is therefore not hard to see that Soviet military planners would have a hard time understanding or accepting such an objective as interpreted within the context of their own doctrine.

An important reason for the difficulty the Soviets had in understanding the reasoning behind the Schlesinger LNO strategy is the distinctively different sources of strategic thinking in the two countries. American strategic thinking, particularly since the early 1960s, has been heavily influenced by highly abstract, "game theory" concepts such as compellence and incremental coercion. These concepts were completely ahistorical and apolitical in their methodology and analysis. When historical examples were used (a rare occurrence), they were carefully selected and interpreted in such a way as to support the assumptions of the game theorists. On the other hand, Soviet military strategy had been developed for the most part by professional military officers, with heavy emphasis on the study of military history and political theory (albeit Marxist-Leninist political theory); therefore, the influence of such "traditional" notions as military effectiveness and warfighting was predominant.[15] If we accept the premise that Soviet political and military analysts of U.S. doctrine are as equally vulnerable to the mirror-imaging fallacy as their U.S. counterparts, then the Soviet reaction becomes much easier to understand.[16]

Soviet observers were plainly not happy about the possibility implied by LNO that the United States might be moving back to a counterforce strategy. Even more unsettling was the prospect of the United States using nuclear weapons first in a crisis situation, thus abandoning its former retaliatory stance. This fear was expressed in the July 12, 1975, issue of *Pravda*, in which it was asserted that:

while talking about some 'hypothetical circumstances' in which the United States might utilize nuclear weapons, Schlesinger is essentially orienting his department not toward the implementation of the agreement on the prevention of nuclear war, but toward a strategy of the possible utilization of nuclear weapons by the United States in any crisis situation.[17] [emphasis added]

The LNO strategy provoked much dismay among Soviet observers; it constituted one of the first instances in which the Soviets began linking it to arms control in one way or another. In the November 1974 issue of *SShA: Ekonomika, Politika, Ideologia*, it was Mil'shtein who equated the LNO strategy with the McNamara strategy of counterforce, claiming that LNO was an attempt "to return to ten-year-old concepts and to apply them under the new conditions on the pretext that a 'limited strategic war' under modern conditions is 'more advantageous' and is supposedly aimed at preventing a nuclear disaster and limiting its scale in every possible way."[18] More specifically, it was claimed that the introduction of LNO would stimulate the arms race in the qualitative sphere, as opposed to merely building large numbers of weapons, and would eventually lead to the U.S. development of a first counterforce strike capability:

> Despite these explanations, it is obvious that the desire to create nuclear forces capable of inflicting effective blows on "military targets" can serve only to encourage the arms race and not to limit arms. And it is understandable why: The introduction of military sites among the primary targets of nuclear weapons justifies the demand to increase the number of warheads, all the more so since anything one pleases can be classed as such targets. [It is interesting that these analysts implied that targeting military installations was somehow a new idea, since Soviet military literature assumed that the U.S. would target military installations.] What is more, the destruction of small military sites will inevitably require the creation of highly accurate nuclear attack facilities, that is, their continuous qualitative improvement. And this is nothing other than the arms race in its most complex and perhaps, most dangerous-QUALITATIVE sphere.[19] [Upper case in original]

Indeed, Arbatov went even further in arguing this point. He contended that any withheld Soviet missiles, "according to Schlesinger's ideas, are in fact the main target of a 'limited' [essentially, disarming] strike by the foe's nuclear forces."[20] In other words, LNO was not only equivalent to counterforce, but to the long-held Soviet concept of the preemptive strike as well,[21] and any qualitative arms improvements made by the United States "are directly linked with the new theory of J. Schlesinger, the Pentagon chief, concerning the 'possibility of making the first nuclear strike, and of a limited nuclear war with the exchange of highly accurate strikes.'"[22]

Well-known military analysts such as Simonyan also drew comparisons between LNO and counterforce. According to Simonyan, the original purpose of the counterforce strategy "was aimed at creating the kind of strategic nuclear forces and at maintaining them at the kind of degree of combat readiness which would enable the United States to deliver a preemptive nuclear strike and achieve victory on this basis. That was its essence."[23] A more clear-cut example of Soviet mirror-imaging would be difficult to find. He then asserted that the LNO strategy "differs little from the essence of the counterforce strategy."[24] This once again illustrates the difficulty Soviet military analysts had in understanding the signaling aspects of LNO, since LNO did not envision a disarming strike with the goal of victory but was instead a means of strengthening U.S. deterrence. Simonyan's argument was not an isolated one, but it was reiterated even in such publications as *Soviet Military Review*:

> In proclaiming the "targeting" concept the Pentagon leaders stated that it does not envisage the creation of forces of the so-called "first capability strike" [sic] but provides only for a more flexible use of the already available strategic offensive forces. It is not hard to see, however, that this statement is an attempt to camouflage the increase in nuclear potential for delivering a massive forestalling nuclear attack.[25]

2. The Soviets believed that the United States might disregard the Soviet threat of uncontrolled escalation and in the event of a crisis employ the use of force on any scale it chose, including selected strategic strikes, without being deterred by the fear of escalation.

This was the aspect of LNO that most profoundly disturbed Soviet analysts, since it added an element of unpredictability to U.S. behavior. This was something that the Soviets obviously felt was the last thing they needed from the United States, since they had enough difficulty making sense out of the public declarations on U.S. doctrine without adding still more uncertainty to it.[26] According to Mil'shtein and Semeyko in the November 1974 issue of *SShA: Ekonomika, Politika, Ideologia*, LNO was part of a continuing effort by U.S. strategists "to seek ways and opportunities to use nuclear weapons, striving here to implant the illusion that it is possible to find a means of doing so without risking the nuclear devastation of the United States itself."[27] This plainly concerned Soviet analysts, because LNO suggested that the United States might not be paralyzed by the fear of escalation and might accept the concept of first use of nuclear weapons, disregarding Soviet warnings of possible escalation. This concern was expressed by Simonyan in the September 28, 1976, issue of *Krasnaya Zvezda*. He argued that by proclaiming a strategic doctrine that emphasized flexibility of options, including a limited counterforce strike, "the strategists across the ocean are hoping not only to convince the potential enemy of the acceptability of a 'limited' nuclear war but also to make him wage it on terms advantageous to the United States."[28]

Although Simonyan implied that the new strategy was a move toward a warfighting posture, he apparently had his doubts about U.S. ability to carry out the strategy in a realistic way. As stated earlier, Soviet observers of U.S. doctrine were aware that the United States had not made any moves toward improving its own war survival capability, not even making anything but the most perfunctory efforts at a civil defense program. In view of the U.S. lack of such protection for its own population and industry in comparison with the Soviet Union's, LNO seemed very awkward to Soviet analysts as a warfighting strategy.[29] Even so, the Soviet perception was still that LNO was a dangerous shift in U.S. doctrine from previous periods.

The reasons for this Soviet concern over LNO were less than unselfish. They had oriented their doctrine to take advantage of the retaliatory nature of U.S. doctrine, which had come to accept the premise for quite some time that nuclear war was both unthinkable and unwinnable.[30] LNO, however, was unsettling for the Soviets because it represented a rejection of many prior assumptions of U.S. doctrine. It postulated not only that the United States might indeed make a first strike on Soviet territory with limited numbers of weapons, but that the United States did not expect that such strikes would inevitably escalate to all-out nuclear war. In effect, the United States was telling the Soviets that it believed them to be as restrained by the fear of escalation as the United States was, and probably more so. Not only did this confront Soviet planners with an unanticipated set of U.S. responses to deal with, but it disrupted the entire picture the Soviets had constructed of expectations of U.S. behavior in a crisis. From the Soviet side of things the United States should have been behaving in a more restrained manner because of the attainment of strategic parity by the Soviet Union with the United States. But instead, the United States was saying that it might ignore such restraints. This concern was reflected in the April 1976 issue of *SShA: Ekonomika, Politika, Ideologia*:

> Discussions of new concepts are taking various directions. However, the main topic of debate in the United States on the revision of military strategic concepts is the new military-strategic concept known as the "Schlesinger doctrine." This concept and the "strategic retargeting" it envisages adds yet another kind of war -"limited strategic nuclear war"- to the spectrum of nuclear wars accepted by the "realistic restraint" doctrine. *"Limited strategic nuclear war" implies a limited exchange of strategic nuclear strikes against a small number of military targets.* The substantiation for this type of war is that both sides would have no interest in expanding the nuclear conflict and would prefer variations offering the possibility of localizing it since their strategic nuclear forces would retain a constant capacity for so-called "assured destruction" -a capacity which has been and remains the basis of the development of strategic nuclear forces in the United States. *In other words, the "retargeting" doctrine provides for an increase in the flexibility and feasibility of the use of strategic nuclear weapons in war.*[31] [Emphasis added.]

Of course, there was supposedly "a principal, determining factor exerting a decisive influence" on the evolution of U.S. doctrine in this particular direction. It was "the further shift in the correlation of forces in the world, including the military-strategic sphere." It was this growth in Soviet strategic power that was "compelling American strategists and politicians to engage in repeated analysis and forecasting taking into account the correlation of forces on both a global and a regional scale and to assess through this prism the effectiveness of previous military-strategic concepts and to formulate new ones."[32]

Although the unwary reader might be tempted to dismiss these Soviet allegations of a U.S. move towards a preemptive strategy as propagandistic, it is clear that the Soviets were reading the logic of their own nuclear warfighting doctrine as the only truly rational, objective, and scientific doctrine onto the LNO strategy. And assuming that the Soviets saw their U.S. counterparts as equally rational, it naturally follows that they would expect the United States to have been considering a preemptive strategy like their own.

Just how seriously Soviet analysts viewed the implications of the LNO strategy was revealed in an article in the April 1976 issue of *SShA: Ekonomika, Politika, Ideologia.* A group of Soviet analysts, among them Georgi Arbatov, the director of the institute that published that periodical, discussed the ramifications of the LNO strategy. Arbatov, in particular, voiced concern over LNO to the extent of proposing that the arms-limitation agreements also include a provision that would prohibit either side from altering its strategic doctrine. Absurd as the proposal was, it nevertheless reflected the degree to which Soviet analysts in general were perturbed by the "unpredictability" of the course of U.S. strategic doctrine. The following passage was a major exception to the general Soviet practice of compartmentalizing their discussions of SALT and U.S. strategic doctrine as separate considerations:

> It is also essential to stress that in works by our research workers the military detente which must reinfoce political detente is often solely identified with the limitation and reduction of arms and armed forces. A broader view obviously must be taken of this problem. *As we see it, the concepts of "military detente" must be extended to military doctrines and military-strategic concepts, which constitute a very important component of the entire mechanism of military policy and one of the factors influencing the arms race-both the quantitative and the qualitative arms race.* Of course, the struggle against imperialist military strategic doctrines and concepts is a complex matter, but there is broad scope here for exposing the dangerous military-strategic theories being formulated by reactionary U.S. circles -theories calculated to wreck the relaxation of international tension and the positive development of Soviet-U.S. relations.[33] [Emphasis added.]

Conclusions

Although the anxiety evidenced in the Soviet reaction to the LNO strategy provided some promising clues to the kind of U.S. doctrine that would best strengthen our national security, it would have been exceedingly trite to say that all the United States need have done was declare that the LNO strategy was part of U.S. strategic doctrine and its problems were essentially solved.[34] The Soviets, as evidenced in this and preceding chapters, also looked for signs that the United States was trying to match its actual capabilities to its declared doctrine. Since the LNO strategy incorporated certain aspects of the Soviet nuclear warfighting doctrine, the Soviets naturally looked for the United States to begin bolstering its strategic defenses in order to attain a credible war survival capability. When it was obvious that the United States had no intention of doing such a thing, LNO lost credibility in the eyes of Soviet observers. During the period in which the LNO strategy was under consideration (1974-1976) and until August 1980, U.S. strategic doctrine was a combination of the mutual assured destruction concept and a watered-down version of the Nixon Doctrine. To put it another way, the United States had the worst of both worlds during the period from 1974 to 1980; it had many security commitments and interests around the world that were vulnerable to Soviet expansionary efforts, but at the same time lacked both the national will to use its military power in defense of these interests and the actual military capability to do so. The Soviets, seeing their opportunity but not wishing to alarm the United States to the point where it might take decisive action, accelerated their use of proxy forces in support of ostensible national-liberation movements in various Third World countries in the Middle East and Africa. In some cases Soviet military advisers alone were present; in others it was a combination of proxy forces supported by Soviet logistics and advisers (see Appendix B). In all cases the Soviets managed to keep a profile low enough that their presence was not viewed as sufficiently threatening to elicit vigorous countermeasures from the West. At the same time, the Soviets kept up the pretense of detente by engaging in SALT talks, Mutual Balanced Force Reductions (MBFR) talks, and the Helsinki accords, and in general paying lip service in their pronouncements to the West on peace, security, respect for human rights, and anything else the Soviets felt the United States wanted to hear. The Soviets obviously felt sufficiently free in their ability to use military power that they decided to use their own troops in an actual intervention in Afghanistan in December 1979 to support a collapsing pro-Soviet regime. Compared to previous periods, this was a definite escalation in the Soviet use of military power in support of foreign policy, and was definitive proof that the Soviet leadership was acting upon its perception of a United States that had been restrained by the growth of Soviet strategic power, thus allowing the Soviet leadership to gradually expand the use of its own military power.

    In July 1980, nearly seven months after the Soviet intervention in Afghanistan, the Carter Administration announced another shift in U.S. nuclear strategy in the form of Presidential Directive 59. This "new" strategy supposedly emphasized the nuclear warfighting aspects of the U.S. strategic doctrine and posture by targeting such things as Soviet missile silos, command posts, and a Soviet warmaking capacity in general. Supposedly this was a step in the right direction; but were the Soviets genuinely convinced?

Notes

1. S. Ivanov, "Soviet Military Doctrine and Strategy," *Voennaia Mysl'* 5 (May 1969), trans. in FBIS, FPD No. 0116/69, 18 December 1969, 49.
2. M. Mil'shtein and L. Semeyko, "The Problem of the Inadmissibility of a Nuclear Conflict (On New Approaches in the United States)," *SShA: Ekonomika, Politika, Ideologia* 11 (November 1974), trans. in JPRS No. 63625, December 10, 1974, 9.
3. G. Arbatov, "Strength-Policy Impasses," *Soviet Military Review* 1 (January 1975): 48.
4. A. Karenin, "Detente and New Variants of Old Doctrines," *Mezhdunarodnaia Zhizn* 5 (May 1975), trans. in FBIS, *USSR Daily Report*, lO June 1975, AA7
5. Ibid., AA8.
6. A. Arbatov and G. Arbatov, "Schlesinger's Ideas in Form and Content," *Novoe Vremya*, No. 30, 25 July 1975, trans. FBIS, *USSR Daily Report,* 14 August 1975, B3.
7. Ibid., B4. See also R. Simonyan, "The Concept of 'Selective Targeting,'" *Krasnaya Zvezda*, 28 September 1976, 3, trans. in FBIS, *USSR Daily Report*, 1 October 1976, B4.
8. Radio Moscow in English to North America, 4 July, 1975, trans. in FBIS, *USSR Daily Report*, 7 July 1975, Bl.
9. R. Simonyan, "'Realistic Deterrence': The Real Implications," *New Times* 10 (March 1977): 19.
10. Bonds, *The US War Machine*, 65-66. See also J. L. Snyder, *The Soviet Strategic Culture: Implications for Limited Nuclear Operations* (Santa Monica, Calif.: RAND, R-2154-AF, September 1977), 1-3.
11. Endicott and Stafford, *American Defense Policy*, 82.
12. The reader is referred to FBIS, *Eastern Europe Daily Report*, January-November 1974.
13. Mil'shtein and Semeyko, "Nuclear Conflict," 6-7.
14. M. Ponomarev and V. Vinogradov, "The Atlanticists' Nuclear Ambitions," *Krasnaya Zvezda*, 8 July 1975, 3, trans. in FBIS, *USSR Daily Report*, 14 July 1975, B2.
15. See John J. Dziak, *Soviet Perceptions of Military Power: The Interaction of Theory and Practice* (New York: National Strategy Information Center, 1981), 20-28, for a detailed discussion of this point.
16. Snyder, *Soviet Strategic Culture*, 6. In his analysis of the Soviet perception of LNO, Snyder does not discriminate among the various Soviet statements on LNO, but tends to take them at their face value.
17. "J. Schlesinger's Strange Position," *Pravda*, 12 July 1975, 4, trans. in FBIS, *USSR Daily Report*, 15 July 1975, B4.
18. Mil'shtein and Semeyko, "Nuclear Conflict," 8.
19. Ibid.
20. Arbatov and Arbatov, "Schlesinger's Ideas," B3.

21. An excellent article showing the consistency of the Soviet "preemptive strike" concept through the 1970s is found in J.M. Caravelli, "The Role of Surprise and Preemption in Soviet Military Strategy," *International Security Review* 6, 2 (Summer 1981): 209-36.
22. Y. Gavrilov and V. Berezin, "The Pentagon: More Billions, More Programs," *Krasnaya Zvezda*, 14 September 1975, 3, trans. in FBIS, *USSR Daily Report*, 2 October 1975, B5.
23. Simonyan, "Selective Targeting," B5.
24. Ibid.
25. P. Sergeyev and V. Trusenkov, "Evolution of the US Military Doctrine," *Soviet Military Review* 11 (November 1976): 53.
26. For an in-depth analysis of this particular problem of Soviet analysis of U.S. doctrine, see L. Goure, "The U.S. 'Countervailing Strategy' in Soviet Perception," *Strategic Review* (Fall 1981): 51-64.
27. Mil'shtein and Semeyko, "Nuclear Conflict," 8.
28. Simonyan, "Selective Targeting," p. B3.
29. See Goure, "U.S. 'Countervailing Strategy,'" 56-57.
30. Bonds, *US War Machine*, 62-63. See also J. Collins, *Military Trends*, 76-78.
31. Editorial, "Certain New Trends in the Development of U.S. Military-Strategic Concepts," *SShA: Ekonomika, Politika, Ideologia* 4 (April 1976), trans. in FBIS, *USSR Daily Report Annex*, 30 April 1976, 3. See also Mil'shtein and Semeyko, "Nuclear Conflict," 5.
32. Editorial, "New Trends," 3.
33. Ibid., p. 8.
34. Dziak seems to imply this in his closing remarks in *Soviet Perceptions of Military Power*, 68. Merely declaring a more "symmetrical" strategic doctrine vis-à-vis the Soviets would not have been enough; it would have to have been supported by military programs which the Soviets themselves would have found credible, otherwise the Soviets would quickly have seen through any such superficial declaration as a mere sham.

9
Toward Nuclear Warfighting? The Soviet View of PD 59

Is It Nuclear Warfighting or Not?

The initial Soviet response to PD 59 was along the lines of their reaction to previous U.S. strategic doctrine. The United States was once again trying to break out of the strategic impasse forced upon it by the growth of Soviet strategic power by devising a "new" strategy that the United States supposedly believed would bring it victory in the event of a nuclear confrontation with the Soviet Union. Soviet analysts allegedly saw indications that were more definitive than ever before that the United States was actively striving for a preemptive strike capability. It seemed initially that PD 59, known later as the countervailing strategy, might actually have given Soviet planners cause to fear a true change in U.S. strategic doctrine.

But there were signs during this most recent period, even in open Soviet publications, that the Soviets were not convinced of the genuine credibility of PD 59 as a serious U.S. move towards a nuclear warfighting doctrine. For one thing, Soviet observers were well aware by this time of the long lead times involved in the U.S. procurement of new weapons systems to support its doctrine. They also knew that the United States was moving even more slowly than usual to obtain the necessary weapons systems to carry out the highly accurate and selective strikes on Soviet missile silos, command posts, and other Soviet nuclear warfighting means called for by PD 59. Second, the U.S. concept of "victory denial" seemed illogical to the Soviets, and a contradiction to the principles of strategy in general and their own nuclear warfighting doctrine in particular. In fact, this latest U.S. proclamation was simply another in a long line of strategic concepts founded on the belief that nuclear war was unwinnable and therefore unthinkable except as a means of "punishing" the Soviets for having started the war. Third, and perhaps most important of all, the Soviets recognized that the U.S. version of nuclear warfighting, even though it envisaged a range of responses less than a massive attack, was lacking in the kind of war survival capability necessary to make the strategy truly credible from the Soviet perspective. Moreover, as Leon Goure had pointed out in a 1981 article in *Strategic Review,*[1] what is convincing to the Soviets is whether there is a concerted effort to match capability to doctrine, and not mere sham declarations of a change in strategy. In fact, the United States made no moves until the declaration of SDI in 1983 to initiate the development of space-based defense systems which would have gone a long way towards giving the United States a credible capacity for war survival and recovery.

Even during this period of U.S. doctrinal development, Soviet propagandists were still trying to obscure their true strategic perceptions with a great deal of rhetoric aimed at the alleged aggressiveness of the countervailing strategy. The purpose here, of course, was to draw attention away from the Soviets' own buildup and use of military power.

The Soviet Propaganda Line

1. *The essence of the countervailing strategy involves the use of a preemptive strike as part of a preventive war against the Soviet Union.*

This line was actually nothing new in the Soviet repertoire at all, as a glance back at Chapter 3 shows. During the latter part of the massive retaliation period, when the United States was considering (albeit briefly) the merits of a preemptive strike strategy against the Soviet Union, this was an extensive theme of the Soviet declaratory deterrence strategy. Although the Soviets were well aware of the fact that a preemptive strike was based purely on military considerations and could be part of a defensive doctrine (which the Soviets themselves claimed for their doctrine), they deliberately sought to distort the political intent behind U.S. doctrine and strategy by asserting that the so-called preemptive strike was really the opening phase of a preventive war against the Soviet Union. Although it is true that a preventive war, based on the political consideration of eliminating a potential long-term enemy by going to war while one still has military superiority, requires the use of a preemptive strike, it is not true that the mere advocacy of a preemptive strike strategy is an intent to undertake a preventive war. Nevertheless, this did not prevent Lieutenant General N. Chervov, in an interview with the Czech newspaper *Rude Pravo* on August 25, 1980, from claiming that "the practical plans for preventive nuclear warfare with the delivery of a preventive strike against the Soviet Union's military facilities have formed the basis of the United States' strategic course for a long time."[2]

An *Izvestiya* commentator argued much along the same lines only a couple of days earlier in the August 23 issue of that newspaper, contending that the aim of U.S. strategy was to create the necessary conditions for the undertaking of a preventive war against them:

> Contrary to what was said in Vienna and in complete contradiction with previous Soviet-American accords, the Washington administration has in effect announced as its main method of conducting international affairs the method of exerting pressure on the USSR in all its forms, including the possible use of nuclear weapons. At the same time attempts are being made to create a political and psychological climate favorable to the adoption by the U.S. leadership, when it is considered expedient, of a decision, in the guise of "defense," to deliver a "preemptive" nuclear strike against the Soviet Union.[3]

The commentator went on to say that world peace would be endangered if the United States were to adopt a preemptive strategy.[4] But since a preemptive strike, in the context of the U.S. countervailing strategy, would be made only if the United States saw that the Soviets were about to launch an attack of their own, there was in fact no increased danger of nuclear war at all. No danger, that is, if in fact the Soviets indeed had defensive and peaceful intentions, in which case they would not have had anything to worry about, since they would never fulfill U.S. conditions for the delivery of a preemptive strike. If, on the other hand, the Soviets harbored truly aggressive and warlike intentions, then a preemptive strike strategy would be the best possible deterrent against Soviet aggression, since the Soviets could not plan on beginning any sort of major war without having to worry about the possibility of U.S. disruption of their plans with a "spoiling" nuclear strike. In either case, the U.S. announcement of the possibility of launching preemptive strikes did not increase the likelihood of war, contrary to Soviet propaganda, since the Soviets alone controlled the trigger cause for the United States making such a strike.

2. *The U.S. countervailing strategy represents another attempt by the United States to stimulate the arms race and attain strategic superiority over the Soviet Union.*

U.S. responsibility for the arms race has long been a standard Soviet theme. The main difference at this time was that the Soviets were emphasizing the fact that the United States had lost superiority and that attempts to regain it were futile. A standard example of this theme was an article in the January 1981 issue of *International Affairs* by Major General Slobodenko:

> The material base for the elaboration of this strategy is provided by the development and sophistication of diverse new arms systems in the United States, with which its government circles hope to achieve military superiority over the Soviet Union. This once again outlines the extreme danger stemming from the arms race, which is continuously being whipped up by aggressive imperialist forces, since the stockpiling and sophistication of weapons do not increase security but, on the contrary, as the "new nuclear strategy" demonstrates, increase the threat for all the peoples throughout the world.[5]

The way in which Soviet commentators managed to conceal the true course of events in the so-called strategic arms race borders on the ingenious. For example, Arbatov noted how "previously, the U.S. relied on its 'nuclear superiority' . . . in its approach" to the political utility of nuclear weapons.[6] Yet he says later on in the article that "the hopes of U.S. ruling circles for achieving an advantage in the strategic arms sphere as they move toward the 'countervailing' strategy are even less well founded, given the present correlation of forces, than the previous American plans of building 'nuclear superiority.'"[7] This statement was corroborated in an article in *Izvestiya* in August 1980, in which the author boldly stated that "the Soviet Union has never permitted anyone to talk to it from a 'position of strength' in the past, nor will it permit this in future. *It is evident that attempts to achieve military superiority over the USSR are even more unfounded now than formerly.*"[8] [emphasis added.] In the case of these particular passages, it was not what was said, but rather implied, that demonstrated the falsity of this Soviet declaratory deterrence theme. In the first statement by Arbatov, it was conceded that the United States had possessed strategic superiority over the Soviet Union. But the latter two statements implied not only that the United States had lost this superiority, but that any attempts to regain it, despite increases in the defense budget, were becoming increasingly unrealistic. This was a tacit recognition of the greater momentum of the Soviet military buildup by Soviet commentators themselves. Yet they couched this recognition in language designed to give the impression that the United States was solely responsible for the arms race.

3. *It is impossible to speak of waging a limited nuclear war, since any use of nuclear weapons, no matter on how limited a scale it might be begun, carries the danger of a massive retaliatory blow by the other side.*

The continuity of the Soviet declaratory deterrence strategy is clearly demonstrated in this theme, since it was used previously against the LNO strategy as proposed by Schlesinger, as well as against the "limited war" concept first espoused back in the mid-1950s. It is the standard Soviet threat of uncontrolled escalation to strategic nuclear war, which Soviet commentators repeatedly used in their efforts to persuade U.S. observers and analysts that the U.S. nuclear arsenal could not be used even in a limited fashion to pursue political goals (such as the enhancement of deterrence against expansionary uses of Soviet military power), without an unacceptable risk of escalation. Slobodenko argued this line in typical fashion in *International Affairs*:

> Arguments that a nuclear war under the present-day conditions can be controlled and waged according to rules imposed on the enemy are utterly false. It is much easier to decide on the non-use of nuclear weapons than to confine their use within certain limits. The use of nuclear weapons even on a small scale can cause a chain reaction and turn what would seem to be a limited nuclear conflict into a nuclear conflagration.[9]

This was a highly presumptuous statement by Slobodenko, since he knew full well that the use of any kind of military power was governed by the political objectives being sought. The nature of these political objectives imposes natural limits on the level of military force employed, whether it be conventional or nuclear. The only objective that would call for the use of all-out nuclear war would be a decisive struggle in which the winner imposed a "Carthaginian peace" on the loser, i.e., effectively destroyed the opponent as a political entity. And if this were the case, then there would be no process of "escalation" to such levels, since one nation (presumably the aggressor) would be trying to gain the advantage of surprise.

Even though Soviet analysts had long since recognized the fact that the United States had retreated in the level of military force it was willing to actively commit according to the tenets of realistic deterrence (see Chapter 8), Soviet commentators nevertheless continued in their efforts to portray the United States in as aggressive a light as possible while inhibiting U.S. willingness to use its strategic arsenal for deterrence purposes. In doing so, they made use of American statements that supported their own declaratory deterrence themes. A prime example of this was in an article by L. Semeyko in a September 1980 issue of *New Times*:

> The inevitability of escalation is not denied even by [Defense Secretary] H. Brown, who has admitted that implementation of the new strategy could lead to an all-out nuclear war. In his message to the NATO countries' defense ministers about the directive he signed, he once again stated with regard to nuclear war: " . . . We have no illusions about the difficulties of limiting its escalation and consequences." That would seem to be a realistic assessment. So why then is there a need for the suicidal concept? Why try to reconcile "limited" and "prolonged" nuclear strikes? After all, even Clausewitz said: Any attempt to limit the use of force in war is ridiculous. But since the collapse of the strategy of "massive retaliation" the United States has been persistently seeking the possibility of the "rational" use of nuclear weapons.[10]

The actual Soviet view of the countervailing strategy as enunciated in PD 59, however, showed that the Soviets were well aware of the intent behind the latest U.S. strategic doctrine, as well as of its shortcomings.

The Real Soviet View

1. *The countervailing strategy represents a new U.S. attempt to adopt a nuclear warfighting doctrine, thus abandoning its pure retaliatory stance.*

This theme was entirely consistent with past Soviet perceptions of previous U.S. doctrinal concepts, beginning with massive retaliation in the 1950s. From the Soviet vantage point, a nuclear warfighting doctrine was the only truly rational doctrine for a state to adopt; they therefore expected the United States also to accept the logic of this proposition and move towards a nuclear warfighting strategy itself. Any public U.S. declarations of deterrence strategies that lacked the elements of a warfighting strategy with the objective of victory, or at least a "favorable war outcome," could not really be trusted, according to Soviet thinking.[11]

In their statements along this line, Soviet analysts concentrated on the renewed emphasis on counterforce and the notion of limited nuclear war in asserting that the United States was again in pursuit of a strategy that would restore the political utility of its strategic arsenal. Slobodenko made this point well in his article in *International Affairs*:

> The new nuclear strategy proceeds from the possibility of waging a "limited" nuclear war and provides for the first nuclear strike at a limited number of the most important military objectives and control centres of the Soviet Union, leaving the forces of "assured destruction" in the reserve, which would prevent the conflict from growing into an all-out war. In point of fact, this is nothing else but a modified version of the previous "target selection" and "counterforce capability" concepts. American political observer J. Anderson noted in *The Washington Post* in an article entitled "Not-So-New Nuclear Strategy": "In fact, Carter's directive is only the latest refinement of a policy that has been on the books for six years." Yet there is something new to it. Thus, it is planned to wage a "protracted but limited nuclear war." This means that there are provisions for a few selective strikes instead of one, which should follow in sequence. The possibility for using nuclear weapons in local wars is also an important innovation.[12]

Actually, Slobodenko was in error in his belief that there was anything new or innovative even in the notion of a "protracted but limited nuclear war"; the idea can be traced to one of the rungs described by Herman Kahn in his book *On Escalation: Metaphors and Scenarios*, in which he describes a limited counterforce war.[13] The logic of the American strategy, tenuous though it was from the Soviet standpoint, was explained concisely by commentator V. Lemeyko during a Moscow radio broadcast of "International Observer's Roundtable":

> And the substance of the new nuclear strategy is that Washington now intends to deal a nuclear blow primarily not at cities but at military targets. In the opinion of the American strategists, this makes it possible, without beginning a universal atomic war, supposedly to inflict a limited preventive [!] strike at particular installations and regions. And here Washington hypocritically asserts that such a strategy must promote the maintenance of peace, since the other side, fearing partial retaliation, will behave more circumspectly and tractably.[14]

L. Semeyko, in a September 1980 issue of *New Times*, not only pointed out the emphasis on counterforce and limited nuclear war, but also emphasized that the new strategy was "a gamble not on preventing nuclear war, as is proclaimed, but on unleashing and actively waging it."[15] But the Soviets were well aware of the slowness with which the United States was moving to implement the tenets of the countervailing strategy. The explanation for this U.S. difficulty was, predictably enough, the continued growth of the Soviet Union's strategic nuclear might, which was restraining the United States from such "adventuristic" plans:

> Wilat occasioned this turnabout in Washington's nuclear strategy? If you consider Directive 59 as a whole, it is a U.S. attempt to get out of the "nuclear impasse" which developed back in the sixties thanks to the creation of the socialist community's mighty defense potential. All this time the strengthening of the USSR's nuclear missile might has curbed U.S. aggressive aspirations. This might is curbing them all the more now that strategic equilibrium exists between the USSR and the United States. Washington is now hoping to secure strategic superiority primarily through the qualitative development of its nuclear forces. At the same time it is not forgetting the quantitative aspect of the matter either.
>
> Hence the new nuclear strategy, which is essentially based on the strategy of "superior countermeasures" announced by the Pentagon 18 months ago.[16]

The most disturbing part about the above passage was Semeyko's reference to the Soviet nuclear missile forces being the main reason for the restraint of U.S. "aggressive aspirations," and not any U.S. desire for peaceful relations or for arms control or disarmament. Given such a perception, there still existed no incentive for the Soviets to engage in anything resembling serious arms-control negotiations other than its potential as a propaganda exercise or for impeding U.S. strategic buildup.

2. *The United States is far more vulnerable to nuclear destruction at any level of nuclear war than the Soviet Union, no matter how limited U.S. strategy might try to make it.*

This theme of Soviet perception was one the Soviets had undoubtedly held in private for a long time, since the lack of U.S. defense against a nuclear attack of any kind had been quite apparent since the mid-1960s. The reason that the Soviets did not make mention of it before this time was that the United States still possessed nuclear superiority until 1969, and then parity until the late 1970s, when the Soviet Union nearly attained a level of marginal strategic superiority. Now that the United States was recognizing its own vulnerability on defense and potential inferiority in strategic offensive forces, Soviet commentators were making the most of their opportunity to remind the United States of this disparity. In doing so, they made frequent use of U.S. calculations concerning the likely number of people in the United States that would be killed as a result of a nuclear war:

> These documents [Presidential Directives 53 and 58] show that the President and his advisers by no means expect that after an American preventive nuclear

attack the Soviet Union will sit idle-handed. They understand that the answer will be appropriate, that the retribution will be inevitable and that the adventurist actions of official Washington will be detrimental to the population of the United States . . . .Other calculations were cited in one of the documents prepared by a number of American governmental departments in 1978. 140 million will die in case of a nuclear conflict- this is more than half of the population of the United States.

Naturally, the question arises: have the architects of the American policy taken into account these calculations while drawing up directive 59? There is every indication that Carter, Brzezinski and Co. are little worried about this. The main thing for them is to survive. And for the purpose it is planned beforehand to "harden shelters for the key persons," to establish a kind of bunker for them.[17]

By pointedly mentioning the disparity in the relative abilities of the United States and the Soviet Union to survive and recover from a nuclear exchange, the Soviets were trying to get the most propaganda value out of it as possible, in the process hoping to restrain the United States from taking any effective action in the event of confrontation with the Soviet Union. In the following passage from an article by doctor of historical sciences V. Zhurkin in the September 1980 issue of *Literaturnaya Gazeta*, the author combines this perception of U.S. vulnerability with elements of declaratory deterrence in an effort to prove that the United States could not safely make use of even so-called limited nuclear strikes, which were less than all-out war:

By threatening to use (still more by using) nuclear warheads against "selected" enemy military targets, Washington would above all jeopardize its own country. After all, confronted by such a truly apocalyptic decision, the other side would make one assumption: that Washington was prepared and was about to follow the path of nuclear escalation to the end. In those conditions the only possible decision for the other side is to respond not according to the "rules" proposed by Washington, but by its own choice. The authors of Presidential Directive 18 conscientiously calculated what a modern nuclear war would mean to the United States: The loss of about 140 million Americans, that is, nearly three-fifths of the population, and about 75 percent of the country's economic potential. When he was just a professor, Henry Kissinger called such an outcome, in brief, "the end of history."[18]

By making such statements regarding the likely level of U.S. fatalities, the Soviets were making one point unmistakably clear: the United States is too vulnerable to nuclear attack or retaliation by the Soviet Union to rationally threaten the Soviets with even a highly selective nuclear attack. Therefore, the so-called nuclear warfighting strategy enunciated in PD 59 cannot be considered credible.

3. *The Soviets continued to mirror image their own concepts of nuclear warfighting with the objective of victory onto U.S. strategy, asserting that the*

actions of the United States made the concept of victory denial too irrational to be truly indicative of U.S. intent.

While mirror-imaging had been a constant of the Soviet perception of U.S. strategy from 1954 on, it played an especially important role in their determination of how believable U.S. doctrine really was. It is important here, however, to make the distinction between Soviet projection of their own intentions onto U.S. doctrine and projection of their own actions in carrying out such a doctrine. Soviet analysts clearly saw a disparity between U.S. words and apparent intentions as opposed to U.S. efforts to match military capability to declared doctrine. Soviet analysts such as Semeyko traced the current alleged U.S. emphasis on victory in a nuclear war back to the signing of Memorandum 242 by then President Nixon on January 17, 1974, which was the initial statement of the Schlesinger doctrine. Schlesinger tried to move U.S. strategic doctrine away from the purely retaliatory doctrine of mutual assured destruction by linking U.S. actions in a nuclear confrontation to postwar political objectives. This was the notion of early war termination, which was later to evolve into the idea of victory denial. In the following passage from his article, Semeyko clearly shows the projection of Soviet doctrinal intentions onto those of the United States:

> In approving plans for waging "limited" nuclear war as it was understood at that time, the memorandum set the objective of "achieving the speediest end to the war on terms acceptable to the United States and its allies." (Let us observe that this formula later migrated into the statements of Defense Secretary H. Brown). But what is meant by "acceptable terms" for ending military actions? There is scarcely any need to guess. This expression has always meant the achievement of particular political war aims, in other words definite success in the war. With regard to a generalized nuclear war, Memorandum 242 contains an even clearer form of words: " . . . to secure for the United States and its allies the most advantageous possible outcome from a war."
>
> Hence it was hardly just, even in the mid-seventies, to accuse American military doctrine of excessive "modesty" or exaggerated emphasis on "deterrence." If the U.S. military and political leadership had been completely denying the idea of possible victory in a nuclear war, the various concepts for fighting it would not, it would seem, have been elaborated in such detail in the seventies. And this is not to mention Presidential Directive 59, adopted in the summer of 1980, with its much more clearly expressed gamble on winning a nuclear clash.[19]

Semeyko had made this assertion even more emphatically in the September 1980 issue of *New Times*, in which he maintained that the change in the types of targets to be attacked in the event of war from population centers to primarily military targets was definitive proof that the United States desired to attain victory in a nuclear war:

Political and military control centers have now been included in the list of vulnerable targets. That is not merely an arithmetical increase in the number of targets (an increase of about 50 percent, according to some American data), but a clear intention of winning a nuclear war, a possibility ostensibly denied by America's leaders themselves in view of the catastrophic consequences of such a war. It is hard to reach any other conclusion since the destruction of the whole complex of strategically important targets is, according to the Pentagon's calculations, capable of paralyzing the enemy and forcing him to capitulate, and not merely of producing an "impression" on him by means of individual selective strikes.[20]

The question that undoubtedly arose in the minds of Soviet analysts, though, was, how credible could the U.S. countervailing strategy actually be, since the weapons systems needed for its implementation would take years to deploy? The answer was given quite clearly by G. Trofimenko, a follower of U.S. strategic doctrinal developments since the late 1960s, in the December 1980 issue of *SShA: Ekonomika, Politika, Ideologia*:

No matter how hard the American civilian and military leaders try to frighten the Soviet Union with their "well orchestrated" strategy of counterforce superiority, the U.S. does not possess this kind of superiority because the majority of the systems on which Directive 59 relies will begin to be deployed only in the second half of the 1980s . . . .Naturally [the USSR] will not change its strategy simply because someone in Washington has tried to perpetrate another bluff by publicizing yet another directive-particularly in view of the fact that U.S. political and military leaders already liave published an excessive amount of various types of "strategic" doctrines, memoranda and directives.[21]

One could not find a more straightforward statement of the Soviet evaluation of the U.S. countervailing strategy. Barely three months after its enunciation, the Soviets were calling the U.S. bluff by declaring, in effect, that the latest development in U.S. strategic doctrine was little more than another ill-disguised sham. And true to Trofimenko's words, the use of Soviet military power to support national-liberation movements, along with the acquisition of increased sealift, airlift, and logistics capabilities to support such military power projection, continued to increase until the mid- 1980s.[22]

Conclusions

Although U.S. doctrine paid a great deal of lip service to the idea of waging a nuclear war with the objective of some sort of acceptable outcome, or victory denial, U.S. actions subsequent to the declaration of PD-59 showed that the United States did not really have its heart in the matter.[23] The Soviets were quick to pick up on this, noting that the United States was making no serious moves towards reducing the vulnerability of its own population to nuclear attack, and hence were undeterred by the new declaration. For declaratory deterrence purposes, however, they denounced any perceived U.S. intent to adopt a nuclear warfighting strategy as "adventuristic." Soviet employment of its military power continued the pattern of gradual but constant increase in scale, while Soviet military programs showed increasing efforts to augment even further the Soviet ability for rapid power projection to such areas as Africa and the Middle East.

It is eminently clear from our analysis of the Soviet reaction to the U.S. countervailing strategy that mere changes in declared U.S. strategic doctrine did little or nothing to enhance the credibility of U.S. deterrence against Soviet-sponsored aggression, particularly against the more subtle form of aggression, employing proxy forces of Soviet minor allies, while the Soviets themselves provided mainly logistical, sealift, and airlift support. The SALT talks, and the virtual U.S. abandonment of them, had no discernible effect on the pace of Soviet military programs, which may serve as an indication of how little seriousness the Soviets gave to such talks as ends in themselves. Indeed, given the Soviet perception that their increased strategic power not only had forced the United States to make more accommodating changes in its strategic doctrine but had compelled the United States to seek arms control negotiations in the first place, it is not surprising to find that SALT had so little effect producing the strategic stability it sought. As other authors have pointed out, the Soviets have no word for stability in the sense that the United States understands it, nor had it appeared anywhere in their literature until very recently.[24]

Notes

1. See Leon Goure, "The U.S. 'Countervailing Strategy' in Soviet Perception," *Strategic Review* (Fall 1981): 59.
2. N. Chervov, "The Threat of the 'Nuclear Directive': What the So-Called New Strategy of the White House Entails," Interview by APN Commentator Vasiliy Morozov, August 20, 1980, trans. in FBIS, *USSR Daily Report*, 25 August 1980, AA1.
3. Kobysh, "On the 'New U.S. Nuclear Strategy,'" *Izvestiya*, 23 August 1980, 5, trans. in FBIS, *USSR Daily Report*, August 28, 1980, AA2.
4. A. Slobodenko, "The Strategy of Nuclear Adventurism," *International Affairs* (January 1981): 26.
5. Ibid.
6. A.G. Arbatov, "Strategic Parity and the Policy of the Carter Administration," trans. in *Soviet Press Selected Translations*, No. 81*2 (February 1981): 53.
7. Ibid., 55.
8. Kobysh, "Nuclear Strategy," AA5.
9. Slobodenko, "Nuclear Adventurism," 30-31.
10. L. Semeyko, "Directive 59: Development or Leap?" *Novoye Vremya*, 38, September 19, 1980, 5-7, trans. in FBIS, *USSR Daily Report*, September 30, 1980, AA2. See

also N. Ponomarev, "In Militarist Intoxication," *Krasnaya Zvezda*, September 6, 1980, 3, trans. in FBIS, *USSR Daily Report*, September 10, 1980, A2.

11. See also Goure, "Countervailing Strategy," 55.

12. Slobodenko, "Nuclear Adventurism," 30.

13. The reader is advised to refer to Herman Kahn's entire discussion of the 44 rungs of the "escalation ladder," including the rung involving limited counterforce war, to gain a better appreciation of the kind of logic used by U.S. planners in formulating PD 59. See H. Kahn, *On Escalation: Metaphors and Scenarios* (New York: Praeger, 1965), 37-195.

14. V. Lemeyko, "International Observers Roundtable," Interview by V. Katin, August 24, 1980, trans. in FBIS, *USSR Daily Report*, August 25, 1980, CC6.

15. Semeyko, "Directives 59," AA3.

16. Ibid.

17. V. Goncharov, "Directives 53, 58, 59," *Tass*, August 12, 1980, trans. in FBIS, *USSR Daily Report*, August 13, 1980, AA2-AA3. See also Goure, "Countervailing Strategy," 60.

18. V. Zhurkin, "In Pursuit of the Impossible Goal: The 'New U.S. Nuclear Strategy,'" *Literaturnaya Gazeta*, September 17, 1980, 14, trans. in FBIS, *USSR Daily Report*, September 22, 1980, AA1. See also G. Trofimenko, "Who Threatens Whom? Discussions with Soviet Generals and Experts of the Military Sciences," interview by Ferenc Vamai, September 23, 1980, trans. in FBIS, *USSR Daily Report*, September 26, 1980, AA3.

19. L. Semeyko, "Strategic Illusions," *Novoye Vremya* 50, December 12, 1980, 12-15, trans. in FBIS, *USSR Daily Report*, December 31, 1980, AA4. See also Chervov, "Nuclear Directive," AA1.

20. Semeyko, "Directives 59," AA2.

21. G.A. Trofimenko, "Washington's Strategic Fluctuations," *SShA: Ekonomika, Politika, Ideologia* 12 (December 1980): 58; See also Goure, "Countervailing Strategy," 60.

22. For an excellent study of Soviet employment of military power, see A.P. Schmid and E. Berends, *Soviet Military Interventions Since 1945* (New Brunswick, N.J.: Transaction, 1985).

23. Goure, "Countervailing Strategy," 60-61.

24. J. Dziak, *Soviet Perceptions of Military Power*, ix. The appearance of the Russian word *stabilnost* in Soviet writings subsequent to this period did not necessarily that the Soviet leadership had a similar concept, particularly since the Soviets had defined strategic nuclear parity as a key restraining factor on the U.S., and therefore the crucial requirement for maintaining *stabilnost*.

Part V

FROM STRATEGIC DEFENSE INITIATIVE TO THE COLLAPSE OF COMMUNISM
(1983-1991)

10
Nightmare Becomes Reality: The Soviet View of SDI

When President Reagan offically launched the Strategic Defense Initiative (dubbed "Star Wars" by the press) in his speech of March 23, 1983, it did not take the Soviet political and military leadership long to realize that this was the realization of their worst fears. It was bad enough that Reagan had accelerated the defense buildup initiated by President Carter in 1979 in response to the Soviet invasion of Afghanistan. What Reagan apparently now proposed to do was to harness American technological superiority for the express purpose of rendering nuclear weapons "impotent and obsolete." Not incidentally, since the Soviets had perceived their attainment of strategic nuclear parity as the key factor compelling the U.S. to behave in ways more accommodating to the Soviet use of its military power for the achievement of Soviet objectives, the Soviet leadership feared an effective U.S. strategic defense eventually would reduce the Soviet Union to a second class power. As a result, during the rest of the 1980s, the West would witness the most strident Soviet *desinformatsiya* campaign against SDI since its highly effective propaganda campaign against deployment of the neutron bomb in Europe back in 1977. What would be even more remarkable than this, however, would be the consistency of key elements of the Soviet perception of SDI across the spectrum of military and political observers, even thru the period leading up to the final collapse of the Soviet Union.

The Soviet Propaganda Line

The most striking aspect of the Soviet *desinformatsiya* campaign against SDI was its greater scope and sophistication compared to previous Soviet efforts. A number of works in recent years have detailed the effectiveness and sophistication of Soviet deception strategy and "active measures" against the U.S.[1] In distinguishing what was the actual underlying Soviet perception of SDI from Soviet *desinformatsiya* themes, one must remember that the objective of the Soviet propaganda campaign was to discredit SDI as the basis for a realistic US deterrence strategy both in the eyes of the Western public and in the perceptions of U.S. policymakers. The major propaganda themes to be discussed here show how the Soviets sought essentially to create a plausible case using U.S. internal arguments against SDI whenever possible in their own statements.

1. *The US is striving for the opportunity to unleash a preventive nuclear war against the Soviet Union.*

This theme of Soviet propaganda has remained virtually unchanged since the United States first declared its "massive retaliation" doctrine in 1954. Regardless of what doctrine the U.S. leaders declared, the Soviets would always claim that the U.S. was inherently aggressive because of the unalterably hostile nature of the capitalist system to Soviet socialism. When Reagan declared the Strategic Defense Initiative, this theme was appropriately modified, as shown in an April 1985 article in *International Affairs*:

> No amount of pseudo-theoretical arguments in the spirit of the "containment through intimidation" doctrine can refute the fact that the USA's "strategic defense initiative" is not meant to strengthen its defenses, but to obtain a first-strike capability which could be used with impunity. Graphic practical proof of that fact is provided by the USA's crash programmes to build up strategic offensive weapons across the whole spectrum . . . .The large scale ABM system itself, intended to enable the aggressor to act with impunity, in terms of the principle on which the weapons being included into it operate, is increasingly converted into an offensive weapon system: according to the US press, the space-based ABM weapons being developed are also to be used to attack "enemy" satellites, aircraft and other targets.[2]

Even after Gorbachev introduced his policies of glasnost and perestroika, the U.S. was still accused of using the "process of preparations for nuclear war to further the ideological, political, and military-strategic interests of their ruling class," of which SDI was considered to be one of the leading tools.[3] It is interesting to note that this particular theme of Soviet propaganda had nearly disappeared by 1990.

2. *No defense is 100% effective; therefore SDI is useless.*

This theme of the Soviet declaratory deterrence strategy has been one of the most cogent of all their *desinformatsiya* themes, since it so skillfully combined truth with falsehood to formulate the classic "all or nothing" argument regarding the political utility of strategic defense. In fact, on the U.S. side, there have been more than substantial arguments and scientific evidence provided in recent years to document the virtual impossibility of creating a "perfect" Ballistic Missile Defense (BMD).[4] As the recent U.S. experience in Desert Storm showed, however, even a rudimentary antiballistic missile defense as embodied in the

Patriot's employment in that role demonstrated the enormous political value that BMD could have for preventing escalation of a conflict.

At the time SDI was first announced, of course, Operation Desert Storm was still nearly eight years in the future, and the Patriot had not yet even been fielded in Germany (January 1985), let alone demonstrated that it could intercept a tactical ballistic missile like the Lance (which would not occur until September 1986).[5] So arguments such as those made by Y. Tomilin in the June 1984 issue of *International Affairs* were quite plausible:

> Naturally, any antimissile defence system will be meaningful only if it 100 percent effectively covers the entire country's territory. The present nuclear missile arsenals are so large that even if the smallest faction (sic) succeeds in penetrating the enemy's antimissile defence, it is capable of producing "unacceptable damage" to the other side, to use American terminology. Can there be an absolute ABM system?[6]

This, of course, was begging the question in the most heavy-handed way. As a corollary to this theme, the Soviets always contended that their response to any attempted U.S. deployment of an SDI system would be to develop "asymmetrical" and comparatively inexpensive countermeasures to penetrate any BMD system. This implied that the Soviet's doctrinal emphasis was on maintaining an alleged "assured destruction" capability, rather than on developing their own ballistic missile defenses. There has been considerable recent literature, however, that argues that the Soviet interest in BMD is at least as great as our own.[7] Nevertheless, this did not prevent commentators like A. Kozyrev from arguing that even the smallest penetration of a BMD system would have catastrophic consequences:

> It is also known that the missile interception system cannot be fully impenetrable. Even the most optimistic forecasts of Pentagon experts expect a system of this kind to intercept no more than 90-95 percent of ballistic missiles should they ever be launched en masse. The 5 to 10 percent that would reach their targets would deliver a sufficient number of nuclear warheads to cause the "disintegration" of the society on which they would be targeted.[8]

What is amazing about the above statement is that it was published in *International Affairs* in May 1985, approximately the same time as a private KGB estimate which gloomily estimated the same level of U.S. effectiveness for SDI, but which additionally stated that there was no way that the Soviet Union would be able to keep up with the U.S. effort![9] This demonstrated that the Soviets did not really believe in the non-utility of strategic defense, otherwise it would have been reflected in their own strategic force structure. The final confirmation that this theme was in fact mere propaganda came on October 5, 1991, when Mikhail Gorbachev expressed interest in creating a mutual system of BMD for protection against limited attack.[10]

3. *SDI extends the arms race into space, threatening to militarize an otherwise peaceful sphere.*

This theme of Soviet *desinformatsiya* was used in tandem with the Soviet argument that SDI was an inherent violation of the 1972 ABM Treaty, a theme that will be discussed in detail below. The purpose of this theme was quite simple: to cast the U.S. once again in the role of warmonger, while at the same time deflecting attention away from the fact that the Soviets were much more heavily engaged in exploitation of space during this period for military purposes, particularly with their emphasis on logging numerous man-hours in earth orbit over extended periods. In addition, the Soviets were emphasizing the development of "heavy-lift" capability in their launch vehicles. This was not necessarily useless for space exploration, but it had considerably more utility for military applications.[11]

Typical of this theme was the use of the classic "action-reaction" argument put forth by Colonel-General V. Lobov in the October 1987 issue of *International Affairs:*

> Time has showed the correctness of that conclusion. The fifteen years that elapsed since the ABM Treaty entered into force have shown that the interrelationship between offensive and defensive weapons exists objectively, no matter what technical level their development has reached. With parity in strategic offensive arms the building of an additional defence potential by either side would be tantamount to gaining unilateral advantages in offensive arms. This would inevitably cause a response by the other side, and so a new round of the arms race, unpredictable in scope, would be provoked.[12]

A. Platonov had earlier made a similar argument in the same journal, arguing that any effort to circumvent existing restrictions on ABM systems by either side would lead somehow to an unrestricted arms race in both offensive and defensive armaments:

> An uncontrolled arms race would inevitably set off greater rivalry in all strategic arms, for the other side would not sit back and wait until the USA achieves overwhelming superiority. As a result, mankind would be faced with the prospect of a continued growth of nuclear confrontation. This does not remove the nuclear threat to people. On the contrary, due to Washington it would grow still bigger, while the international situation would become still more unstable.[13]

As noted above, however, this line of propaganda asked that one believe not only in the action-reaction argument, but that the building of strategic armaments was some mechanistic, uncontrollable process once set in motion, ungovernable by such "irrelevant" factors as political decisions by the national leadership in accordance with its strategic doctrine. Given the target audience of Soviet propagandists, however, lines of argument such as this found ready listeners in the West, at least until recently.

4. *SDI violates the 1972 ABM Treaty.*

This by far was the most useful element of the Soviet propaganda campaign against SDI, mainly because the argument itself was quite plausible to many in the West who were neither Soviet sympathizers nor opponents of U.S. defense preparedness. The issue, of course, hinged on the interpretation of the provisions of the 1972 ABM Treaty. If one chose a narrow interpretation of the Treaty provisions, as the Soviets did, then such advanced BMD research and deployment as called for by the SDI program would be prohibited. If one chose a broad interpretation, as did the Reagan and Bush administrations, then such research and deployment were permissible. Since the validity of this propaganda theme depended so much on legal interpretation, it was an extremely effective theme for the Soviets to exploit, as was done so well by A.G. Arbatov, in his book *Lethal Frontiers:*

> It is obvious that the "broad interpretation" of the treaty contradicts its letter and spirit, a conclusion reaffirmed by Senator Sam Nunn's report in early 1987. To carry out the development and testing of BMD systems within the framework of the "broad interpretation" would be incompatible with the principle of the inviolability of the ABM Treaty regime. It would destroy the treaty and make strategic offensive arms reductions impossible. Fortunately this understanding was reflected as well in the U.S. Congress's resolution on FY 1988 SDI appropriations. Indeed, this approach to the ABM Treaty was fixed in the joint Soviet-U.S. declaration at the Washington summit in December 1987, at which the participants expressed their goal to reach an agreement during a certain period not to withdraw from the ABM Treaty "as it was signed in 1972."[14]

This theme occupied central importance in the Soviet *desinformatsiya* strategy against SDI and the subsequent GPALS program (Global Protection Against Limited Strikes). Since, as mentioned above, the Soviets lacked confidence in their own ability to compete effectively against the U.S. SDI program, then it became paramount for the Soviets to interpret existing treaty obligations as strictly as possible to prevent the U.S. from unilaterally neutralizing the Soviet offensive nuclear arsenal. If that occurred, the Soviet strategic position, from the Soviet perspective, would deteriorate rapidly.

Rather than stating this rationale baldly, another common variation on this theme employed by Soviet commentators was the importance of the 1972 ABM Treaty for maintaining a state of "mutual deterrence" between the superpowers, as stated by S. Menshikov in a June 1986 article in *International Affairs:*

> In the first place, any nuclear state has offensive nuclear weapons. Approximate strategic parity between the sides is a guarantee that none of them would risk

being the first to use nuclear arms, for this would mean risking a catastrophic retaliatory strike. If any of the sides having offensive weapons begins to protect itself from retaliation with an antimissile shield, there is a real danger that it will be tempted to be the first to use such nuclear weapons with impunity. The 1972 ABM Treaty was concluded precisely to exclude such a situation. By committing themselves not to develop total ABM systems the sides thereby created a favourable atmosphere for the limitation and subsequent reduction of offensive strategic arms.[15]

As discussed below, however, this argument was false. By adhering to strict limits and a narrow interpretation of the ABM treaty, the US in fact was giving the Soviet leadership what it really had wanted: continued political leverage over U.S. foreign policy and strategic doctrine thru the maintenance of U.S. strategic vulnerability to Soviet nuclear weapons. Given the actual Soviet perception of SDI and the factors which the Soviets perceived as influencing U.S. policy, one could argue that imposing strict limits on BMD deployment under SDI actually *impeded* serious progress on arms control until shortly before the collapse of Communism and the Soviet Union itself.

The Actual Soviet View

As in the past with the actual Soviet perception of all previous U.S. strategic doctrines, the real Soviet perception of U.S. strategy can be identified by their "mirror-imaged" projections of Soviet strategic doctrine and cultural biases onto the mindsets of US planners and policymakers. These are not merely "misplaced views" (as one well-known analyst contends),[16] which can be corrected by reeducation as to the "correct" view, but a perceptual prism through which all American strategic concepts and doctrine are filtered in the process of interpretation. These perceptions have not only been consistent over time, but they have been held across the spectrum of the Soviet political and military leadership.

1. *SDI is part of a US nuclear warfighting strategy.*

To the Soviet leadership, President Reagan's declaration of the Strategic Defense Initiative was the fulfillment of a continually recurring Soviet nightmare: the fear that the U.S. would employ its technological superiority to engage the Soviets in a contest they could not hope to win. The Soviets already had their own strategic concepts of nuclear warfighting, war survival, as well as the concept of what constituted meaningful political victory in a nuclear war, should one occur. By declaring the SDI, the U.S. had reached the logical culmination of its strategic doctrinal development, from the Soviet perspective. According to one Soviet political analyst:

> . . . SDI is part and parcel of the US nuclear strike forces, preparation for US aggression against the Soviet Union, and a provision for its impunity. The US administration speaks a great deal about the amorality of a guaranteed mutual annihilation if a large-scale conflict breaks out. However, it is not so much worried by moral considerations as by its inability to wage a nuclear without risking its own survival. That is why SDI is an attempt to ensure victory for itself that would entail minimal losses.[17]

This line of thinking was not an isolated one; it was echoed by representatives of the Soviet military leadership such as Lobov, who contended that "Washington still stakes on the possibility of winning a nuclear war and on using nuclear arms as an instrument of foreign policy,"[18] and Slobodenko. Soviet military commentators engaged in the mirror-imaging fallacy as much as their political counterparts did; the difference was in degree, not in kind. The following commentary by Slobodenko was a classic projection of traditional Soviet nuclear warfighting doctrine onto American intentions:

> . . . Furthermore, the US rulers are out to create an international military-strategic situation in which it could use nuclear weapons unhampered. In other words, they would like to threaten other countries, including the Soviet Union, with nuclear weapons, impose their will upon them and use these weapons if necessary without jeopardising their own existence. They believe they can destroy the Soviet Union and survive, thereby achieving victory.[19]

Slobodenko detailed U.S. plans for strategic force improvements, interpreting them all within the context of a nuclear warfighting mindset. From the Soviet viewpoint, strategic defense was not a convenience; it was a vitally necessary component of their traditional nuclear warfighting doctrine. The Soviet strategic defense force structure was not designed to absorb a full-scale U.S. first strike; of this the Soviet leadership was all too well aware. The only context in which Soviet strategic defense made any degree of sense would be as a makeshift shield to absorb a weakened U.S. retaliatory strike in response to a Soviet preemptive strike. As discussed below, this logic was also projected onto the rationale for the US SDI.

2. *The preemptive strike concept is central to the SDI.*

From the Soviet perspective, SDI was simply a U.S. improvement on how the Soviets would themselves employ strategic defense in the event of a nuclear war: to parry the retaliatory strike of the opponent after having delivered a preemptive strike, presumably against the opponent's offensive nuclear capability. This is a logical extension based on the premise that since mirror-imaging is mostly an unconscious fallacy that is often committed without the guilty party being totally aware of his mistake, Soviet military and political commentators were often expressing the biases of their own strategic culture in their analyses of SDI. Given this premise, the following statement in *International Affairs* takes on more significance:

> Still, the Pentagon believes that a large-scale ABM system with space-based elements could weaken the power of, or even neutralise, a retaliation blow, for most enemy ballistic missiles would be destroyed in their silos during a so-called preemptive attack. All these calculations, however, run counter to the assurances given by Washington official spokesmen that the new programme of space weapons deployment is "defensive." the use of the word "defensive" is no more than a play on words to mislead the public.[20]

Soviet commentators often elaborated at length on the notion that SDI was to be employed as the "shield" behind which a U.S. preemptive strike could be delivered with impunity. The following discussion of "space-strike" weapons (as the Soviets termed them) is significant:

> Strike space weapons (SSWs) are primarily offensive arms designed to deliver a first strike against the USSR and its allies ... SSWs can also be used to destroy important targets *in the atmosphere and on the surface of the earth.* ... Finally, SSWs used as an "integrated" potential can sharply increase the offensive potential of nuclear weapons and give them a dangerous quality -the ability to deliver a first strike in the hope of impunity, in the hope that the other side's weakened counter strike can be repulsed with antimissile defence weapons. In other words, there is an objective interconnection between defensive and offensive potential which is expressed in the fact that a greater ability to neutralize a counter strike means a simultaneous increase in offensive force.[21] [Emphasis in original.]

The reason that such seemingly esoteric discussions were significant is that they often reflected the likely direction of future Soviet strategic thinking. In the example above, the Soviets were projecting their own concepts of how they would employ an SDI-type system onto their discussions of U.S. doctrine. In case one may be skeptical, the following statement by General Major V. Ivanov of the Academy of the General Staff in August 1990 was revealing, since he contended that Soviet military reform should:

> include the currently existing Strategic Rocket Forces, and units and large units of Military Aviation, the Navy, and Air and Anti-satellite forces, equipped with nuclear weapons and weapon delivery vehicles which are to be consolidated into Nuclear forces and also *Space Forces, whose units and large units will be provided with systems capable of destroying the enemy's installations from space."* [Emphasis added.][22]

   3. *SDI represents another U.S. attempt to break the strategic stalemate imposed by the Soviet attainment of strategic parity, which is an objective factor restraining U.S. aggression.*

This theme was emphasized in Soviet pronouncements right up to the collapse of the Soviet Union in 1991. Unlike the previous two themes, which occurred less frequently in Soviet statements after 1989 when it seemed that the U.S. was not going to pursue a full-scale SDI program, this theme of Soviet perception appears to be part of the "core perception" of U.S. strategy (and the political utility of nuclear weapons) that survived the breakup of the Soviet Union. This perception appeared to motivate Gorbachev's willingness to adhere to the "narrow" interpretation of the 1972 ABM Treaty until the breakup of the union changed the strategic picture entirely. While the Soviet Union still had unified control of its nuclear arsenal, this arsenal provided considerable return in the form of international prestige as a superpower and political leverage over the U.S. This leverage had come at a considerable cost, since it was the Soviet attainment of parity in land-based ICBMs in 1969 that was a decisive event for them in Soviet-American relations. Any attempt to neutralize this strategic parity by building a BMD system naturally was seen as a "destabilizing" development, as stated by Lobov in the February 1987 issue of *International Affairs:*

> In other words, while declaring its readiness to destroy nuclear arms with the help of a large-scale ABM system with space-based elements, Washington is speedily building its first-strike potential, and the nationwide ABM system is going to be one of its elements. A large-scale ABM system would be a supplement to the nuclear first-strike offensive forces, but in no way would it be opposed to them. One complements the other, and taken together, these two directions of the arms race stimulate each other. Their integration sharply increases the risk of a nuclear war, aggravates crisis situations, and leads to greater world tensions. Therefore the US actions to hamstring the ABM Treaty, interpreting its provisions so that it would not restrict the testing of space-based ABM components, should be regarded as an attempt to upset the existing military-strategic parity.[23]

The majority of Soviet spokesmen and commentators who espoused this theme in particular tended to be leading officers in the Soviet military. This did not mean, however, that the Soviet political leadership held views that were incompatible with this theme, or that their perceptions of the "U.S. threat" were any less pessimistic. Both military and political commentators, for example, agreed with Major General Y. Lebedev's view that "the core of the military and strategic parity is the rough balance in Soviet and US strategic armaments" in addition to the rough overall balance between the forces of NATO and the Warsaw Pact (while it still existed).[24] Given the importance of strategic nuclear parity to the Soviet leadership, Lebedev's assessment of SDI was not only predictable, but widely held among both political, military, and even academic observers:

The realities of today are such that the economic, scientific, technological, and other capabilities of industrialised states do not permit any single country or a group of states to count on gaining military superiority. It is not fortuitous that the U.S. nuclear policy, i.e. the position-of-strength policy, has now ended up in a deadlock. But the main thing is probably that because of the inevitability of a nuclear retaliatory strike all Washington's hopes of winning a nuclear war also become pointless. Under those conditions, the USA and some of its NATO allies, unwilling to comprehend the realities of the nuclear and space age, attempt to find a way out of the "nuclear impasse" through outer space. The masters of the White House are fooling themselves with a belief that through "star wars" they would allegedly be able to rush ahead militarily and to dictate their will to the Soviet Union . . . Reliance on outer space and on space weapons based on new physical principles is utterly groundless. The Soviet Union possesses necessary material and intellectual capabilities to foil US attempts at acquiring military supremacy. *The military and strategic parity has been and continues to be an objective factor of containment.* [Emphasis added.][25]

4. *SDI threatens to neutralize the main means of Soviet political leverage over the U.S.*

It is this last theme of the actual Soviet perception that underlay the Soviet fear of SDI, which drove the entire Soviet propaganda campaign against it, and which was the basis for Soviet insistence on rigid adherence to a narrow interpretation of the 1972 ABM Treaty. With a deployed SDI system, commentators such as Lobov argued in *International Affairs* that the U.S. would be able "to use nuclear weapons as a decisive argument in its foreign policy." Taking his argument still farther in the same article, he wrote:

So, the "purely research" character of the work conducted in the SDI framework clearly coincides with Washington's plans to escalate the qualitative arms race, and fits into the borader strategy of gaining military technological superiority over the USSR. This is not chance coincidence, of course. It is a carefully calculated policy whose ultimate aim is to upset the military strategic parity at all levels, from nuclear to conventional arms, and to return to US imperialism its "position of strength" in international relations. It would be dangerous to underestimate this most aggressive aspect of the SDI programme.[26]

Even members of the Soviet academic community recognized the potential dangers of SDI to Soviet influence, and were not particularly reticent about criticizing it. R. Ovinnikov's statement in an August 1985 issue of *International Affairs* revealed a high degree of Soviet paranoia over SDI:

The aim is to neutralise those types of Soviet strategic weapons which, for geographic and historical reasons, are the backbone of its defence might. It is easy to see that under this scheme the USA has superiority in submarine-based nuclear weapons and strategic bombers which are left untouched, as are long-range nuclear cruise missiles. In practice, says R. Bowman, President of the US Institute for Space and Security studies, the aim of the "star wars" plans is to hamstring that type of strategic arms which enables the Soviet Union to maintain parity. "We are tired of this equality business," he admits. "The only way we can regain our political leverage . . . is to regain absolute military superiority."

Thus, the "star wars" programme in its exposed form is extremely aggressive. It is a desperate attempt on the part of US imperialism to "stake its all" in the nuclear age. The stake is on making full use of the colossal military might of the USA and, if possible, the military potentials of its main allies, to check the course of history in one stroke, take social revenge worldwide, and destroy socialism. In practical terms, two interconnected tasks are set to this end: to regain invulnerability for the United States and, on the other hand, to render the Soviet Union extremely vulnerable.[27]

According to the contentions of military analysts such as Lebedev and Podberezkin in *Voennaia Mysl'*, once the U.S. succeeded in nullifying strategic parity between the US and the Soviet Union through the SDI, it would then be able "to unleash a broad offensive against the forces of socialism and the national liberation movement."[28] It should be kept in mind that these perceptions were not the isolated paranoid ravings of rabid "hawks" or the self-interested rationalizations of a "military-industrial complex"; these views were characteristic of a broad spectrum of the Soviet military, political, and academic leadership. As earlier noted, even the KGB had gloomily estimated in April 1985 that the U.S. would eventually be able to block 90 percent of Soviet strategic missile with SDI systems, and that there was little chance of Soviet SDI research keeping pace with the United States.[29] Given this combination of pessimistic worst-case evaluations of U.S. ability to implement SDI with the steadily worsening Soviet economic situation, it is small wonder that the Soviet Union began attempting to link promises of arms control concessions to U.S. willingness to forego a full-scale SDI program; there was little else the Soviet leadership could do to buttress its steadily weakening power position vis a vis the U.S.

Conclusions

The Soviet perceptions of SDI during this period reflected the paranoia of the Soviet military and political leadership that the US was finally utilizing its technological and economic superiority to engage the Soviet Union in a contest it could not hope to win; a contest to develop effective space-based ballistic missile defense. The Soviets had little confidence in their own BMD effort being able to keep up with the U.S.; indeed, it was this lack of confidence that had motivated the Soviet Union to negotiate the 1972 ABM Treaty with the U.S. in the first place. The ABM Treaty was the only thing in the Soviet view that was keeping the U.S. from nullifying the Soviets' last true means of political leverage.[30] Gorbachev, recognizing that the U.S. was not going to abandon SDI altogether, decided to pursue the second best option, which was to negotiate large mutual cuts with the U.S. while still maintaining some form of strategic parity. Once the Soviet Union itself collapsed after August 1991, however, even Gorbachev recognized that strategic parity was no longer practical, particularly with the separate republics vying for control over various portions of the Soviet nuclear arsenal.[31] Ironically then, Gorbachev began expressing interest in cooperating with the US in establishing some form of mutual strategic defense system with the US.[32] It is reminiscent of the Soviet Union's efforts between the two world wars to establish some form of collective security arrangement within Europe. Only now it would be collective security against an as yet unknown number of independent nuclear powers.

Even with the final collapse of the Soviet Union only a few months away, the Soviet leadership was keenly aware of the key role played by its nuclear arsenal in exerting leverage internally as well as internationally and for gaining prestige as a great power. The view expressed by V.N. Mikhaylov (at this writing still deputy minister of nuclear energy and industry) in an interview in early 1991, is indicative of the decisive hold that nuclear weapons still had in the minds of the Soviet military and political leadership:

> The nation's nuclear arsenal was created by the entire people, all republics contributed to it. The idea of dividing it is quite absurd from the political, economic, scientific, and technical points of view. No single republic has either the economic or the scientific and technical capabilities for this.
>
> ... We must foresee any possible scenario and not allow such a development of events, because that would mean the collapse of our state. The nuclear-missile shield was built by the efforts of the entire nation, the entire country. This mighty potential makes us an influential world power, serves as a guarantee of our safety, a guarantee of the integrity of the state. It is one of the forces cementing the federation.[33]

Even after the formal dissolution of the Soviet Union and the subsequent formation of the Commonwealth of Independent States (CIS) under the nominal leadership of Boris Yeltsin as *primus inter pares*, the importance to the Russian republic, at least, of nuclear weapons as instruments of political leverage and prestige has not diminished; indeed, Yeltsin's strenuous efforts to maintain at least joint, if not wholly unified, control over the former Soviet nuclear arsenal is proof of this.[34] But now that there is no longer a Soviet Union wielding a unified nuclear force as its only formidable instrument of coercion, its ability to exert influence on U.S. policy in any significant fashion has all but disappeared. This is evidenced by the U.S. decision in January 1992 to exclude the 1972 ABM Treaty from the list of major arms control accords to which, it has told the former Soviet republics, they should adhere.[35] How will the formation of the CIS affect the future strategic relationships among its component republics and with the U.S., particularly as the CIS struggles with trying to balance the development of democratic, free-market institutions against the need for order arising from the growing chaos of a collapsing economy? This will be the focus of our concluding chapter.

Notes

1. Three works of significant value in this area have been L. Bittman, *The KGB and Soviet Disinformation: An Insider's View* (McLean, Va.: Pergamon Brassey's International Defense Publishers, 1985); R.H. Shultz and R. Godson, *Desinformatsia: Active Measures in Soviet Strategy* (Washington, D.C.: National Strategy Information Center, 1984); and B.D. Dailey and B.J. Parker, eds. *Soviet Strategic Deception* (Lexington, Mass.: D.C. Heath & Company, 1987).

2. A. Platonov, "Towards The Geneva Talks," *International Affairs* 4 (April 1985): 21-22.

3. S. Sanakoyev, "Peaceful Coexistence in the Context of Miltary Strategic Parity, *International Affairs* 2 (February 1988): 80. This line was echoed in the 27th Party Congress of the CPSU. See A. Sovetov, "27th Congress of the CPSU on Imperialism's Aggressive Policy," *International Affairs* 8 (August 1986): 11.

4. The literature, in fact, is too overwhelming to document in detail here. Three works that provide a good balanced look at SDI overall are S.J. Cimbala, ed., *The Technology, Strategy, and Politics of SDI* (Boulder, Co.: Westview Press Inc., 1987); M. Charlton, *The Star Wars History* (London: BBC publications, 1986); and J. Rhea, *SDI: What Could Happen* (Harrisburg, Pa.: Stackpole Books, 1988).

5. The author served as the Brigade S-2 (Intelligence Officer) of the 10th Air Defense Artillery Brigade (HAWK/PATRIOT), the first operational unit to deploy the Patriot in Germany, at the time of the initial deployment of the first two Patriot battalions in 1984-1985. At the time of my duty in Germany as Brigade S-2, I followed Soviet military journals to see if there were any articles dealing with Patriot. As it turned out, not only was this the case, but the Soviets were already crediting Patriot in 1985 with an antiballistic missile capability in an article entitled "Antiaircraft Rocket Systems for Medium and High Altitudes," *Vestnik Protivovozdushnoi Oborony* (Herald of Antiaircraft Defense) 1 (January 1985): 89-90. The article went even further, envisioning its "employment for the antimissile defense (PRO) [ProtivoRaketnoi Oborony] of some objectives of the territory of the USA."

6. See Y. Tomilin, "To Avert the Threat of Militarizing Outer Space," *International Affairs* 6 (June 1984): 63. This author uses a similar argument in a later article, "Space: Confrontation or Cooperation?" *Mirovaia Ekonomika i Mezhdunarodnaya Otnoshenia* 9 (September 1987): 3-4.

7. An excellent paper that documents and analyzes the case for Soviet BMD is B. Parrott, *The Soviet Union and Ballistic Missile Defense* (Boulder, Co.: Westview Press, 1987). A recent book that argues relative similarity between US and Soviet strategic doctrine is R. Garthoff, *Deterrence and the Revolution in Soviet Military Doctrine* (Washington, D.C.: The Brookings Institution, 1990)

8. A. Kozyrev, "For Peaceful Outer Space," *International Affairs* 5 (May 1985): 123-4.

9. See C. Andrew & O. Gordievsky, *KGB: The Inside Story* (London: HarperPerennial, 1991), 607.

10. S. Schmemann, "Gorbachev Matches U.S. on Nuclear Cuts and Goes Further on Strategic Warheads," *New York Times*, October 6, 1991: 1.

11. See the Congressional report, *Soviet Space Programs: 1981-87. Space Science, Space Applications, Military Space Programs, Administration, Resource Burden, and Master Log of Spaceflights* (Washington, D.C.: Senate Committee on Commerce, Science, and Transportation, April 1989).

12. V. Lobov, "The ABM Treaty: Apprehensions and Hopes," *International Affairs* 10 (October 1987): 21.

13. A. Platonov, "Militarization of Outer Space- A Threat to Mankind," *International Affairs* 2 (February 1985): 31.

14. A.G. Arbatov, *Lethal Frontiers: A Soviet View of Nuclear Strategy, Weapons, and Negotiations,* trans. by Kent D. Lee (New York: Praeger Publishers, 1988), 248.

15. S. Menshikov, "What is Behind the Star Wars Debate," *International Affairs* 6 (June 1986): 69.

16. Raymond Garthoff, in *Deterrence and the Revolution in Soviet Military Doctrine,* acknowledges that Soviet mirror-imaging does take place in their analyses of American doctrine and strategy, but dismisses these analyses out of hand as misplaced views. See R. Garthoff, *Deterrence and the Revolution in Soviet Military Doctrine* (Brookings Institution: Washington, D.C., 1990), 64.

17. Y. Shashkov, "Space Shield: Myths and Reality," *International Affairs* 3 (March 1987): 24.

18. V. Lobov, "The ABM Treaty," *International Affairs* 10 (October 1987): 22. Other examples of articles offering a similar argument are L. Lyubimov, "New Thinking and Soviet-American Relations," *MEMO* 3 (March 1988): 10; L. Tolkunov, "Nuclear Disarmament-Demand of the Times," *MEMO* 12 (December 1987): 7; and especially A.A. Kokoshin, "American Plans for the Militarization of Space," *Voennaia Mysl'* 4 (April 1987): 78-79. Interestingly enough, these and other articles of a similar nature are not cited by Raymond Garthoff in *Deterrence and the Revolution in Soviet Military Doctrine,* as they tend to weaken his argument regarding the underlying similarity of the U.S. and Soviet strategic outlooks.

19. A. Slobodenko, "The US Military Doctrine: Reliance on Force," *International Affairs* 9 (September 1987): 39-40.

20. A. Kozyrev, "For Peaceful Outer Space," *International Affairs* 5 (May 1985): 124. See also A. Platonov, "Towards The Geneva Talks," 21.

21. Yu. Lebedev and A.I. Podberezkin, "SDI-A New Stage of the Arms Race," *International Affairs* 2 (February 1987): 62-63, passim. The authors made virtually the same arguments at greater length in "The Imperial Ambitions of Washington - Main Obstacle on the Path to Nuclear Disarmament," *Voennaia Mysl'* 1 (January 1987): 3-12. See also V.G. Andreyev and S.V. Skorokhodov, "Third Generation Nuclear Weapons in the American Plans of 'Star Wars,'" *Voennaia Mysl'* 9 (September 1986): 73-79.

22. Attributed to General Major Ivanov, August 1990. Cited in briefing by F.X. Kane and J.R. Howe, "Emerging Soviet Views on Future Warfare," August 27, 1991. For an excellent discussion of Soviet views on the future of warfare, see also Mary C. Fitzgerald, "The Soviet image of Future War: 'Through the Prism of the Persian Gulf," *Comparative Strategy* 10 (October-December 1991): 393-435.

23. V. Lobov, "The ABM Treaty," 22-23. See also Editorial, "Star Wars: Illusions and Dangers," *Voennaia Mysl'* 9 (September 1985): 15; and D. Klimov, "Threat to Strategic Stability," *KVS* 23 (December 1988): 82.

24. Y. Lebedev, "Military and Strategic Parity and the Realities of the Nuclear and Space Age," *International Affairs* 7 (July 1986): 26.

25. Ibid., 26. This same argument was reiterated at greater length in more authoritative journals such as *Voennaia Mysl'*. See V.F. Andreyev, "Military-Strategic Parity- An Objective Factor in Restraining Aggressive Forces," *Voennaia Mysl'* 2 (February 1989): 45-53, for a detailed exposition of this theme. Interestingly enough, this article also is not cited by Garthoff in *Deterrence*, probably because it contradicts his main thesis assuming essential similarity between U.S. and Soviet strategic thought. One of the most publicized Soviet expositions on strategic parity as a restraining factor on US policy can be found in A. Arbatov, *Lethal Frontiers*. Contrary to the assertion of Lee, the book itself is not remarkably original in its perceptions, since these have been stated at length by various Soviet commentators over the entire period since 1954, particularly since 1970, and were obvious to anyone who cared to study them. What is truly remarkable is the book's sophisticated use of all elements of the Soviet *desinformatsiya* themes described in this chapter, which makes Arbatov one of the most effective spokesmen for attempting to influence the U.S. debate.

26. Lobov, "The ABM Treaty," 25. This argument is expanded on by Lebedev and Podberezkin in "Imperial Ambitions," 4-5.

27. R. Ovinnikov, "'Star Wars' Programme- A New Phase in Washington's Militaristic Policy," *International Affairs* 8 (August 1985): 19-20.

28. Lebedev & Podberezkin, "Imperial Ambitions," 5.

29. Cited in Andrew and Gordievsky, *KGB: The Inside Story,* 607.

30. There is considerable evidence to indicate that the 1972 ABM Treaty was an excellent example of Soviet strategic deception strategy in operation. See B.D. Dailey, "Deception, Perceptions Management, and Self-Deception in Arms Control: An Examination of the ABM Treaty," cited in B.D. Dailey and P.J. Parker, eds, *Soviet Strategic Deception,* 225-59.

31. F. Hiatt, "Soviet Republics See A-Weapons as Bargaining Chips," *Washington Post*, October 24, 1991, A41.

32. S. Schmemann, "Gorbachev Matches U.S.," 1.

33. Interview by L. Chernenko with V.N. Mikhaylov, "The Keys From the Nuclear Arsenal," in *Pravitelstvennyy Vestnik* 12 (March 1991): 12. Trans. in JPRS-UMA-91-013, May 20, 1991, 39-40.

34. M. Dobbs, "Nuclear Command Shifted to Yeltsin," *Washington Post,* December 26, 1991, A1.

35. R.J. Smith, "U.S. Moves Away From ABM Treaty," *Washington Post*, January 26, 1992, A1.

11
The Future of U.S. and Russian Strategy

For most of the post-World War II period prior to the accession of Gorbachev to power in the Soviet Union, the Soviet perception of U.S. strategy was both consistently hostile to the notion of arms control as an end in itself and confident in the power of its strategic nuclear arsenal to provide it both leverage and cover for the use of its own military power to further its interests in the Third World. The Soviet perception could be defined by three major themes, two of which, as we shall see, still have great significance for the future policies of the independent republics which now comprise the Commonwealth of Independent States.

The first major theme of Soviet perception during this period was that Soviet analysts continued to project their own strategic concepts of nuclear warfighting with the objective of meaningful political victory onto the intentions of U.S. strategic planners. U.S. statements regarding deterrence and the essential "unwinnability" of nuclear war were dismissed as propaganda by Soviet analysts, who evaluated U.S. doctrine and associated capabilities in terms of their nuclear warfighting potential rather than by the U.S. criterion of deterrence. This is not surprising, since the Soviet military has its own firmly held beliefs about what is rational in strategic planning. From the Soviet standpoint, a nuclear warfighting doctrine based on the capacity for nuclear war survival, war waging, war winning, and subsequent recovery was the only logical doctrine in accordance with the "laws of war," as defined by the Soviets. This being the case, if one assumes that Soviet analysts saw the United States as equally rational (albeit "aggressive" and "adventuristic"), it was only natural that Soviet analysts expected U.S. planners to adopt and implement a nuclear warfighting doctrine similar to their own. Just as a number of U.S. analysts have made the error of mirror-imaging U.S. strategic thought onto Soviet planners and decision makers, so too have Soviet analysts committed the same ethnocentric error, as has been shown throughout this book.

The consequences of Soviet mirror-imaging have been much different for Soviet doctrine and military programs, however, than has been the case for the United States. This had been particularly true with respect to arms control. For while Soviet analysts and commentators had compartmentalized their discussions of arms control and strategic doctrine as separate considerations, the former merely being a tool of the latter to restrain U.S. strategic growth, U.S. arms control advocates have pursued SALT, START, and other disarmament talks as ends in themselves, confidently believing that the Soviets also shared their convictions about the political non-utility of nuclear weapons. Few U.S. advocates of arms control had ever given the Soviet perspective concerning U.S. doctrine and programs any serious consideration, or felt that it really mattered much.

Despite the Soviet emphasis on "reasonable sufficiency" during the Gorbachev regime, examples of Soviet mirror-imaging can be found throughout the entire period of their pronouncements on U.S. strategic doctrine. The earliest and most consistently found example was the Soviet reaction to U.S. discussion of a preemptive strike strategy in the late 1950s. The Soviets themselves had endorsed privately the concept of a preemptive strike strategy as early as May 1955,[1] although they only alluded to such a strategy in their public pronouncements. The Soviets were concerned, however, over the possibility that the United States might also adopt a preemptive strike strategy, since this would have negated the effectiveness of their own warfighting strategy and created a highly unstable situation. This same concern was reflected in later Soviet reactions to counterforce, Schlesinger's Limited Nuclear Options strategy, and the U.S. countervailing strategy, since from the Soviet standpoint all of these were attempted moves toward a nuclear warfighting orientation in U.S. doctrine.

Another element of Soviet mirror-imaging was the projection of the objective of victory in a nuclear war as a primary consideration in U.S. strategic doctrine. This was a logical continuation of the Soviet military's own warfighting mindset. After all, if a state were going to adopt a warfighting strategy, then it made sense for some sort of conditions for defining victory to be established. In a nuclear war, the Soviets conceived of victory in the following terms:

1. Though damaged, the Soviet Union continues to function politically, economically, and militarily after the initial exchange.
2. Prosecution of the war continues until all enemy forces are destroyed or defeated.
3. Europe is occupied.
4. The Soviet Union recovers in a reasonable time and Soviet-directed socialism prevails in the world.[2]

The Soviets saw a particularly significant step in this direction in the LNO strategy, in which Schlesinger linked deterrence to post-nuclear war political objectives. To the Soviets, this was a great leap away from the pure deterrence objective of war avoidance with its subsequent objective of early war termination should deterrence fail. (This was later to evolve into the notion of victory denial in the U.S. countervailing strategy.)

This Soviet predilection for mirror-imaging conflicted with the second major theme of Soviet perception, which emerged near the end of the massive retaliation period in 1960. This was that the Soviets increasingly began to admit, in both public as well as private analyses, the likelihood and the necessity of having to wage limited wars with the use of conventional and/or nuclear weapons. This was contradictory to the Soviet projection of their warfighting strategy onto U.S. planning. If the Soviets had really believed that the United States was moving toward a preemptive strike strategy, then Soviet readiness levels would have reflected a high degree of anticipation of such a strike. Yet it was not until recent years that Soviet strategic forces were raised to a level that would have made launch on warning or launch under attack in response to an attempted U.S. first strike possible.[3] Further indications of the lack of Soviet readiness were repeated calls for efforts to raise the readiness of the armed forces to a high degree, thus implying that such a condition did not in fact exist.[4]

Rather, the buildup of Soviet nuclear and conventional forces across the board shortly after the accession of the Brezhnev regime to power in 1964 demonstrated that the Soviets were in fact striving for a flexible offensive capability similar to that postulated by the United States in its flexible response doctrine. The shift by the United States during the 1960s and early 1970s towards a pure deterrence stance based on mutual assured destruction (MAD), with its associated objective of war avoidance, helped convince the Soviets that the United States was being increasingly restrained in its range of potential responses to Soviet actions by its fear of uncontrolled escalation to total war. In the Soviet view, the two major exceptions to this trend were the escalation concept as espoused by Herman Kahn and the LNO strategy as enunciated by Schlesinger. Although the former was never really a part of U.S. strategic doctrine and the latter was never officially adopted, both concepts were highly disturbing to Soviet analysts in terms of their implications for the credibility of the Soviet desinformatsiya campaign against LNO. Part of the deterrent value of the Soviet strategic posture was its implied threat that any local conflict that involved the Soviet Union might escalate uncontrollably into a total nuclear war. Both the escalation concept and the LNO strategy, as well as the limited nuclear war options of the subsequent countervailing strategy, strongly implied that the United States might ignore the Soviet threat of uncontrolled escalation and thus employ the use of force at whatever level it chose. Other than these exceptions, the Soviet perception until the mid-1980s was that the likelihood of limited war was growing relative to that of total nuclear war.

There was a discrepancy, therefore, between the first two themes of Soviet perception. Since the Soviet projection of its own strategic concepts onto U.S. doctrine was quite apparent, Soviet observers had to reconcile this to the fact that the United States, however much it ostensibly desired to adopt a nuclear warfighting strategy, was nevertheless moving in the opposite direction, to a deterrence strategy geared to the waging of more limited conflicts and the notion of MAD. This discrepancy was resolved by the third major theme of Soviet perception, which concluded that the evolution of U.S. strategic doctrine was the result of a *forced* response to the growth of Soviet strategic power. Soviet analysts had previously credited the development of the Soviet ICBM as having been a significant factor in the U.S. shift from massive retaliation to flexible response. They attributed similar status to the attainment of strategic parity with the United States in 1969, which they saw figuring prominently in the U.S. abandonment of flexible response in favor of realistic deterrence, as well as in the U.S. willingness to engage in SALT.[5] Whether the Soviets arrived at this conclusion by reasoned analysis or simply used it as a convenient rationalization for the buildup of Soviet military power is a moot point. The fact remains that this conclusion provided a self-sustaining impetus for the buildup of Soviet military power throughout the 1960s, the 1970s, and the first half of the 1980s with no clear definable upper limit. Until Gorbachev, there was neither a stated nor an implied penalty for too much military buildup. This perception was not dependent on ideological adherence to Marxism-Leninism, since the cultural milieu and methods of expressing concepts in the Russian language largely predetermined the Soviet interpretation of U.S. strategy throughout this period.

The correlation of these perceptions to the use of military power in support of Soviet foreign policy objectives was quite high. During the massive retaliation period (1954-1960), when the United States possessed a demonstrable strategic superiority over the Soviet Union, Soviet use of its military power consisted of little other than threatening to use it or engaging in military maneuvers near the area in dispute. The one major exception to this, of course, was suppression of the Hungarian Revolution in 1956, which can be explained by the fact that it occurred in an area tacitly conceded to be under Soviet influence, so that the Soviets felt obliged to use force to support what they considered a vital interest; in this case, it was the suppression of so-called "counterrevolutions."

During the flexible response period (1961-1968), however, a noticeable change in the character of Soviet military behavior took place. In addition to the general pattern of threats and maneuvers, the Soviets began to provide logistical support on an ever increasing scale to its clients in the Third World. This pattern was most noticeable during the latter half of the 1960s. Two major aberrations from this pattern took place during the flexible response period. The first was the Cuban missile crisis, in which Khrushchev prematurely attempted to attain strategic parity with the U.S. by installing intermediate range ballistic missiles in Cuba. As discussed previously, this was a natural outgrowth of his campaign of strategic bluffing concerning the actual size and scope of the Soviet ICBM program in the late 1950s and early 1960s. The other was the Soviet intervention in Czechoslovakia in 1968. Like the earlier intervention in Hungary, this could be rationalized as a Soviet-perceived protection of vital interests as proclaimed in the subsequently declared Brezhnev Doctrine, which reserved the Soviet right to protect socialist regimes from the threat of counterrevolution. Then, too, by this time the Soviet ICBM force was on the verge of attaining its historic state of strategic parity with the U.S., and so the Soviets doubtless saw themselves as having relatively greater freedom of action to intervene, particularly with the U.S. at the height of its involvement in Vietnam.

The level of Soviet military activity increased even more significantly in scale during the realistic deterrence period (1969-1982). Aside from continued major supply efforts to North Vietnam and the Middle East, the Soviets supported Cuban proxy forces in armed interventions in Angola, Ethiopia, and Yemen, and sent Soviet "advisers" to Mozambique, Syria, Libya, and Algeria. This Soviet activity reached its post-war peak with its armed intervention in Afghanistan in 1979, in that it marked the heretofore unprecedented use of Soviet troops outside of its generally recognized East European sphere of influence. Until the Reagan Administration came to power in 1981, the trend during this period had been an increasingly greater Soviet willingness to use its logistical airlift and sealift capability in support of its proxies in "national-liberation movements" not contiguous with Soviet territory. The overall trend during the period 1954-1980 could therefore be summarized as a fairly constant, if very gradual, increase in scale of the use of Soviet military power in support of its foreign policy objectives. This usage paralleled the Soviet perception of a United States increasingly restrained by its forced accommodation to an unfavorably altered strategic balance.

During the 1980s, however, this trend began to reverse itself. The causes for this are several, and no one cause can be considered predominant over any other. The first was the resurgence of U.S. political resolve under the Reagan and Bush administrations to expand and use U.S. military power to oppose what they perceived as Soviet-sponsored "national-liberation movements" in the Western Hemisphere, with Grenada and Nicaragua being the premier examples. The U.S. also began to supply rebel forces in Afghanistan with the weapons and ammunition they needed to sustain their resistance. In particular, the supplying of Stinger antiaircraft missiles to the rebels rendered the Soviet Air Force almost completely ineffective for close air support and helped create the military standoff that ultimately forced Gorbachev to announce the Soviet withdrawal from Afghanistan in early 1988. This steady increase in U.S. political resolve, bolstered by the largest peacetime military buildup of the entire Cold War period, was further accentuated during the Bush administration by the U.S. operations in Panama and Operation Desert Storm. From the Soviet perspective, only the "nuclear-missile shield" of the Soviet state kept the U.S. from being even more aggressive.[6]

The second cause of the Soviet reversal in use of military power did not become apparent until after the rise of Gorbachev in 1985 and his subsequent declaration of the doctrine of "reasonable sufficiency"; the Soviet economic system was becoming less and less able to support the demands of the Soviet military machine coupled with an adventuristic foreign policy. When the U.S. declared its Strategic Defense Initiative in 1983, the Soviets mounted the largest desinformatsiya campaign in post-World War II history to discredit it and dissuade the U.S. from deploying a large-scale SDI system. The KGB privately estimated that the Soviet Union would not be able to match the U.S. effort in SDI.[7] Moreover, Soviet military and political analysts concluded that such deployment would effectively disrupt "strategic stability," thus removing the one independent means of political leverage the Soviet Union had over the U.S.: its offensive nuclear forces. When it had become apparent that the U.S. would continue its SDI research regardless of what the Soviets said or threatened, the Soviet leadership saw that its bluff had been called. Rather than allow its strategic power to be unilaterally eroded to no benefit, Gorbachev pursued his second best option; that of negotiating deep cuts in strategic offensive forces for both sides in such a way as to preserve the relative political leverage of Soviet strategic forces. At the same time, the Soviets continually sought to tie SDI into arms control negotiations, which the U.S. steadfastly refused. The "reasonable sufficiency" doctrine, in retrospect, was a tacit recognition by the Soviet leadership that it no longer could pursue its foreign policy objectives as vigorously as before by simply giving free rein to the demands of the Soviet military machine; the inherent economic weakness of the Communist system was finally catching up with Soviet ambition.

Even the belated declaration of the "reasonable sufficiency" doctrine, however, was not enough to offset the third cause of the Soviet reversal, which was the discrediting of Marxism-Leninism as a credible revolutionary alternative to capitalism and democracy. By the 1980s the abject failure of the Communist economic model was becoming readily apparent to all but the most die-hard advocates of Communism in the West, and the threat of "Eurocommunism" gaining a foothold in the NATO alliance was receding. Without a viable alternative to offer the peoples of its empire, the legitimacy of the Soviet leadership rested solely in the coercive power of the KGB and the Soviet armed forces. Once Gorbachev declared his policies of *glasnost* and *perestroika*, the ideological floodgates were opened. The internal dissent that was unleashed inhibited Gorbachev's freedom of action in the foreign policy arena, making his withdrawal announcement from Afghanistan in early 1988 seem more a bow to the inevitable than a peace-loving initiative. As internal pressures mounted within the Soviet Union, the Soviet leadership found itself both unwilling and unable to employ military power to suppress the uprisings in Eastern Europe in 1989 and 1990. As dazzling as the collapse of the Eastern European Soviet empire and the subsequent formal dissolution of the Warsaw Pact alliance in 1991 was to Western observers, it was the impotence of the ideologically conservative Soviet military to suppress the revolution in the Soviet Union itself in August 1991, followed by its final dissolution on December 31, 1991, that demonstrated the ultimate bankruptcy of Communist ideology.

The Implications of the Soviet View

What are the lessons, then, that can be drawn about the past Soviet mindset regarding U.S. strategic doctrinal development? First of all, it is clear that the Soviet perception prior to the mid-1980s, which provided a self-sustaining motivation for the buildup of its conventional and strategic power, gave the Soviets no serious incentive to engage in arms control or disarmament negotiations with the United States for its own sake. Indeed, since the Soviets saw favorable changes for them in U.S. strategic doctrine as having resulted mainly from increases in Soviet strategic power, coupled with the fact that they believed this increased power also to have been responsible for compelling the United States to seek arms-control negotiations with them, there was practically no reason why the Soviets should have ceased their buildup as long as they had the capacity to support it. This buildup continued regardless of any unilateral action the United States might have taken. The only action taken by the U.S. which had a demonstrable effect on Soviet willingness to negotiate was, ironically enough, its commitment and steadfast adherence to the SDI. By threatening to neutralize the one independent means of political leverage the Soviets possessed, the U.S. in turn gained leverage over Soviet willingness to negotiate real arms control, although, we must remember, not as an end in itself.

The political significance of strategic defense and its effects on the Soviet perception of U.S. strategy and on Soviet willingness to negotiate is the other major lesson for U.S. foreign policy and defense planning; only when the perceived political utility of nuclear weapons as symbols of prestige and instruments of coercion has been nullified can true arms control take place. And a comprehensive strategic defense program was the only credible means of doing so from the Soviet perspective. This is why the Soviet government pursued its strategic defense program with all means available, and conversely why they so vigorously opposed the development of SDI in the US until recently.

This lesson applies in the current situation. Despite all of the lip service that has been paid to arms reduction proposals on both sides, the fact of the matter is that the collective Commonwealth republics still possess the power to destroy the United States in 30 minutes with a preemptive nuclear strike. By voluntarily foregoing a full-scale SDI with the objective capability for neutralizing a potential first strike, the U.S. had given the former Soviet leadership under Gorbachev what it really wanted: continued political prestige as a nuclear superpower, in addition to preserving the leverage value of the Soviet nuclear arsenal as a restraint on U.S. freedom of action. It was this ability to "restrain" the US that was the main requirement for strategic stability as defined by the Soviets, not arms control.

This perception has profound implications for the future development of military doctrine and programs in the Commonwealth republics, and most particularly the Russian republic, assuming that the current political and economic upheavals can be resolved and a measure of stability regained. It means that the former Soviet military and political leadership of the Russian republic, despite the collapse of the Soviet Union, will continue to develop third-generation nuclear weapons in an effort to enhance the political as well as military utility of their arsenal. Moreover, since control of strategic nuclear weapons amounts to potential "great power" status in their perspective, it will be impermissible for control of the former Soviet nuclear arsenal to come under the control of more than one authority. The following statement by Viktor N. Mikhaylov, deputy minister of nuclear energy and industry, on 12 March 1991, was particularly revealing of this attitude (not to mention highly prophetic):

> The nation's nuclear arsenal was created by the entire people, all republics contributed to it. The idea of dividing it is quite absurd from the political, economic, technical, and scientific points of view. No single republic has either the economic or the scientific and technical capabilities for this. And then, imagine that instead of one nuclear power-the Soviet Union-there would suddenly appear fifteen states possessing nuclear weapons . . . We must foresee any possible scenario and not allow such a development of events, because *that would mean the collapse of our state. The nuclear-missile shield was built by the efforts of the entire nation, the entire country. This mighty potential makes us an influential world power, serves as a guarantee of our safety, a guarantee of the integrity of the state. It is one of the forces cementing the federation.* (Emphasis added.)[8]

It is this attitude, prevalent throughout the viewpoint of both the former Soviet military and political leadership, which will ultimately thwart any prospect for total disarmament in the absence of a strong U.S. strategic defense against nuclear attack. This does not mean that any one or more of the independent Commonwealth republics would seek to threaten the US with its portion of the nuclear arsenal. It does mean that the political benefits of nuclear weapons, both in terms of prestige and leverage vis-à-vis one another, are just too tempting for the leadership of the individual republics to resist. By the same token, this perception is virtually certain to result in a struggle for control over Soviet strategic and tactical nuclear weapons. The independent republics, particularly Ukraine, Belarus, and Kazakhstan on the one hand, by now realize the benefits, and ultimately the necessity, of possessing their own independent nuclear arsenals free from central control if they are to successfully maintain their autonomy from Yeltsin's Russian republic, which already possesses the majority of strategic and tactical nuclear weapons within its own territory. Failing this, they would at least want to have "veto power" over the use of any portion of the former Soviet nuclear arsenal. This explains the existence of "joint control" by the four republics over the nuclear arsenal; it is not so much to facilitate the use of the nuclear arsenal against an outside power as to prevent its use as an instrument of political coercion against any of the individual republics. On the other hand, Yeltsin (or any who succeed him) by now must also realize that anything less than unified control of all Soviet nuclear forces under a single national authority is unacceptable if Russia is to have any hope of reunifying the republics in the future under its leadership. *In the absence of any outside restraining factors, the goals of the breakaway republics and the Russian republic, therefore, will ultimately prove to be incompatible and irreconcilable by any means short of armed conflict.* This potential danger explained Gorbachev's apparent willingness to engage in deep strategic cuts in the Soviet nuclear arsenal beyond those stipulated in the new START agreement. His announcement on October 5, 1991 of a substantial unilateral reduction in the Soviet arsenal to approximately 5,000 weapons was aimed more at reducing the nuclear weapons available to the breakaway republics such as Ukraine, Belarus, or Kazakhstan rather than at attaining genuine arms control as the end in itself, since such disarmament will require outside inspection and verification. His move also paralleled President Bush's in that he was proposing to reduce those nuclear forces that are either militarily obsolete or which do not translate directly into political leverage over either the independent republics or the U.S. This desire to reduce the potential leverage value of the republics' nuclear arsenals also explains the recent Soviet reversal on SDI and its desire to participate in expanding strategic defenses.

It is not difficult to see how this will affect Russian military programs for the foreseeable future. The weakness of the republics' economies will not permit the former Soviet defense establishment to pursue the broad range of military technology or to challenge U.S. supremacy across the board in high technology warfare, much as they would like to do so. Instead, the Russian military will "play to strength" by continuing to develop those areas where it has the best chance to obtain selective parity, or even superiority. The development of third-generation nuclear weapons will enable a reduced Russian military to compensate for technological inferiority in other areas. It is similar in some ways of how Khrushchev attempted to substitute nuclear firepower for manpower as the justification for his reduction of the Soviet military in the 1950s and early 1960s. The only difference is that the Russians now are being compelled to follow this course as much out of economic weakness as out of compensation for technological inferiority.[9]

Aside from nuclear weapons, the only other area of comparative Soviet strength is their military exploitation of space. This also comes as no surprise, since the Soviets had stressed the importance of military utilization of space since Sokolovskiy's *Voennaya Strategia* in the early 1960s. This belief was reinforced by the Soviet observations of Operation DESERT STORM, which essentially concluded, among other things, that the Persian Gulf War was confirmation "of the emergence of 'air-space warfare' and 'maneuver by fire' to replace conventional operations," and that "the most central target becomes the opponent's system of C2 (Command and Control)."[10]

More recently, the role of space in Soviet military reform was emphasized by General Major V. Ivanov of the Academy of the General Staff, who said that military reform should

> include the currently existing Strategic Rocket Forces, and units and large units of Military Aviation, the Navy, and *Air and Anti-satellite Defense Forces,* equipped with nuclear weapons and weapon delivery vehicles which are to be consolidated into Nuclear Forces *and also Space Forces, whose units and large units will be provided with systems capable of destroying the enemy's installations from space.*"(Emphasis added.)[11]

The Future of the Independent Republics: Four Scenarios

The situation within the former Soviet Union after its dissolution is being driven by two main factors: the progressively deteriorating economic situation that threatens to kill off the democratic reform movement before it has a chance to take hold in the republics, and the ongoing dispute over decentralized versus unified control of the vast Soviet nuclear arsenal. The ultimate outcome of the interaction between these two forces is likely to be one of four possible scenarios:

Scenario I: Reunified Republics & Economic Recovery

This is the "best case" scenario from the standpoint of both the Commonwealth republics and the rest of the world. It presupposes that the republics are able to resolve the question of nuclear weapons control without fear of sacrificing their own autonomy from Moscow. Moreover, an economic recovery, or at least stabilization, within the republics would go a long way towards preventing the return of authoritarian or extremist regimes and give the peoples of the republics the best chance to establish democratic traditions. It is practically a given that democracies have a difficult time surviving, let alone flourishing, in a situation involving significant external threats and internal economic collapse.

What is the principal concern for the U.S. in this scenario? Certainly not imminent nuclear attack, although strategic defenses for both the U.S. and the reunified republics would still be mandatory to deter the unknown number of emerging Third World nuclear powers that will be on the scene. It appears that the main security problem for the U.S. will be ongoing espionage efforts by individual republics, although this effort has been recognized as focusing more on industrial espionage rather than on gaining strategic or military secrets. As in the past, however, even this latter goal cannot ever be totally discounted.[12] The prospects for arms control and disarmament, on the other hand, should be the best of all possible scenarios, since the political objectives of a stable and prosperous Commonwealth of Independent States with democratic governments would have the least use for a large strategic nuclear arsenal. The new Commonwealth could join the US in progressively paring back such forces to virtually symbolic levels, even while building up or improving their respective strategic defenses to discourage the aforementioned emerging nuclear powers.

The problem with this best case scenario is that virtually everything has to go right in order for it to occur, and "Murphy's Law" still reigns supreme in international affairs as in virtually every other aspect of life. The independent republics, the Ukraine in particular, already have recognized the political leverage value of strategic nuclear weapons as a guarantor of sovereignty from the unwelcome dominance of the Russian republic. And unless the nations of the West are able to act in concert to stabilize the rapidly deteriorating economy within the republics, the stage is being set for yet another coup or series of coups within the various republics by as early as the spring of 1992.

Scenario II: Independent Republics and Economic Recovery

This scenario constitutes the next best case of the four possible scenarios, and is at least somewhat more likely than the admittedly utopian first scenario.

This scenario presupposes that the independent republics are able to gain control of their own nuclear forces (or at least prevent unified control by one authority), and that the Russian republic does not resort to armed force in an effort to seize control of the individual arsenals. The likely makeup of these independent republics will be a mixture of democratic and authoritarian regimes, depending on the cultural proclivities of the individual republics and how well their individual economies fare in the recovery.

Just as inevitable, however, will be the rise of several independent nuclear states of widely varying strengths and technological capability for research and development. Depending on the perceptions of the individual republics concerning the utility of nuclear forces, this will greatly complicate arms control negotiations. For even if the individual republics do not perceive the U.S. as the main threat, they will still wish to maintain, if not improve, their individual nuclear arsenals and conventional forces as their guarantor of sovereignty against a would-be "empire builder" among the republics, the Russian republic being the most obvious candidate. This will lead to a period of the most byzantine "divide and conquer" diplomatic maneuvering in the history of Russia, as the independent republics strive to maintain their sovereignty versus one another by forming alliances with each other as well as with outside powers.

The drawback to this scenario is that it presupposes the absence of armed conflict over the issue of nuclear weapons or control of military forces; that the Russian republic will allow the rise of several independent nuclear states among the republics, which numerous Soviet leaders, Gorbachev included, had said would be an unacceptable development. Historical experience has also shown the general unwillingness of peoples to voluntarily surrender their sovereignty to a central authority if it can be avoided. (The historical experience of the United States from the Revolutionary War through the Civil War is a prime example.) Moreover, the "economic miracle" of a recovering Soviet economy has shown no sign of appearing. As in the first scenario, much depends on what the nations of the West do or fail to do in this area. And one must consider the likelihood that the economies of the republics are already too far gone to avert widespread collapse.

Scenario III: Reunified Republics and Economic Collapse

This is the next-to-worst-case scenario, which assumes that either the Russian republic has been able to reestablish unified control over the breakaway republics, which in turn presupposes that unified control over the entire Soviet nuclear arsenal has been regained. Unfortunately, the economic collapse envisioned in this scenario also heralds the rise of a hostile extremist regime which blames the West in general, and the U.S. in particular, for its economic woes. While such a regime would not mean a return to the Marxist-Leninist revolutionary ethos, neither would it preclude a resurgence in influence and prestige for the former Soviet military and the KGB, who have been convinced all along that the U.S. has been poised to exploit their weakness, just as they themselves would have done if roles were reversed.

The effect of this situation on arms control will be far from salutary; in fact, arms control efforts will all but disappear, since the military hard-liners will reemphasize the strategic and political importance of strategic nuclear weapons. The principal concern for the U.S. will be to avoid as much as possible being stampeded into another costly arms race while safeguarding U.S. security. This will prove a difficult, but somewhat familiar, diplomatic balancing act for the U.S.; so much so that this scenario could be dubbed "Cold War II."

This next-to-worst-case scenario is also the second most likely to occur. Its only problem lies in the fact that a confederation of reunified republics with single control over nuclear weapons is unlikely to occur by totally peaceful means—not with several republics, the Ukraine and Kazakhstan in particular, having already recognized the political leverage and prestige value of independent nuclear forces vis-à-vis each other as well as the West. Reunification during a period of economic collapse is likely to come only as the result of a protracted armed struggle over nuclear weapons control.

Scenario IV: Independent Republics and Economic Collapse

This is the worst-case scenario of the four projected outcomes for the former Soviet republics. This scenario presupposes either that the West fails to provide sufficient economic aid to avert widespread economic collapse, or that the aid provided will prove ineffectual. It also assumes that the Russian republic will be unable to regain full control over the remainder of the Soviet nuclear arsenal now situated within the breakaway republics, and that these republics will be able to more firmly establish their sovereignty as a result.

Under these conditions, democracy is unlikely to survive for long, if at all. The economic deprivation within the republics will foster the rise of a number of extremist regimes, some armed with nuclear weapons, all striving to maintain their independence and expand their influence vis-à-vis one another, and all seeking to get the maximum diplomatic, economic, and military support from outside powers. Of major concern here is the possibility that some of the republics with large Moslem populations such as Kazakhstan, once in firm possession of even a few tactical nuclear weapons, might use those weapons as bargaining chips with other Moslem nations such as Iraq, who could certainly provide the former Soviet Moslem republics with much-needed expertise in nuclear weapons production and development. Worse yet, the exchange could also take place in reverse, as many Soviet nuclear researchers attempt to seek gainful employment outside the former Soviet Union. This will only accelerate the proliferation of nuclear powers.[13]

Again, this is the scenario which is most likely to lead to armed conflict among the former Soviet republics. With the larger number of nuclear powers involved, the pressures and temptations to use these weapons would become extremely difficult for the leadership of any given republic to resist, particularly if it perceives that it is losing its struggle for independence and lashes out in desperation. By the same token, if past Soviet military doctrine and war plans are guide to the probable intentions of the Russian republic in this hypothetical "war of reunification," preemptive nuclear strikes on selected high value military targets (primarily nuclear weapons and their associated delivery systems and storage sites) cannot be ruled out entirely.[14]

The implications for the U.S. are obviously the most profound and dangerous of any possible scenario. Additional arms control agreements in this situation will be not only impossible to negotiate, but irrelevant. And without a credible strategic defense to discourage nuclear coercion by an unknown number of independent nuclear powers, it will be virtually impossible for the U.S. to remain neutral in a conflict that would be in its best interests to avoid.

The Future of U.S. Strategic Doctrine

Given the foregoing, how should the U.S. leadership respond to the challenges posed by a loose Commonwealth of independent republics in possession of a still considerable strategic nuclear force? In formulating such a response, one would do well to reconsider the goals of U.S. grand strategy in an international environment in which it is the only true global superpower, at least for now.

Grand strategy is designed to attain an ultimate long-range objective, toward whose achievement all the energies, resources, and planning of a given nation are directed. A grand strategy states an ideal; it is rare that a nation actually carries out its grand strategy with a single-minded sense of purpose and organization, although some nations have done so more effectively than others. The former Soviet Union's grand strategy could have been characterized best as the establishment of *bezopasnost*; of total safety, for Soviet-directed socialism. Such a total kind of security implied a corresponding lack of security for those nations whose social systems were perceived by the Soviets as unalterably opposed to the establishment of bezopasnost, the United States having been chief offender in this regard. The ideological and economic collapse of Communism resulted in the defeat of the bezopasnost grand strategy of the former Soviet Union. Formulation of a new grand strategy will be subordinated in the near term to the reestablishment of a new union of the republics under the aegis of a single national authority. This likely will be the intermediate goal of the Russian republic under Boris Yeltsin and his successors. The United States, on the other hand, successfully pursued the grand strategy of containment as advocated by George Kennan in the July 1947 issue of *Foreign Affairs*. Containment demonstrated, on the grand strategic level, the truth of Clausewitz' observation that the defense is the inherently stronger form of warfare. By striving to maintain the international status quo, the U.S. did not have to defeat Communism, in Kennan's thinking; all the U.S. had to do was prevent the Soviet Union from achieving thru military aggression or political subversion what it could not achieve through economic superiority or ideological revolution, and Communism inevitably would buckle under the stresses of its own internal contradictions. History has proven Kennan right.

The international situation that has now emerged, however, has rendered the containment strategy obsolete. Moreover, given the growing proliferation of Third World powers with nuclear potential, if not actual capability, and the very real prospect of several former Soviet republics becoming nuclear powers in their own right, U.S. grand strategy is dangerously out of focus.[15] An implied objective of every nation's grand strategy is the preservation of its security and well-being against all foreign threats. The central concern of the U.S. until the collapse of the Soviet Union was the deterrence of strategic nuclear conflict involving direct attack on U.S. territory.

With the potential rise of many smaller nuclear powers, a number of which may have interests hostile to those of the U.S. and the West, it is no longer practical to speak of deterrence in terms of "mutual assured destruction." Countries such as Iraq have demonstrated their willingness to commit seemingly irrational acts of destruction in an effort to attain their objectives. If such powers acquire intercontinental nuclear delivery capability, their political leverage will increase out of all proportion to the damage they can inflict, for the detonation of even one nuclear weapon on U.S. territory would be an unparalleled disaster. Without a strong and active strategic defense to block such attempted strikes, no U.S. government could run the risk of confrontation with one or more such states. And no U.S. government would want to be in the odious position of having to make an example of such a state by imposing a nuclear "Carthaginian peace" in retaliation for a single nuclear strike on U.S. territory.

The arguments of those who favor arms control or disarmament center around the notion that a nuclear war cannot be survived, cannot therefore be won, and should be avoided at all costs. Their supporting arguments are based on the current superiority of the means of nuclear attack over the means of defeating it. In the case of strategic nuclear war with a unified Soviet Union, this argument was quite true. In the emerging situation, it is becoming less so. The proliferation of smaller nuclear powers, while complicating the problem of deterrence in the classic sense, has simplified the problem of strategic defense. It is no longer necessary to block a massive nuclear attack by a unified power; it is instead necessary to prevent a concerted attack by a combination of smaller powers or block the attack of any single "renegade" power that attempts to carry out its nuclear threat. The current thinking of arms control advocates is a classic example of the error of allowing available means to dictate overall strategy, instead of formulating strategy in accordance with a properly understood grand strategic objective. This latter approach aims at acquiring the eventual means to implement the strategy fully. The former Soviet Union had taken this course during the 1950s and 1960s. It first adopted a preemptive strike concept as the best means it then had available for negating as much as possible a U.S. nuclear attack's effectiveness. It then adopted civil defense as another major means, along with extensive antiaircraft defenses and a limited antiballistic missile defense around its main center of government. Soviet military thinkers have never abandoned the concept of strategic defense, even under their concept of reasonable sufficiency. Nor is it unreasonable to expect in the future that individual republics, particularly the Ukraine, will attempt to develop credible strategic defenses for both defense against limited nuclear strikes and as a means for neutralizing the coercive value of the Russian nuclear arsenal.

The U.S. notion of the unwinnability of nuclear war has been dictated by the observation that the *present* means of nuclear attack are superior to those available for defense against it. To say, however, that the attainment of the capability for defeating a nuclear attack and thus rendering it ineffective is technologically impossible is highly presumptuous, to say the least. It is reminiscent of those who claimed at the turn of this century that man would never fly. In considering what course future U.S. strategy ought to take, some reflection on the new realities of the U.S. geopolitical position is in order.

The Geopolitical Reality and Future U.S. Strategy

Mackinder first postulated the notion that control of the "world island" of the continents of Europe, Asia, and Africa was tantamount to world domination. Since many of the world's natural resources are still concentrated in this world island, this makes preventing the domination of the world island by a hostile power or coalition a paramount concern of the United States. This was also a consideration in Mahan's advocacy of global sea power for the United States as an essential element of national security.

For the entire history of the United States until the acquisition of an intercontinental nuclear delivery capability by the Soviet Union in 1957, the United

States was able to rely on the expanses of the two oceans surrounding it as a buffer against foreign powers. So long as powers friendly to the United States controlled the seas surrounding it, the United States could, without fear of interference, mobilize its resources in order to deal with any foreign threat. This situation enabled the United States to be the decisive influence on the outcome of both world wars in this century. But once the Soviet Union had acquired the capability to breach the oceans with its ICBM, sea control as the basis of U.S. security was effectively neutralized. No longer could the United States mobilize its national strength without fear of interference; it now stood as naked to attack and devastation as any other country.

Great Britain was able to preserve its security during the 19th and 20th centuries by pursuing a "balance of power" policy with respect to the continent of Europe, allying against any power or combination of powers that threatened to dominate the continent. As the world's only true global superpower at present, the United States is in an analogous geopolitical position, although on a much larger scale. The United States today is to the world island of Europe, Asia, and Africa what Great Britain was to the continent of Europe during the nineteenth and early twentieth centuries; it is the insular power that bases its security and well-being on the prevention of any hostile power or combination of powers from dominating the world island.[16]

The advent of space travel regrettably has done far more than merely open up new vistas for man's exploration; it has also opened up a new arena for man's conflicts. Although present technology is still far from perfected, it is entirely possible, indeed inevitable, that one nation or a coalition of nations will devise and deploy space-based defenses capable of defeating a nuclear attack however it is launched, whether by bombers, submarine or land-launched ballistic missiles, or even cruise missiles. Given such potential for the nation or coalition that succeeds in establishing such space-based defenses, the implication for the United States is clear; space is simply the modern geopolitical equivalent of the sea. It is just as real an avenue of attack for an enemy's missiles and spacecraft as an undefended shoreline is for an enemy's naval fleets and amphibious landing craft. Therefore, the geopolitical demands imposed by the strategic potential of space-based defenses require that the United States have the capacity to dominate space in the event of a military conflict, and conversely have the ability to deny its use to any prospective opponent or coalition (See Appendix C). Such a requirement is merely the logical modern extension of Mahan's earlier advocacy of sea power with the objective of global sea control as the means of ensuring U.S. security. With such dominance of space, and with the acquisition of credible strategic defenses against intercontinental nuclear attack, the U.S. would then be able to maintain international stability even with greatly reduced standing military forces; it would once again become the insular geopolitical "balancer," relatively secure against physical attack, and able to use its military power, economic resources, and political influence together with its allies to prevent the domination of the world island by any hostile power or coalition of powers. Able to defeat any attempts at nuclear attack against its territory, the United States, and the world as well, would be freed from the inherent insanity of mutual assured destruction, and the United States would be in the best position in its history to preserve the rights of nations to seek freedom and self-determination from the depredations of would-be imperial powers, no matter what their nationality or ideology.

A Foundation for Future U.S. Strategic Doctrine

Any future strategic doctrine for the U.S. ought to be considered within the context of an overall grand strategy. Since containment has become outmoded as an overall concept following the demise of Communism as a revolutionary ideology, one should start with the formulation of the grand strategic objective.

The grand strategic objective of the United States ought to be the creation of an international environment that best promotes the freedom and prosperity of the greatest number of people. This implies the promotion of democracy as the preferred method of government wherever possible, and free market capitalism as the preferred economic mechanism for achieving prosperity within any given nation, although this is not an absolute. The geopolitical manifestation of this objective is the prevention of world island domination by any power or combination of powers hostile to American ideological principles or economic interests.

The main threat to U.S. security in the 1990s and early 21st century will be the attempted nuclear coercion of U.S. policy by an unknown number of independent nuclear powers, both from the fragmented republics of the former Soviet Union as well as the newer Third World members of the nuclear club. These powers should be prevented from forming an effective coalition that could act in concert to employ their combined nuclear forces as instruments of political leverage against the U.S. or the West in general. U.S. strategic doctrine, therefore, should include the following components:

Strategic Defense. This component was also advocated in the first version of this book as the most effective means of deterrence from the Soviet perspective, since it would have neutralized their main perceived means of leverage over U.S. strategic doctrine and foreign policy.[17] In a future world of nuclear proliferation with an unknown number of independent nuclear powers, a strong, active strategic defense will be more vital than ever to the national security of the United States -far more vital, in fact, than the maintenance of large offensive strategic nuclear forces. The potentially decisive impact that BMD will have on the nature of future operational warfare will make both land and space-based defenses against nuclear attack an indispensable component of U.S. strategic doctrine.

Power Projection. With smaller and presumably higher quality military forces than our prospective opponents, it will be necessary for the U.S. to maintain superior capability for rapidly projecting not only military manpower and equipment, but firepower and logistical capability for sustained operations as well. Operation DESERT STORM showed what can be accomplished with a comparatively undisturbed U.S. buildup; we cannot count on this kind of luxury in the future. Therefore, any military force that is required for action in the "world island" or its periphery must be assembled, transported, and sustained as rapidly and efficiently as possible. Superior logistical support capacity also will be indispensable for the U.S., whether acting alone or as part of a coalition.

Phased Arms Control. In a world of nuclear proliferation and a larger number of nuclear powers, arms control will be far more difficult than it has been in the past, but not impossible. The key to arms control in the future will depend on the progressive neutralization of nuclear weapons as instruments of political leverage through the phased buildup of strategic defenses by the larger nuclear powers, including the U.S. By linking the buildup of strategic defenses of the larger nuclear powers to a progressive "builddown" of their remaining offensive nuclear forces, it should become possible to negotiate the formation of a multinational Worldwide Strategic Defense Matrix (WSDM) which can frustrate the attempts of smaller nuclear powers to use their nuclear weapons as instruments of terror or intimidation. WSDM conceivably could act under the aegis of the United Nations as a collective security organization for strategic defense against nuclear attack by a renegade power as well as for discouraging the formation of a coalition of hostile powers. This will prove especially useful in dealing with the various independent Soviet republics, particularly if the Moslem republics attempt to form a nuclear alliance with such nations as Iraq. Simply pursuing arms control as an end in itself will not be enough; nations must be made to recognize their own inherent self-interest in the neutralization of nuclear weapons as instruments of political prestige and leverage before they will willingly agree to get rid of them. The recent U.S. decision in late January 1992 to move away from the 1972 ABM Treaty will pave the way for the creation of a collective strategic defense system modeled after the WSDM.[18]

It has not been our purpose here to raise anew a hue and cry about a prospective CIS threat in the traditional sense; such a threat, if it ever comes about, will not materialize at least until well into the twenty-first century. What we have tried to demonstrate is the fact that the history of the past Soviet perception of U.S. strategy and the factors which influenced it are far from irrelevant in trying to understand the future of the various independent republics and their likely perceptions vis-à-vis each other as well as the U.S. and the West. We believe that these perceptions are vitally important in predicting the likely attitudes and behavior of the separate republics toward nuclear weapons and their political utility. If we understand how this perception has affected past Soviet policies toward us, it will be an indispensable guide in the formulation of future U.S. policy. This ability "to see ourselves as others see us" will, to further paraphrase poet Robert Burns, "from many a blunder free us, and foolish notion."

Notes

1. "World-wide Historic Victory of the Soviet People," *Voennaia Mysl'* 5 (May 1955): 12-13, trans. by J.R. Thomas (Santa Monica, Calif.: RAND, T-110, 1959), 25.
2. J. Dziak, *Soviet Perceptions of Military Power*, 28.
3. J. Collins, *American and Soviet Military Trends Since the Cuban Missile Crisis* (Washington, D.C.: Center for Strategic and International Studies, 1978), 84-85. Even until the very collapse of the Soviet Union itself, however, the Soviet strategic readiness posture generally has been conceded to be weaker than that of the United States, notwithstanding the unilateral cutbacks announced by Gorbachev on October 5, 1991. See R. Jeffrey Smith, "Gorbachev Ends Era of Strategic Equality," *Washington Post*, October 7, 1991, A15.
4. Examples of this Soviet call for attaining a high state of readiness are found in Editorial, "The Tasks of Soviet Military Science in Light of the Decisions of the 24th CPSU Congress," *Voennaia Mysl'* 8 (August 1971), trans. in FBIS, FPD No. 0011/74, February 28, 1974, 6. See also V.D. Sokolovskiy and M. Cherednichenko, "Military Strategy and Its Problems," *Voennaia Mysl'* 10 (October 1968), trans. in FBIS, FPD No. 0084/69, September 4, 1969, 37.
5. This same admission of the importance of the Soviet attainment of strategic parity was made on the American side as well, although its relative importance was downplayed. See J. Newhouse, *Cold Dawn: The Story of SALT* (New York: Holt, Rinehart, & Winston, 1973), 66-102.
6. See Chapter 10 on the role of strategic parity as a critical factor in maintaining strategic stability. See also L. Chernenko, "The Keys From the Nuclear Arsenal," trans. in JPRS-UMA-91-013, May 20, 1991, 41.
7. C. Andrew and O. Gordievsky, *KGB: The Inside Story* (New York: HarperCollins Publishers, 1991), 607.
8. L. Chernenko, "The Keys From the Nuclear Arsenal," 40-41.
9. This observation about the decreased ability of the Soviet economy to produce the defense technologies needed to compete successfully was made by Major General Slipchenko, USSR General Staff Academy, at a March 1991 conference at the U.S. National Defense University. Additional corroboration of this projected trend for Soviet planning concerning the nature of future war is found in M.C. Fitzgerald, "The Soviet Image of Future War: 'Through the Prism of the Persian Gulf,'" *Comparative Strategy* 10 (October-December 1991): 393-435.

10. Quoted from Major General Slipchenko, ibid. Cited in briefing by F.X. Kane & J.R. Howe "Emerging Soviet Views on Future Warfare," August 27, 1991.
11. Cited in Ibid.
12. See G. Lardner, Jr., "Experts Say Soviets Are Still Spying in U.S.; Warsaw Pact Isn't," *Washington Post*, October 30, 1991, A6.
13. Viktor N. Mikhaylov, deputy minister for nuclear power and industry, and Yevgeny Primakov, chief of Soviet foreign intelligence, voiced this worry, and it has already become a major issue of concern for the West. See F. Hiatt, "Third World Woos Soviet Arms Experts," *Washington Post,* November 28, 1991, A61, A66.
14. See report by Lothar Ruehl, "As Late as in 1990 the National People's Army Aimed at Western Germany and the Benelux Countries," trans. in FBIS-WEU-91-109, August 2, 1991, for a description of the Soviet plans for employing preemptive nuclear strikes in the event of a war against NATO as late as June 1990.
15. The potential rise of several former Soviet republic nuclear powers is no longer speculation; it is a real threat. See F. Hiatt, "Soviet Republics See A-Weapons as Bargaining Chips," *Washington Post*, October 24, 1991, A41.
16. Henry Kissinger used a similar argument in *Nuclear Weapons and Foreign Policy* (Garden City, N.Y.: Doubleday & Co., 1958), although he subsequently claimed that it was no longer valid. The theme is explained briefly in S.R. Graubard, *Kissinger: Portrait of a Mind* (New York: W.W. Norton & Co., 1973), 65-66.
17. See J.S. Lockwood, *The Soviet View of US Strategic Doctrine*, 180-2.
18. Smith, "U.S. Moves Away From ABM Treaty," *Washington Post*, January 26, 1992, A1.

Appendix A

Comparison of US/USSR ICBM/SLBM/Bomber Deployments
1960-1991

	United States			Soviet Union		
Year	ICBM	SLBM	Bombers[1]	ICBM	SLBM[2]	Bomber
1960	18	32	1845	35	0	140
1962	294	144	1705	75	0	140
1963	424	224	1218	100	0	140
1964	834	416	1092	200	0	140
1965	854	496	882	270	0	140
1966	904	592	644	300	0	140
1967	1054	656	588	460	0	140
1968	1054	656	560	800	80	140
1969	1054	656	560	1028	196	140
1970	1054	656	550	1299	304	140
1971	1054	656	450	1510	440	140
1972	1054	656	450	1530	560	140
1973	1054	656	450	1527	628	140
1974	1054	656	397	1575	720	140
1975	1054	656	397	1618	784	135
1976	1054	656	387	1527	845	135
1977	1054	656	373	1477	909	135
1978	1054	656	366	1400	1015	135
1979	1054	656	365	1398	1028	156
1980	1054	656	338	1398	1003	156
1981[3]	1052	576	316	1398	989	150
1982	1052	520	316	1398	989	150
1983	1045	568	272	1398	980	143
1984	1037	592	241	1398	981	143
1985	1023	640	241	1398	979	170
1986[4]	1010	640	260	1398	983	160
1987	1000	640	317	1418	967	165
1988[5]	1000	640	337	1386	978	175
1989[6]	1000	608	372	1451	960	195
1990	1000	624	277	1398	930	175
1991	1000	640	277	1388	912	177

1. Early figures include medium bombers based in Western Europe.
2. Only Polaris-type SLBMs (intercontinental range) included.
3. Phaseout of Titan II begins.
4. B-1 bomber operational.
5. MX missile operational.
6. Trident D-5 refit.

Sources: *The Military Balance* (1965-1991); *Statistical Abstract of the United States, 1961-1968*; Bonds, *The US War Machine*, 1978; Bonds, *The Soviet War Machine*, 1976.

Appendix B

Chronology of Major Events Involving Use of Soviet Military Power
1954-1991

MASSIVE RETALIATION

1955   Formation of Warsaw Pact
1956   Soviet suppression of Hungarian Revolution
Threat of military force used in Polish crisis
Soviets threaten Great Britain and France with nuclear weapons during Suez crisis
1957   Development of Soviet ICBM
Military response threatened by Soviets in the event of Turkish attack on Syria
1958   Soviets announce military maneuvers in Transcaucasus and Bulgaria in response to U.S. intervention in Lebanon
1959-61   Demands on Berlin repeated-no other action taken
1957-62   Khrushchev engages in "strategic bluffing" involving Soviet ICBM capability and deployment

FLEXIBLE RESPONSE

1962   Khrushchev attempts to install Soviet IRBMs in Cuba-United States responds with naval quarantine of Cuba
1967-72   Soviets supply North Vietnam by sea and rail—military advisers also sent
Soviet military advisers present in Egypt
Massive resupply effort of Egyptian forces mounted by Soviets after Arab defeat in 1967 Arab-Israeli war
1967-68   Soviet supply effort to Yemen
1968   Soviet intervention in Czechoslovakia

REALISTIC DETERRENCE

1973   Soviets engage in threatening military maneuvers during Yom Kippur War-later resupply Egyptian forces
1972-79   Buildup of Soviet military power in Cuba through shipment of nuclear-capable MIG-23 warplanes and installation of Soviet combat brigade
1975-76   Cuban "proxy army" transported and supplied by Soviets in intervention in Angolan civil war
1977-78   Cuban forces intervene with Soviet support in Ethiopia-Somalia conflict
1978   Soviets supply arms to Vietnam prior to Vietnamese invasion of Kampuchea
1979   Soviet military advisers and Cuban forces train and support South Yemen forces in invasion of North Yemen
1979-82   Soviet troops invade Afghanistan and set up puppet government in unprecedented use of Soviet forces outside Eastern Europe. Soviet advisers withdraw from Egypt
1981-82   Soviets employ military maneuvers in Polish crisis

STRATEGIC DEFENSE INITIATIVE

1985   Gorbachev declares doctrine of "reasonable sufficiency"

1988   Gorbachev announces decision to withdraw Soviet troops from Afghanistan;
            later announces unilateral reduction of 500,000 troops in Soviet armed forces
1989   Shevardnadze announces that the 50,000 troops to be withdrawn from Eastern
            Europe will take their tactical nuclear weapons with them; Soviets complete
            withdrawal from Afghanistan; Gorbachev announces cuts of 14.2 percent
            in defense budget, with even larger cuts slated in procurement and troop
            strength
1989-90   Eastern European regimes overthrow Communist governments in rapid
            succession; Soviet government begins withdrawing its troops from Eastern
            Europe
1991   Dissolution of Warsaw Pact July 1
            Soviet military fails to support coup plotters in overthrow of Gorbachev.
            Republics declare independence; Soviet Union collapses
            Struggle begins for control of Soviet nuclear arsenal by various republics;
            joint control established.
            Soviet military forces sent to suppress secession attempt by Chechen-Ingush
            in Russian republic
            Soviets cut off military aid to Cuba and begin negotiations to withdraw
            its combat brigade.
            Commonwealth of Independent States established on December 31

Sources: Wolfe, Thomas W., *Soviet Power and Europe, 1945-1970*, *U.S. News and
           World Report*, January 14, 1980

           Defense Electronics, January 1982.

           W.C. Green and T. Karasik, *Gorbachev and His Generals: The Reform of
           Soviet Military Doctrine* (Appendix B)
           Washington Post, July-December 1991.

Appendix C

The Impact of Ballistic Missile Defense on Operational Warfare[1]

The performance of the Patriot as an anti-tactical ballistic missile (ATBM) system in the Desert Storm operation of 1991, flawed as it might have been in the eyes of some critics, was nevertheless a major breakthrough in the technology of operational warfare. At the very least, Patriot demonstrated the enormous political value that even an imperfect Ballistic Missile Defense (BMD) can have for imposing restraint on the potential escalation of a regional military conflict. Given the recent collapse of the Soviet Union in 1991 and the rise of a democratic reform movement within the republics, it seems that the prospect of a cataclysmic nuclear confrontation with the former Soviet Union is more distant now than at any time since it first acquired its atomic bomb in 1949.

This is not cause for euphoria, however. The continued proliferation of nuclear weapons technology among Third World nations such as Iraq, India, and Pakistan portends ill for any future military conflict involving these or any other nations which may acquire such technology, particularly if the U.S. should choose to intervene, either alone or as part of a coalition. One of the lessons that a future opponent inevitably will have drawn from Operation Desert Storm is that it is suicide to allow the United States the time and opportunity to build up a logistics base in theater so that its full technological and military superiority can be brought to bear. There will be enormous incentive and temptation for any future Third World opponent to resort to first use of missile-delivered mass destruction weapons on arriving U.S. or coalition forces in theater. To run the risk of retaliation in a bid for quick victory would be preferable to such an opponent rather than accept the certain defeat that would follow the completion of an undisturbed U.S. buildup. Lt. Gen. Charles Horner, commander of U.S. Central Command tactical air forces, had these observations:

> Patriot success also has exposed a hole in the allied arsenal . . . Patriot is a point-defense weapon; areas (defended) in Saudi Arabia are concentrated in a few small clusters. If the allied military targets had been spread out, there wouldn't have been enough Patriots in the world to defend . . . .When very accurate missiles with mass destruction warheads are available to Third World nations, the United States will need a regional, wide-area defense force to duplicate on a grand scale the Patriot's pivotal role in defanging the Scud."[2] (Emphasis added.)

Moreover, there is no guarantee that individual Commonwealth republics might not attempt in the future to develop their own organic capabilities and delivery means for weapons of mass destruction in an effort to increase their individual political prestige and/or leverage vis-à-vis one another or the West. It is in light of these future possibilities that we should examine the impact of BMD technology on future operational warfare in the 21st century if its full potential is realized.

THE STRATEGIC CONTEXT

In spite of the momentous political and economic upheavals in the former Soviet Union, the abortive coup against Gorbachev and the subsequent collapse of the power of the Communist Party demonstrated, if anything, the fragility of the foundation on which Soviet democracy was ostensibly being built. If the defeat of the reactionary forces did not guarantee the future continuance of Gorbachev in power, neither does it guarantee the success of a democratic regime in the new Commonwealth of Independent States, particularly as the economic situation within the former Soviet Union has continued to deteriorate. As one Washington Post editorialist put it, future coup plotters may simply have learned to "shoot first and make announcements later."[3]

Given the continued existence of a relatively powerful Soviet defense establishment with its own interpretation of the requirements for bezopasnost (literally, "without danger"; a more absolute interpretation of security than is generally understood in the West), it is necessary to understand that Soviet strategic doctrine and theory, for virtually the entire period since its formal declaration in the three editions of Sokolovskiy's *Voennaya Strategia*, had been dominated by an obsession with nuclear weapons.[4] Until Gorbachev, the Soviets saw nuclear weapons as not only being a potentially decisive war-winning instrument in the event of a conflict with the West, but also as having enormous political value in exerting restraint on the U.S. and compelling it to change its doctrine and policy in ways favorable to Soviet foreign policy objectives and its use of military power to support them.[5] After Gorbachev's accession to power, Soviet commentators no longer emphasized the nuclear warfighting, war-survival aspects of Soviet military doctrine and publicly eschewed any possibility of attaining victory in a nuclear war. They still implicitly placed a high value on strategic parity, however, as exerting a decisive restraining influence on U.S. policy (at least, arguably, until Operation Desert Storm), and steadfastly resisted any attempts to neutralize the offensive nuclear forces that enabled them to attain such parity. Moreover, the West German discovery in 1990, shortly after reunification and the subsequent seizure of East German/ Soviet war plans and diaries, of an operational war plan based on nuclear first use as early as the second day of a conflict with NATO, cast serious doubt on the so-called "defensive" nature of "reasonable sufficiency."[6]

Indeed, the Soviet obsession with nuclear weapons goes beyond their mere theoretical utility in a nuclear warfighting doctrine or as an instrument of political leverage in foreign policy. To the past Soviet leadership, long dominated by a "siege mentality" and sense of inferiority regarding the West, strategic nuclear parity gave the psyche of the collective Soviet leadership a sense of assurance that it was a nation worthy of respect. Regardless of whether the nuclear arsenals in the various former Soviet republics eventually come under the control of one central authority, as before, or of several republics, it is this long-standing outlook that will ultimately undermine any prospects for real arms control, President Bush's recent unilateral proposals notwithstanding.[7] In terms of the former Soviet Union, it was the possession of strategic nuclear parity that made them a superpower in any respect at all.

On the U.S. side, President Reagan's declaration of the Strategic Defense Initiative on March 23, 1983, signaled the start of "the counterrevolution in military affairs."[8] Reagan intended SDI as a repudiation of the doctrine of mutual assured destruction espoused by Defense Secretary McNamara. But President Reagan went still further in his March 23, 1991 speech, declaring that the ultimate purpose of SDI was to render nuclear weapons "impotent and obsolete." Presumably then, it would be comparatively easy to achieve arms control through obsolescence. In spite of this, although a number of promising technologies have been developed as a result of SDI research, the U.S. still has no deployed strategic defense of any scale against nuclear strikes. In light of the growing likelihood of future military conflicts involving Third World nations possessing primitive nuclear weapons with ballistic missiles of short or intermediate range, President Bush has endorsed the concept of a modified form of the SDI known as GPALS (Global Protection Against Limited Strikes).[9]

The Soviet Perspective

From the Soviet viewpoint then, the declaration of SDI was undoubtedly the fulfillment of a recurring nightmare within the minds of the Soviet leadership. The Soviets had long tended to perceive U.S. doctrine and intentions within the context of a mirror-image mindset, they projected their own concepts and logic regarding the political and military utility of nuclear weapons onto the intentions of U.S. policymakers and planners, fully expecting the U.S. to arrive eventually at a nuclear warfighting doctrine similar to their own. When the U.S. failed to live up to this mirror-imaged expectation, Soviet commentators and analysts concluded that it was the quantitative and qualitative growth of Soviet offensive strategic nuclear forces that had compelled the U.S. to change its strategic doctrine and foreign policy in ways favorable for Soviet objectives.[10] When the Soviets achieved strategic nuclear parity in 1969 (recognized officially by President Nixon), the Soviets regarded this as a major landmark in their international relations, and have done so ever since.

What SDI threatened to do at one stroke was nullify the one factor that gave the Soviet Union political leverage over U.S. foreign policy, the one factor that gave the Soviets (until the early 1980s) relative freedom of action to use their own military power in support of their objectives in the Third World, and what is now the one factor that gives them any semblance of equality in the eyes of the U.S. Small wonder, then, that the Soviet Union mounted the most vigorous *desinformatsiya* campaign of any they had conducted to date in their denunciation of SDI and the alleged threat it presented to strategic and political stability. Indeed, if a deployed SDI system truly managed to live up to an April 1985 KGB estimate that it would eventually be able to block 90 percent of Soviet missiles in a nuclear attack, then from the Soviet standpoint SDI would definitely have destabilized the Soviet strategic position.[11] With the collapse of the Soviet Union and the subsequent formation of the Commonwealth of Independent States, however, this point has become moot.

Much the same could be said for the Soviet perception of Airland Battle doctrine, which is the name given the U.S. Army's operational warfare doctrine as expressed in FM 100-5, and which guided the U.S. Army's operational planning for Operation Desert Storm. The same mirror-imaging tendencies that existed in their view of U.S. strategic doctrine and the SDI were equally prevalent in their view of Airland Battle doctrine. In particular, Soviet analyses of Airland Battle doctrine reflected a preoccupation with preemptive strikes in depth, implying first use of nuclear weapons in an offensive role. Soviet analysts also recognized, however, the critical importance of "reconnaissance-strike complexes"(the Soviet term) and precision guided munitions (PGM) to the success of Airland Battle operations.[12] As Operation Desert Storm demonstrated, the doctrine was not without merit.

How BMD Influences Operational Warfare

The following discussion is based on a theoretical model derived from Hegelian "dialectic reasoning" i.e., the use of logic based on the concept of one idea, or "thesis," giving rise to its dialectic opposite, the "antithesis," and being transformed by this clash of opposites into a new "synthesis," which then becomes the basis for a new thesis, and so on in a theoretically never-ending historical cycle.[13] Using the four Airland Battle concepts of Synchronization, Initiative, Agility, and Depth as the framework, the impact of BMD on each concept is discussed below within the context of a "perfect" BMD. Assuming that an operationally perfect BMD (the antithesis) were to be deployed on the battlefield by one or both sides to block missile-delivered weapons of mass destruction (the thesis), what would be the "practical" effect in terms of each concept (the synthesis)? This discussion is followed by a description of four scenarios that outline the implications of BMD deployment for one or both sides.

Synchronization and the Concept of "Interlocking Shields"

Synchronization on the operational level can be described as an interactive, cooperative, combined-arms effort in which the capabilities of all combat and combat support arms are used to complement each other to produce the maximum combat power on the battlefield at the right moment. In terms of ballistic missile defense against aircraft or missile-delivered mass destruction weapons, this translates into a system of "interlocking shields" consisting of the following elements:

- Air Defense Artillery (against nuclear-capable aircraft).
- Ground-based ATBM Defense (e.g., Advanced Patriot ICW ground-based lasers against cruise missiles and short-range ballistic missiles).
- Air Force (counterair against nuclear-capable aircraft and missiles).
- Space-based Defense (reconnaissance and defense against longer-range missiles).

In a perfectly operating system of interlocking shields, there will be a constant flow of intelligence and targeting information between the adjoining shields in order to ensure that missiles and aircraft not engaged by one shield will be engaged by the next. This is so because even an ideal system will not await passively incoming aircraft or missiles; even the successful penetration of the shields by one or two strikes with mass-destruction weapons will result in the rapid progressive collapse of the entire system of interlocking shields, eventually exposing the entire depth of the battlefield to enemy strikes. As a result, continuous reconnaissance and offensive air operations against opposing missile launch and control facilities will be conducted. The concept of interlocking shields, therefore, represents a fully integrated, active air defense and BMD system engaged in a constant and dynamic process of offensive strikes and defensive intercepts against enemy delivery systems.

Operation Desert Storm demonstrated the validity of the interlocking shield concept, albeit in rudimentary form, since the full potential range of BMD technologies has yet to be fielded. Nevertheless, even such a rudimentary interlocking shield system had enormous political value, both for neutralizing the psychological value of Iraq's missile force as a terror weapon and for preventing the likely escalation of the conflict that would have resulted from Israeli reprisals against Iraq. Such a system will become even more valuable in future conflicts employing smaller U.S. forces.[14]

The Impact of BMD on Initiative

On the AirLand battlefield of today, the side possessing the initiative is able to conduct offensive operations at a time and place of its own choosing, and does not have its course of action being dictated by the opponent. Looking at a hypothetical twenty-first century battlefield in which one or both sides have deployed perfect interlocking shield systems, it becomes apparent that this greatly reduces, if not eliminates, the potential decisiveness of a theater-wide first strike with aircraft and missiles, since the attacker's efforts will initially be blunted by the opponent's shields. The campaign will then become a dynamic struggle by both sides to wrest the operational initiative from one another in order to mount a successful offensive. But unless one side is able to collapse the other's shields quickly and decisively, it will be impossible to mount an offensive operation in theater without significant losses. Ironically enough, even though current disarmament initiatives declare that these weapons are no longer militarily useful, the mass-destruction delivery systems that will have the best chance of not being intercepted under these conditions will be artillery; artillery shells have the shortest "flight time" and the smallest physical signature, and are likely to be the most numerous. Unfortunately, they also will be located closest to the front line relative to all other mass destruction delivery systems, and therefore will be most vulnerable to counterbattery fire. The effect thus will be to create a potential low-yield nuclear "no man's land" in the area between the two opposing forces not covered by the interlocking shields of either side. To employ a somewhat overused metaphor, the effect on initiative will represent a contest of the mass-destruction "sword" versus the BMD "shield"; seizure of the initiative will depend on who can destroy the other's shield first.

Impact of BMD on Agility

Agility, within the context of Airland Battle doctrine, is best defined as the ability to conduct operations more rapidly than the opponent, thus rendering his responses irrelevant. On the contemporary battlefield as illustrated by the Desert Storm campaign, the C3I (Command, Control, Communications, and Intelligence) system played a vital role in assuring a decisive victory for coalition forces.[15] It will become even more so on the hypothetical twenty-first century battlefield. The ability to conduct effective interlocking shield operations under dynamic conditions in which both sides are engaged in efforts to seize the initiative by means of deep missile strikes will be critically dependent on timely intelligence prediction, continuous monitoring of the battlefield to the entire depth of the enemy's defenses, and virtually instantaneous reporting of critical information between each layer of the system. Assuming relative parity in the technological capability of both sides, a future conflict involving opposing interlocking shield systems will be characterized by an effort to collapse the opposing shield system while maintaining the integrity of one's own. This mutual struggle will be waged at an astonishingly rapid pace, even by today's standards, and so will leave virtually no margin for error by either side.

The converse of this dynamic struggle will be waged in the electromagnetic spectrum, whether it is an advanced form of Command, Control, and Communications Countermeasures (C3CM) or Radioelectronic Combat (REC). Since the ability to intercept and destroy enemy missiles will depend on virtually instantaneous passage of critical information between the elements of the shield system, delays of seconds or even fractions of a second caused by disruption of friendly use of the electromagnetic spectrum may result in successful enemy strikes with mass destruction weapons, and thus may lead to the total collapse of the shield system. Just as the ability to operate "within the enemy's decision cycle" is a combat multiplier on contemporary battlefields, it will be an even more decisive factor on the twenty-first century battlefield.

Impact of BMD on Depth

Probably the most radical effect of BMD in its ultimately perfected form will be on the depth of the twenty-first century battlefield. On one hand, while the interlocking shield systems of both sides are still relatively intact, it will not be possible to deliver effective strikes of any kind to the entire depth of the opposing defense, whether with conventional PGMs or weapons of mass destruction. The net effect will be to shorten the linear battlefield to the extent of limiting the area for effective delivery of combat power to either the immediate line of contact between opposing forces or, at most, to the range of massed artillery fire. This will have the potential for creating a World War I-style deadlock on the battlefield for as long as the opposing interlocking shield systems remain unbroken, with the unfortunate result that both sides will suffer unprecedented casualty rates in the no man's land area of the battlefield if an offensive is attempted in this situation. In fact, if the interlocking shield systems remain intact for a prolonged period, the eventual result will be a rapid exhaustion of both sides and a subsequent prolonged stalemate. The issue will then be decided, as in previous world wars, on the basis of superiority of materiel and political resolve of one side over the other.

On the other hand, the converse effect that "perfect" BMD will have on the future battlefield will be to extend the vertical battlefield into space. This will naturally result from the overlapping, dynamic, and continuous conflict between the opposing layers of the interlocking shield systems. In such a conflict, just as the gaining of air superiority provided a major advantage to either side in the two world wars, whichever side is first able to establish firm and undisputed control of earth orbital space will have a decisive advantage in the struggle to collapse the opposing shield system. Because of the speed at which an opposing system will collapse once a decisive breach is made and exploited, reestablishing its integrity will be nearly impossible if the attacking side is able to exploit its advantage decisively with a theater-wide offensive. So it is clear that even the smallest and most temporary tactical advantage provided by technological "breakthroughs" can prove decisive.

In this "dialectical model" in which the thesis of missile-delivered weapons of mass destruction is altered by the antithesis of BMD to produce the synthesis of opposing systems of interlocking shields, the potential effects of BMD on a future battlefield are quite radical. This is particularly true if BMD technology is developed to its full potential. Four scenarios involving the presence or absence of BMD on the battlefield are discussed below.

Scenario I: No BMD

This first scenario requires no imagination or dialectic leaps of faith; it has existed for all of the post-war period prior to the deployment of Patriot in Operation Desert Storm. In situations where neither side has an effective interlocking shield system in place, yet both sides possess mass destruction weapons, a high premium is placed on the successful delivery of a theater-wide preemptive strike with such weapons. The more decisive the political objective pursued by one or both sides, the greater the temptation to preempt. Since both sides are vulnerable to deep missile strikes throughout their entire operational depths (which in some cases will be quite shallow if the attacker has made an amphibious or airborne invasion), seizure of the operational initiative by means of such strikes will largely predetermine the winner.

Insofar as the pre-war period is concerned, however, deterrence under conditions of no BMD on either side would be highly unstable, since deterrence would then depend on the credibility of mutual assured destruction in order to keep such a conflict from breaking out in the first place. If deterrence failed, then the situation would become even more unstable, since there would be the aforementioned strong incentive to preempt with mass-destruction weapons. Since BMD technology is already moving beyond its nascent stages, however, this first scenario will exist only during the period of initial deployment by amphibious or airborne forces into the theater of operations. For obvious reasons, this window of vulnerability must be closed as quickly as possible, and preferably eliminated by ensuring that the upper layers of the interlocking shield system protect the deploying force at all times until additional ATBM-capable forces can be deployed with the ground forces. The only alternative to this is to have ATBM capability organic to the initially deploying forces in theater.

Scenario II: Enemy BMD Superiority

This scenario must be avoided at all costs, for obvious reasons. If the opponent is able to achieve BMD superiority in theater while denying us that same capability, we will be unable to inflict significant damage on the opponent's rear areas. This would negate the effectiveness of Airland Battle doctrine. On the other hand, the opponent will have virtually complete freedom of action to attack the entire depth of our defenses with missile-delivered mass-destruction weapons. If such superiority occurs when our forces have just arrived in theater or are still in the process of building up, this will lead rapidly to the destruction or forced evacuation of our forces.

Under what circumstances could this nightmare scenario occur? Given present U.S. superiority in battlefield high technology, it is hard for one to imagine our forces being caught in such a predicament, especially so soon after Desert Storm. Unfortunately, neither technology nor politics stands still. An enterprising future opponent or coalition of opponents could nullify present U.S. supremacy in selected areas enough that the United States could be taken by surprise if its strategic intelligence is not up to its mission or its leadership becomes complacent. There are enough historical precedents for both occurrences that we ought not to let our recent victory make us smug and think ourselves unbeatable.

Scenario III: U.S./Allied BMD Superiority

This scenario is not too hard to imagine: it was just experienced for the first time in Operation Desert Storm. The mere presence of Patriot as a demonstrably effective ATBM system changed the whole complexion of the campaign by completing a rudimentary interlocking shield system over the Iraqi theater of operations. With his air force grounded and his missile force being intercepted or destroyed on the ground, Saddam Hussein was unable to escalate the conflict as he had hoped by bombarding Israel and thus provoking retaliation. The effectiveness of Airland Battle doctrine was significantly enhanced by the resulting virtually undisturbed buildup.

It is clear that any future operational doctrine adopted by the U.S. Army must take the significance of BMD superiority into account. If both sides have sophisticated interlocking shield systems in place, the suppression of the other side's shields will be the necessary prelude to any theater-wide offensive. With the early attainment of BMD superiority during the initial deployment, U.S.

forces will have the best chance of completing the necessary logistical buildup to bring its full combat power to bear in theater. If the opposing shield system can be suppressed, or at least unable to inflict deep missile and air strikes with mass- destruction weapons, the U.S. will have much the same freedom of action it possessed during Desert Storm, able to defeat numerically superior forces. And as an added bonus, a demonstrably superior battlefield BMD capability will enhance the U.S. prewar deterrence posture, lessening the likelihood of war in the first place.

Scenario IV: BMD Parity

This is certainly not the most desirable scenario, but one that one must eventually expect if an enemy nation or coalition is able to achieve parity in BMD technology. The foregoing discussion has already presaged much of what will occur in this scenario. As stated before, as long as both sides possess an effective interlocking shield system extending over the entire depth of their own defenses, then it will be impossible to mount successful offensives in theater without sustaining unprecedented casualties in the low-yield nuclear no man's land separating the two opposing forces. The development of third-generation nuclear weapons will give a defender a significant advantage over an attacker who has not succeeded in first breaching the defending shield system.[16] Once such a deadlock occurs on the battlefield, a major doctrinal revision will be required.

The appearance of PGMs, in combination with the future development and deployment of third-generation nuclear weapons, also means that there will be a much closer interface between conventional and nuclear weapons than ever before; their use will become virtually interchangeable. Chemical and biological weapons, while they will still be threats to defend against, will be comparatively less effective as defensive medical technology catches up by developing better countermeasures and immunizing serums against these agents. It is the third generation of nuclear weapons that will prove to be the decisive land weapon in this scenario; as long as the standoff between the interlocking shield systems continues, these weapons will be used in ever greater numbers in conjunction with PGMs in an effort to achieve a decisive breakthrough. The result will then be something that neither side wanted or anticipated: high-intensity battles with low-yield nuclear and other mass-destruction weapons.

What of deterrence in a scenario like this? One has to conclude that its effects on deterrence will be mixed. On one hand, BMD parity would seem to enhance pre-war deterrence by introducing greater uncertainty into the planning of a potential attacker. The greater the uncertainty, the less likely an opponent will be to attack at all. On the other hand, opponents might become emboldened, especially if acting as part of a coalition, to gamble on achieving quick victory if their relative level of BMD and space technology gave them parity with us. Then, too, they might simply miscalculate, which has caused more than one war in the past. Pre-war deterrence in this scenario may well hinge on which side has the apparent capability to dominate earth orbital space, for it is this layer that absolutely must be controlled if an interlocking shield system is to be maintained or reconstituted.

Conclusions

This dialectical model has shown the effects BMD technology might have on a future battlefield if developed to its full potential. This model assumed a perfect BMD, which is widely recognized as not currently feasible. But the more BMD technology continues to progress, the closer it will come to the conditions described in the model.

BMD is, in fact, the counterrevolution in military affairs—the antithesis to missile-delivered nuclear weapons, which had been described by the Soviets in the late 1950s as heralding the "revolution in military affairs."[17] The introduction and successful employment of Patriot in Operation Desert Storm demonstrated that BMD can have a significant effect on the course and outcome of a conflict. By blunting the effectiveness of ballistic missiles as a battlefield threat or as a potential instrument of terrorism, BMD has increased the importance of conventional forces and maintained the utility of the ability of the United States to project military power to any part of the world. As BMD technology continues to progress under the aegis of GPALS (if not a full-scale SDI), it will also strengthen the U.S. pre-war deterrence posture versus those prospective opponents that might possess missile-delivered mass destruction weapons, nuclear or otherwise.

This dialectical model has also shown that BMD will have its most radical effect on the depth of the future battlefield, making space the decisive arena if both sides possess sophisticated interlocking shield systems with which to blunt each other's air and missile strikes. The employment of nuclear weapons will also be drastically affected, necessitating lower yields and shorter ranges if employed along the line of contact between opposing forces not covered by interlocking shields. But if the standoff between opposing shield systems continues for a prolonged period, battlefield deadlock will ensue. The prerequisite for a successful theater offensive will then be the suppression or destruction of the opposing shield system while maintaining the integrity of one's own. If an offensive is attempted without this suppression, the result will be a high-intensity duel along the line of contact with low-yield nuclear and other mass-destruction weapons, with correspondingly high casualties.

In order to prevent U.S. forces from being trapped in this kind of nuclear cauldron, it will be necessary to revise doctrine, force structure, and tactics before it becomes apparent that an opponent or coalition has achieved BMD parity. One can expect that as the pace of technological change continues to accelerate, doctrine and tactics will become obsolete more often. This, in turn, will increase the potential for one side to achieve operational surprise over the other in a future war by introducing some unanticipated technological breakthrough on the battlefield. To prevent this, the U.S. must make every effort to develop and refine its current joint and space operations doctrine as well as BMD technology so that it maintains undisputed superiority in this area. In a future world of nuclear proliferation and ever-changing political alliances, BMD will be the decisive edge for the United States and its allies.

Notes

1. This is an updated version of the original briefing entitled, "The Impact of SDI on Airland Battle," presented to HQ US Army Europe staff as an Officer Professional Development presentation on 16 February, 1988, in Heidelberg, Germany.
2. Cited in H. Cooper, "The Changing Face of SDI," *Defense 91*, May-June 1991, p. 4.
3. Jim Hoagland, "Another Round in a Long Struggle," Washington Post, 22 August, 1991, p. A23
4. For a comparison of the three editions of *Voennaia Strategia* in translation, see H.F. Scott's translation of V.D. Sokolovskiy, *Soviet Military Strategy* (New York: Crane, Russak, & Co., 1968).
5. Lockwood, *Soviet View of US Strategic Doctrine*, 1983.
6. Aeppel, "East German Papers Yield War Scenario," 13. See also Ruehl, "People's Army Aimed at Western Germany," trans. in FBIS-WEU-91-149, August 2, 1991, 4-6.
7. A. Devroy and R.J. Smith. "President Orders Sweeping Reductions in Strategic and Tactical Nuclear Arms," *Washington Post*, September 28, 1991, A23.
8. This phrase is a play on a Soviet phrase first employed in the late 1950s in the General Staff journal *Voennaya Mysl'* and later used in the title of a book in the Officers Library series, *Scientific-Technical Progress and the Revolution in Military Affairs*. The phrase was meant at first to denote the new state of affairs in operational warfare because of the development of nuclear weapons, particularly missile-delivered. According to this earlier view, nuclear weapons were seen as having the potential to achieve decisive results by themselves, eliminating the need to mass forces in a relatively small area in order to achieve decisive superiority on a chosen sector of the enemy front.
9. For a detailed exposition of this new program and its official rationale, see Cooper, "The Changing Face of SDI," 2-9.
10. See Lockwood, *The Soviet View of US Strategic Doctrine*, 171-6.
11. Andrew and Gordievsky, *KGB: The Inside Story*, 607.
12. A typical example of this type of Soviet analysis is found in Col A.A. Zhuravlev, "On the Air-Land Operation," *Voennaya Mysl'* 7 (July 1990), trans. in JPRS UMT-90-007-L, September 21, 1990, 78-80.

13. The process of dialectic reasoning is borrowed from Hegel; Hegel's notion of the dialectic, however, was supposed to be a progression of all mankind towards the state of "Absolute Spirit," which is fine if your aim is utopian philosophizing. A more practical use of dialectic reasoning as applied to military theory is found in Colonel A.A. Sidorenko's *The Offensive* (trans. under the auspices of the U.S. Air Force, (Washington, D.C.: Superintendent of Documents, 1973).

14. The value of BMD for future conflicts is already being recognized by contemporary experts. For an example, see James Blackwell, *Thunder In The Desert: The Strategy and Tactics of the Persian Gulf War* (New York: Bantam Books, 1991), 224-5.

15. The conflict also demonstrated, however, that there is still considerable room for improvement in C3I. See Blackwell, *Thunder In The Desert*, 228-9.

16. The Soviets, true to their emphasis on the decisiveness of the nuclear weapon, have been working on third-generation nuclear weapons themselves. See L. Chernenko, "Keys From the Nuclear Arsenal," interview with Professor Viktor Nikitovich Mikhaylov, Deputy Minister of Nuclear Energy and Industry, cited in JPRS-UMA-91-013, May 20, 1991, 39-40.

17. See Colonel-General N.A. Lomov, *Scientific-Technical Progress*, 40-64.

SELECTED BIBLIOGRAPHY

The following is a list of Soviet books from the Officer's Library series translated by the U.S. Air Force, along with Joint Publications Research Service (JPRS) and Foreign Broadcast Information Service (FBIS) translations of *SShA: Economika, Politika, Ideologia* and *Voennaia Mysl'*, respectively. JPRS translations of any Soviet books are also listed. With few exceptions, most periodicals and books will be referred to by their Russian titles.

Arbatov, G.A. "American Foreign Policy at the Threshold of the 1970's." *SShA: Economika, Politika, Ideologia* 1(January 1970). Trans. JPRS No. 49934, February 26, 1970: 13-26.

Davydov, Yu. *Doktrina Niksona*. Moscow: Izdatelstvo Nauka, 1972. Trans. JPRS No. 58317, February 26, 1973.

Dzhelaukhov, Kh. "The Evolution of US Military Doctrine." *Voennaia Mysl'* 9 (September 1967). Trans. FBIS, FPD No. 0132/68, September 5, 1968: 93-98.

Editorial. "On Guard for Peace and the Building of Socialism." *Voennaia Mysl'* 12(December 1971). Trans. FBIS, FPD No. 0003/74, January 17, 1974: 1-19.

_____. "The Party of Lenin: The Fighting Vanguard." *Voennaia Mysl'* 3(March 1971). Trans. FBIS, FPD No. 0020/74, March 29, 1974: 1-14.

_____. "The Tasks of Soviet Military Science in Light of the Decisions of the 24th CPSU Congress." *Voennaia Mysl'* 8(August 1971). Trans. FBIS, FPD No. 0011/74, February 28, 1974.

Ivanov, S. "Soviet Military Doctrine and Strategy." *Voennaia Mysl'* 5(May 1969). Trans. FBIS, FPD No. 0116/69, December 18, 1969: 40-51.

Kalachev, N. "Attack without the Employment of Nuclear Weapons." *Voennaia Mysl'* 2(February 1973). Trans. FBIS, FPD No. 0045/73, November 20, 1973: 93-101.

Kruchinin, V. "Contemporary Strategic Theory on the Goals and Missions of Armed Conflict." *Voennaia Mysl'* 10(October 1963). Trans. FBIS, FPD No. 965, July 20, 1966: 13-25.

Krylov, N. "The Nuclear-Missile Shield of the Soviet State." *Voennaia Mysl'* 11(November 1967). Trans. FBIS, FPD No. 0157/68, November 18, 1968: 13-21.

Kvitnitskiy, A., and Ym. Nepodayev. "The Theory of the Escalation of War." *Voennaia Mysl'* 9(September 1965). Trans. FBIS, FPD No. 952, March 2, 1966: 14-27.

Larionov, V.V. "The Transformation of the 'Strategic Sufficiency' Concept." *SShA: Economika, Politika, Ideologia* 11(November 1971). Trans. JPRS No. 54676, December 10, 1971: 33-44.

Lomov, N.A., ed. *Scientific-Technical Progress and the Revolution in Military Affairs.* Moscow: Voennoe Izdatelstvo, 1973. Trans. and published U.S. Air Force. Washington, D.C.: U.S. Government Printing Office, 1973.

Lukonin, S., and A. Migolat'yev. "The 24th CPSU Congress on Current Problems in the Building of Communism and the Strengthening of the Defensive Might of the USSR." *Voennaia Mysl'* 5(May 1971). Trans. FBIS, FPD No. 0016/74, March 18, 1974: 1-24.

Mal'yanchikov, S. "On the Nature of Armed Struggle in Local Wars." *Voennaia Mysl'* 11(November 1965). Trans. FBIS, FPD No. 953, March 8, 1966: 12-24.

Marxism-Leninism on War and Army. Moscow: Progress, 1972. Trans. and published U.S. Air Force. Washington, D.C.: U.S. Government Printing Office, 1972.

Milovidov, A.S., and V.G. Kozlov, eds. *The Philosophical Heritage of V.I. Lenin and Problems of Contemporary War.* Moscow: Voennoe Izdatelstvo, 1972. Trans. and published U.S. Air Force. Washington, D.C.: U.S. Government Printing Office, 1972.

Mil'shtein, M., and L.S. Semeyko. "The Problem of the Inadmissibility of a Nuclear Conflict (On New Approaches in the United States)." *SShA: Economika, Politika, Ideologia* 11(November 1974). Trans. JPRS No. 63625, December 10, 1974: 1-12.

Perifilov, V. "Limited Warfare in U.S. Foreign Policy." *Voennaia Mysl'* 4(April 1971). Trans. FBIS, FPD No. 0019/74, March 25, 1974: 105-120.

Petrovskyiy, V.F. "The Evolution of the 'National Security' Doctrine." *SShA: Economika, Politika, Ideologia* 11(November 1978). Trans. FBIS, *USSR Daily Report Annex*, November 17, 1978: 2-13.

Samorukov, B. "Combat Operations Involving Conventional Means of Destruction." *Voennaia Mysl'* 8(August 1967). Trans. FBIS, FPD No. 0125/68, August 26, 1968: 29-41.

Selected Soviet Military Writings, 1970-1975. Trans. and published U.S. Air Force. Washington, D.C.: U.S. Government Printing Office, 1977.

Semenov, G., and V. Prokhorov. "Scientific-Technical Progress and Some Questions of Strategy." *Voennaia Mysl'* 2(February 1969). Trans. FBIS, FPD No. 0060/69, June 18, 1969: 23-32.

Sevast'yanov, K., N. Vasendin, and N. V'yunenko. "Comments on the Article 'Augmenting Strategic Efforts in Modern Armed Conflict.'" *Voennaia Mysl'* 9(September 1964). Trans. FBIS, FPD No. 896, March 2, 1965: 34-43.

Sokolovskiy, V.D., and Cherednichenko, M. "Military Strategy and Its Problems." *Voennaia Mysl'* 10(October 1968). Trans. FBIS, FPD No. 0084/69, September 4, 1969: 32-43.

Stepanov, K., and Ye. Rybkin. "The Nature and Types of Wars of the Modern Era." *Voennaia Mysl'* 2(February 1968). Trans. FBIS, FPD No. 0042/69, April 25, 1969: 68-80.

Tolstikov, O. "Civil Defense in Nuclear-Rocket War." *Voennaia Mysl'* 1(January 1964). Trans. FBIS, FPD No. 939, August 4, 1965: 28-37.

Trofimenko, G.A. *SShA: Economika, Politika, Ideologia* 12(December 1971). Trans. JPRS No. 54971, January 19, 1972: 1-15.

_____. "Some Aspects of U.S. Military and Political Strategy." *SShA: Economika, Politika, Ideologia* 10(October 1970). Trans. JPRS No. 51895, December 1, 1970: 14-31.

Vasendin, N., and N. Kuznetsov. "Modern Warfare and Surprise Attack." *Voennaia Mysl'* 6(June 1968). Trans. FBIS, FPD No. 0005/69, January 16, 1969: 42-48.

Yermakov, S. "Counterinsurgency Plans in the System of Military Plans of Imperialism." *Voennaia Mysl'* 5(May 1968). Trans. FBIS, FPD No. 0013/69, February 4, 1969: 60-68.

Primary Soviet Sources

The following primary Soviet sources are grouped by periodicals. The periodicals *Soviet Military Review, International Affairs*, and *New Times*, having been translated into English by the Soviets themselves, are listed by their English titles. A list of Soviet books used appears at the end of the bibliography.

International Affairs

Abarenkov, V. "SDI: A Course Towards Intensified Militarisation." 7(July 1987): 52-59.

AAAndreyev, O., and Lvov, L. "The Arms Drive Strategy Cannot Win." 11(November 1960): 62-67.

Baryshev, A. "New US Doctrines, Same Old Aims." 12(December 1969): 12-16.

Baturin, M. "Peace and the Status Quo." 1(January 1958): 71-76.

Beletsky, V. "What Lies Behind the European Defense Initiative Project." 6(June 1989): 49-55.

Chernyshov, M. "Star Peace vs. Star Wars." 9(September 1986): 53-59.

Dadyants, G. "Cold War: Past and Present." 6(June 1960): 5-10.

Dmitrichev, T. "Today's Realities and the Nuclear Deterrence Doctrine." 10(October 1986): 56-63.

Fyodorov, L. "International Relations and the Battle of Ideologies." 3(March 1960): 7-16.

Gerasimov, G. "The First Strike Theory." 3(March 1965): 39-45.

———. "Pentagonia, 1966." 5(May 1966): 24-30.

Glagolev, I., and V. Larionov. "Soviet Defence Might and Peaceful Coexistence." 11(November 1963): 27-33.

Gromov, L., and V. Strigachov. "The Arms Race: Dangers and Consequences." 12(December 1960): 14-18.

Gromyko, Anat., and A. Kokoshin. "US Foreign Policy Strategy for the 1970s." 10(October 1973): 67-73.

Kamenev, V. "The Big Lie About 'Small' Atomic Wars." 9(September 1956): 61-70.

Katasonov, Y. "Military and Political Strategy of the USA Today." 11(November 1983): 75-82.

Konenenko, A. "U.S. Military Doctrines." 9(September 1956): 61-70.

———. "Present-day U.S. Military Thinking and the Arms Drive." 3(March 1958): 31-35.

Konovalov, Y. "The Tentacles of 'Bases Strategy'." 7(July 1963): 47-52.

Kortunov, V. "Arms Race Policy Historically Doomed." 10(October 1976): 3-13.

———. "Imperialist Power Politics and the Realities of the Present-Day World." 6(June 1986): 31-40.

Korionov, V. "The Crisis of the 'Positions of Strength' Policy." 3(March 1958): 31-35.

Kozyrev, A. "For Peaceful Outer Space." 5(May 1985): 122-9. Kuzmin, V. "The Guam Doctrine: Old Objectives, New Techniques." 12(December 1971): 32-37.

Larionov, V. "The Doctrine of 'Flexible' Aggression." 7(July 1963): 46-51.

Lebedev, Yu. "Military and Strategic Parity and the Realities of the Nuclear and Space Age." 7(July 1986): 23-28.

Lebedev, Yu., and A.I. Podberezkin. "SDI-A New Stage of the Arms Race." 2(February 1987): 60-67.

Lobov, V. "The ABM Treaty: Apprehensions and Hopes." 10(October 1987): 20-26.

Matveyev, V. "Washington's 'New' Doctrines." 4(April 1971): 25-31.

Melnikov, Y. "U.S. Foreign Policy: A Threat to Peace." 1(January 1967): 64-70.

Menshikov, S. "What is Behind the Star Wars Debate." 6(June 1985): 67-77.

Migolatyev, A. "The Military-Industrial Complex and the Arms Race." 11(November 1975): 63-71.

Mil'shtein, M. "A Dangerous Anachronism." 2(February 1960): 26-30.

Oleshchuk, Y. "'Small Wars' and the Aggression in Viet-Nam." 5(May 1966): 35-39.

Ovinnikov, R. "Star Wars Programme: A New Phase in Washington's Militaristic Policy." 8(August 1985): 13-22.

Pechorkin, V. "The Theory and Practice of Counter-Guerrilla Warfare." 10(October 1963): 26-31.

———. "About 'Acceptable' War." 3(March 1963): 20-25.

———. "Crisis of Imperialism's Military Doctrines." 7(July 1962): 32-37.

Platonov, A. "Militarization of Outer Space: A Threat to Mankind." 2(February 1985): 28-36.

———. "Towards the Geneva Talks." 4(April 1985): 17-25.

Proektor, D. "Military Detente: Primary Task." 6(June 1976): 35-43.

Prokopyev, N. "Problems of War and Peace in Our Age." 12(December 1967): 57-62.

Rubinstein, M. "U.S. Bases: An Instrument in the Struggle for World Domination." 3(March 1955): 71-82.

Sanakoyev, S. "Peaceful Coexistence in the Context of Military-Strategic Parity." 2(February 1988): 75-85.

Semyonov, V., and B. Surikov. "The ABM Treaty: Barrier to Star Wars." 8(August 1987): 19-26.

Shashkov, Y. "Space Shield: Myths and Reality." 3(March 1987): 22-29.

Slobodenko, A. "The US Military Doctrine: Reliance on Force." 9(September 1987): 38-46.

Somov, M. ""Star Peace, Not Star Wars." 3(March 1986): 54-62.

Sosnovsky, L. "Strategy of U.S. Neocolonial Wars." 10(October 1971):34-38.

Sovetov, A. "Complete Elimination of Nuclear Weapons- The Soviet Programme." 4(April 1986): 12-22.

———. "27th Congress of the CPSU on Imperialism's Aggressive Policy." 8(August 1986): 3-15.

Talensky, N. "Atomic and Conventional Arms." 1(January 1955): 23-29.

———. "The Military Aspect of Co-existence." 7(July 1960): 64-66.

———. "On the Character of Modern Warfare." 10(October 1960): 23-27.

———. "The Late War: Some Reflections." 5(May 1965): 12-18.

———. "'Preventive War': Nuclear Suicide." 9(September 1962): 10-16.

———. "The 'Absolute Weapon' and the Problem of Security." 4(April 1962): 22-27.

_____. "Prevention of a Surprise Attack." 8(August 1958): 53-55.

_____. "Military Strategy and Foreign Policy." 3(March 1958): 26-30.

Teplinsky, B. "The Strategic Concepts of U.S. Aggressive Policy." 12(December 1960): 36-41.

_____. "Some Aspects of US Global Strategy." 5(May 1970): 70-75.

_____. "U.S. 'Grand Strategy.'" 2(February 1964): 24-29.

_____. "U.S. Military Programme." 8(August 1967): 46-51.

_____. "Military Bases and American Strategic Doctrine." 9(September 1959): 79-85.

Tomilin, Y. "To Avert the Threat of Militarizing Outer Space." 6(June 1984): 61-67.

Trofimenko, G. "Anti-Communism and Imperialism's Foreign Policy." 1(January 1971): 49-54.

_____. "From Confrontation to Coexistence." 10(October 1975): 33-41.

Vasilyev, V. "The U.S.A. Thwarts Solution of Surprise Attack Problem." 2(February 1959): 56-60.

Vronsky, B. "An 'Agonizing Reappraisal' of Dulles Legacy." 4(April 1960): 50-56.

Yazov, D. "The Military Balance of Strength and Nuclear Missile Parity." 4(April 1988): 15-22.

Yeremenko, A. "The Strategic and Political Value of Military Bases." 11(November 1960): 57-61.

Yermashov, I. "The Crisis of American 'Atomic Age Strategy'." 1(January 1960): 48-56.

_____. "The Doctrine of 'Acceptable War': Illusions and Reality." 11(November 1960): 15-21.

Yudin, Y. "A Chain of Miscalculations." 7(July 1957): 34-45.

Zhilin, P., and Y. Rybkin. "Militarism and Contemporary International Relations." 10(October 1973): 23-29.

Kommunist Vooruzhennykh Sil (Communist of the Armed Forces)

Bochkarev, K. "On the Character and Types of Wars of the Contemporary Epoch." 11(June 1965): 8-17.

Fedulayev, Ye. "Strategy of Reckless Adventurism." 16(August 1962): 83-87.

Glazov, V. "Concerning Some Peculiarities of Conducting Military Operations in a Nuclear War." 3(February 1964): 41-46.

Khvatkov, G. "Problems of War and Peace and the Revolutionary Process." 1(January 1970): 28-35.

Klimov, D. "Threat to Strategic Stability." 23(December 1988): 81-85.

Kondratkov, T. "Limited War: Instrument of Imperialist Aggression." 8(April 1969): 24-31.

Konstantinov, S. "The Military Doctrines of American Imperialism." 23(December 1962): 78-85.

Korzun, L. "Strategy of Aggression." 3(February 1967): 90-92.

Kovalevski, N., and G. Korotkov. "Star Wars Without Screens." 17(September 1986): 84-88.

Levin, V. "The Europe of Our Days and NATO." 19(October 1975): 77-82.

Lipkin, R., and V. Tsema. "The Nuclear Forces of American Imperialism." 20(October 1970): 82-85.

Lomov, N. "On Soviet Military Doctrine." 10(May 1962): 11-21.

————. "The Influence of Soviet Military Doctrine of the Development of Military Art." 21(November 1965): 15-24.

Lukava, G. "The Factor of Security in the Aggressive Policy of Imperialism." 11(June 1986): 23-29.

Malyanchikov, S. "The Character and Peculiarities of a Nuclear-Rocket War." 21(November 1965): 70-74.

Migolat'yev, A. "The Aggressive Essence of the Military-Political Strategy of American Imperialism." 10(May 1971): 78-84.

Palevich, D., and I. Poznyak. "The Peculiarities and Character of a World Nuclear-Rocket War." 20(October 1964): 77-82.

Ponomarev, N. "Crisis of Bourgeois Theories of War and Peace." 16(August 1964): 9-17.

————. "The Changing Relationship of Forces in the World and the Crisis of the Military Doctrines of Imperialism." 14(July 1971): 13-20.

————. "Adventurism of Military-Political Concepts of Imperialism." 1(January 1966): 42-48.

Roshchupkin, V. "Reykyavik and the Orbits of Star Wars." 23 (December 1986): 84-88.

Rybkin, E. "On the Essence of a World Nuclear-Rocket War." 17 (September 1965): 50-56.

Sablukov, A. "Imperialist Aggressors: The Bitterest Enemies of Peace, Democracy, and Socialism." 9(May 1965): 75-83.

Shmuratov, V. "Doctrines of Aggression and Piracy." 15(August 1965): 75-80.

Volkov, N. "Imperialism: Enemy of the Peoples and of Social Progress." 13(July 1975): 68-76.

Yesikov, G. "The Most Burning Problem of the Present." 7(April 1962): 60-68.

Mirovaia Ekonomika i Mezhdunarodnaye Otnoshenia (MEMO)
(World Economy and International Relations)

Arbatov, A. "Preserving Reductions of Strategic Armaments." 4 (April 1988): 10-22.

Bogdanov, O. "Nuclear Weapons and the Problem of World Security." 8(August 1958): 3-15.

Bykov, O. "Concerning Some Features of the Foreign Policy Strategy of the USA." 4(April 1971): 53-64.

Chernov, I., and Iu. Yudin. "The Insolvent Policy of Military Blocs (Concerning the Tenth Anniversary of the North Atlantic Alliance)." 4(April 1959): 68-80.

Dikin, L. "Problems of USA Military Policy and Strategy in the Reports of the Rockefeller and Gaither Committees." 7(July 1958): 94-101.

Inozemtsev, N. "'Atomic Diplomacy' of the USA: Plans and Activities." 3(March 1958): 29-43.

Kirshin, Yu. "Policy and Military Strategy in the Nuclear Age." 11(November 1988): 35-45.

Konenenko, A. "'Local Wars' in the Policy and Strategy of the USA." 10(October 1958): 16-25.

Larionov, V. "The Development of the Armed Means and strategic Concepts of the USA." 6(June 1966): 74-81.

Lyubimov, L. "New Thinking and Soviet-American Relations." 3 (March 1988):3-14.

Mil'shtein, M. "Concerning Certain Military-Strategic Concepts of American Imperialism." 8(August 1962): 85-95.

————. "American Military Doctrine: Continuity and Modifications." 8(August 1971): 30-41.

————, and Slobodenko, A. "The Aggressive and Adventuristic Character of the Strategic Concepts of the USA." 3(March 1957): 76-89.

————. "Problems of the Correlation of Policy and War in Contemporary Imperialist Ideology." 9(September 1958): 58-73.

Sadreyev, R., and S. Rodionov. "Concerning the Question About Strategic and Economic Developments of SDI." 5(May 1986): 15-20.

Tolkunov, L. "Nuclear Disarmament - Demand of the Times." 12 (December 1987): 3-11.

Tomilin, Yu. "Space: Confrontation or Cooperation?" 9 (September 1987): 3-11.

New Times

Dashichev, Vyacheslav. "Theory and Practice of 'Little Wars.'" 37(October 1957): 7-10.

Fyodorov, Mikhail. "New Message, Old Doctrines." 10(March 1971): 8-9.

Glazov, V. "The New 'Local War' Conceptions." 48(November 1964): 6-8.

Golikov, F.I. "Who is Advocating 'Preventive' War and Why." 17 (April 1958): 5-6.

Iordansky, V. "Atomic Blackmail: A Futile Weapon." 19(May 1955): 12-15.

Isayev, F. "The 'Small Atomic Weapons' Myth." 13(March 1955): 7-10.

————. "Fallacies of the Policy of Strength." 10(March 1955): 4-9.

Krementsov, M. "The U.S. Atomic Business." 22(May 1954): 7-10.

Krementsov, M., and G. Starko. "Military Bases in Foreign Territories." 21(May 1955): 18-21.

Mil'shtein, M. "Bases and Security." 6(February 1958): 6-7.

Mil'shtein, M., and A. Slobodenko. "'Limited War': Weapons of Unlimited Aggression." 40(October 1958): 13-15.

Rovinsky, L. "The Rocket and Peace." 37(September 1957): 14-16.

Rubinstein, M. "The Atom Business: Calculations and Miscalculations." 25(June 1954): 16-20.

Simonyan, R. "'Realistic Deterrence': The Real Implications." 10(March 1977): 18-20.

————. "The Pentagon's Nuclear Strategy." 35(September 1977): 22-24.

Starko, G. "Crisis of America's 'Peripheral Strategy'." 33 (August 1960): 19-22.

Teplinsky, B. "Polaris and U.S. Strategy." 8(February 1963): 6-9.

Zorin, Valentin. "The Three McNamara Doctrines." 3(January 1963): 12-14.

Soviet Military Review

Arbatov, G. "Strength-Policy Impasses." 1(January 1975): 46-48.

Glazov, V. "Strategic Concept of the Aggressors (Substance and Content of the Theory of Escalation." 4(April 1967): 47-50.

————. "The Evolution of U.S. Military Doctrine." 11 (November 1965): 56-57.

Khomenko, E. "Wars: Their Character and Type." 9(September 1965): 7-9.

Kondratkov, T. "What is a 'Limited War'?" 8(August 1973): 48-49.

Kulikov, N. "On Just and Unjust Wars." 3(March 1977): 8-10.

Matsulenko, V. "The 'Small War' Theory at the Service of the Imperialists." 4(April 1966): 53-55.

Mochalov, V. "What Lies Behind the Theory of 'Limited' Wars?" 8(August 1969): 54-56.

————. "Concerning the 'Theory of Limited Wars.'" 2 (February 1965): 40-42.
Redko, Y. "Anti-Guerrilla Doctrines." 3(March 1965): 54-55.
Sergeyev, P., and V. Trusenkov. "Evolution of the US Military Doctrine." 11(November 1976): 52-54.
Simonyan, R. "Doctrine of the American Aggressors." 1 (January 1969): 50-52.
Sokolovskii, V.D. "On the Soviet Military Doctrine." 4 (April 1965): 6-9.
Zavyalov, V. "Flexible Response Strategy: Theory and Practice." 5(May 1965): 36-38.

Vestnik Protivovozdushnoi Oborony (Herald of Antiaircraft Defense)
Klimovich, E. "Air Defense Missile Systems at Medium and High Altitudes," 1(January 1985): 88-90.

Voennaya Mysl' (Military Thought)
Andreyev, V.F. "Military-Strategic Parity - An Objective Factor for Restraining Aggressive Forces." 2(February 1989): 45-53.
Andreyev, V.G., and S.V. Skorokhodov. "Nuclear Weapons of the Third Generation in the American Plans of Star Wars." 9 (September 1986): 73-79.
Chervov, N.F. "Disarmament: Who is Against It?" 12(December 1983): 3-15.
Editorial "Star Wars: Illusions and Dangers." 9(September 1985): 15-28.
Khorkov, A.G. "About the Question of the Threatening Period." 3(March 1986): 18-25.
Kokoshin, A.A., and M.I. Gerasov. "American Plans for the Militarization of Space." 4(April 1987): 69-80.
Kozlov, M.M. "Preservation of Military-Strategic Parity -Serious Factor for Preserving Peace and International Security." 12(December 1986): 3-13.
Lebedev, Yu. V., and A.I. Podberezkin. "Imperial Ambitions of Washington - Main Obstacle on the Path to Nuclear Disarmament." 1(January 1987): 3-12.
Levadov, L.V. "On a Dangerous Path." 3(March 1986): 72-77.
Nikanorov, S.N. "Armed Forces of the USA - Instrument of Aggressive, Adventuristic Policy of American Imperialism." 6(June 1983): 27-33.
Savinkin, A.E. "Some Dangerous Tendencies in the Contemporary Policy of the USA." 9(September 1986): 63-72.
Simonyan, R.G. "On Offensive Operations in the Armies of the USA." 1(January 1989): 69-77.

Voenno-Istoricheskii Zhurnal (Military-Historical Journal)
Nikitin, N. "The Evolution of the Military Doctrines and Strategic Concepts of the USA after the Second World War." 4(April 1977): 64-69.
Potapov, I. "The Evolution of the Strategic Concepts of Imperialism in the Postwar Period." 5(May 1971): 42-50.
Shavrov, I. "Local Wars and Their Place in the Global Strategy of Imperialism." (Part I) 3(March 1975): 57-66.
————. "Local Wars and Their Place in the Global Strategy of Imperialism." (Part II) 4(April 1975): 90-97.

Voennyi Vestnik (Military Herald)
Garin, V. "Atomic Weapons of the Army of the USA (According to Material in the Foreign Press)." 11(November 1954): 77-81.

Karpovich, B. "The Ideological Preparation of the American Soldier for Atomic War." 6(June 1955): 78-84.
Pukhovskii, N. "The Creative Character of Soviet Military Science." 1(January 1954): 17-24.

Soviet Books and Monographs
Arbatov, A.G. *Lethal Frontiers: A Soviet View of Nuclear Strategy, Weapons and Negotiations* Trans. by Kent D. Lee. New York: Praeger Publishers, 1988.
Dmitriyev, Boris. *Pentagon i Vneshniaia Politika SShA* (The Pentagon and U.S. Foreign Policy). Moscow: Izdatelstvo Instituta Mezhdunarodnikh Otnoshenii, 1961.
Grechko, A.A. *The Armed Forces of the Soviet Union*. Moscow: Progress, 1977.
Konenenko, A. *Atomnoe Oruzhie v Voennykh Planakh SShA (Atomic Weapons in the Military Plans of the U.S.A.)*. Moscow: Voennoe Izdatelstvo, 1957.
Kulakov, V.M. *Ideologia Aggressii (Ideology of Aggression)*. Moscow: Voennoe Izdatelstvo, 1970.
Mil'shtein, M.A., and Slobodenko, A.K. *O Burzhuaznoi Voennoi Nauke (On Bourgeois Military Science)*. Moscow: Voennoe Izdatelstvo, 1961.
Sokolovskii, V.D. *Voennaia Strategia (Military Strategy)*. 1st ed. Moscow: Voennoe Izdatelstvo, 1962.
_____. *Voennaia Strategia (Military Strategy)*. 2nd ed. Moscow: Voennoe Izdatelstvo, 1963.
_____. *Voennaia Strategia (Military Strategy)*. 3rd ed. Moscow: Voennoe Izdatelstvo, 1968.
Trofimenko, G.A. *Strategia Globalnoi Voiny (Strategy of Global War)*. Moscow: Izdatelstvo "Mezhdunarodnaye Otnosheniia," 1968.
_____. *SShA: Politika, Voina, Ideologia (U.S.A.: Politics, War, Ideology)*. Moscow: Izdatelstvo 'Mysl'," 1976.

Index

231

Breinigsville, PA USA
06 October 2009
225307BV00001B/4/P